time money happiness

FOR MY GRANDPARENTS, JOAN AND JOHN,
WHO KNEW THE VALUE OF GOOD THINGS

Thank you to everyone who shared their ideas and opinions
with me, especially those who answered a long questionnaire
on their attitudes to time, money and happiness, and whose
generous replies form the vox pops.

Thank you once again to the staff of Murdoch Books
for being so considerate and courteous to work with,
especially over the ironies of grappling with a deadline
on a book about time use.

Thank you to Samuel French Ltd for permission
to use the excerpt from Kathleen Rich's *Rhymes and Jingles*.

time money happiness

balancing the scales for improved health and happiness

ALISON HAYNES

MURDOCH BOOKS

Let no one be slow to seek wisdom when he is young nor weary in the search thereof when he is grown old. For no age is too early or too late for the health of the soul. And to say that the season for studying philosophy has not yet come, or that it is past and gone, is like saying that the season for happiness is not yet or that it is now no more ... So we must exercise ourselves in the things which bring happiness, since, if that be present, we have everything ...

EPICURUS (341–270 BC), 'LETTER TO MENOECEUS'

CONTENTS

The beyond is not what is infinitely remote, but what is nearest at hand.

DIETRICH BONHOEFFER (1906–1945),
LETTERS AND PAPERS FROM PRISON, 1971

1. THREE GOOD THINGS

TIME IS THE STUFF LIFE'S MADE OF—BUT WHICH DOMINATES, THE BIOLOGICAL OR THE MECHANICAL CLOCK? MONEY CAN'T BUY YOU LOVE, BUT STILL, YOU CAN'T LIVE WITHOUT IT. CASH CAN BE EARNED AND LOST AND EARNED AGAIN. TIME SEEMS REPLENISHABLE AS EACH NEW DAWN CHASES THE NIGHT, BUT IT CAN'T BE REPLACED. IN THE END, WHICH MATTERS MORE IN THE QUEST TO BE HAPPY—TIME OR MONEY?

THE PURSUIT OF HAPPINESS

Within the constraints of the material world, we strive for a happy life. If time is the stuff of life, money is the business of modern life. If money represents our material wants, perhaps time says more about our spiritual needs. The decisions we make in how to spend our time impact on our happiness—whether we work overtime to earn security or spend time with friends and family nurturing relationships and interests outside the financial realm.

We all want to be happy. But what does it mean anyway? Is it gleaned from a life of leisure and pleasure, or one of sustained effort and honed skill? Would we be happier pursuing time or money?

Our desire to be happy—however the word is defined—is famously enshrined in the Declaration of Independence, which was presented in the American Congress on 4 July 1776: 'We hold these truths to be self-evident, that all men are created equal, that they are endowed by their Creator with certain unalienable Rights, that among these are Life, Liberty and the pursuit of Happiness.'

Whichever way you look at it, time and money are central to modern life and a desire for happiness is fundamental to the human condition. We regard time and money as commodities to be measured, earned, saved and managed. Their key position in our lives explains why we often feel so unhappy about them. Misjudge or mismanage time too often or badly and you're at risk of missing deadlines and important occasions, failing exams or even losing jobs. Lack of planning in monetary affairs can have many different effects on your life, from your electricity being cut off, to having large debts, to limiting the support you can offer your children, and this can create a great deal of anxiety in your life, adversely affecting your happiness.

Not for the first time in history, it seems, people feel the need to claw back some personal and family time from work. Meanwhile, promises of happiness are everywhere: workshops, books, reports, conferences and businesses. Has happiness been reduced to a commodity? Witness the increasing popularity of the self-help movement and therapy industries, the growth of positive psychology and hedonics (the study of pleasure). The world today seems preoccupied with time and money and they both seem important in our desire to be happy. We talk of time as money and sometimes in the happiness equation they seem interchangeable: do we want more time at the expense of money? Or will more money buy us time?

Time has been measured since the first humans struggled to find a rhythm in the waxing and waning of the moon and the very essence of money is measurement. Now, in our human drive to chop things up into smaller and smaller elements, we are even prepared to try and measure happiness just as we measure time and money. Inevitably the question surfaces—what is the best way to use our time on Earth and the money in our bank balances to best pursue happiness?

TIME

Time is a slippery concept.
RUSSELL G FOSTER AND LEON KREITZMAN, *RHYTHMS OF LIFE*, 2004

We mark time, make time, spend it, save it, do time, watch time, keep time and measure it. Time is compelling because through it we taste our own mortality, both in the knowledge that we have a limited time in this world, and that its constraints test our abilities to make a difference or simply 'get things done' while we're here.

What's in a word? Time

Nae man can tether Time nor Tide.
ROBERT BURNS, 'TAM O' SHANTER', 1790

The word 'time' comes from Old English, with the idea of a limited stretch of continuous existence. '*Timi*', an Old Norse word, means 'good time' or 'prosperity'. The word 'tide' also comes from a portion of time or season, as in eventide (evening) or noontide (the middle of the day).

We are constantly buffeted against the reality of time: the worn stone step of an ancient building, the cat asleep on our lap that we remember as a kitten, a burnt dinner, and laughter lines in the mirror. Time has fascinated philosophers for at least as long as they have made lasting records. Is it like a river, with us on a boat, moving ever forwards with the current? Is it circular and rhythmical, returning again and again to the same seasons and moments? Or, is it like a pie, to be divided up in hours and minutes and seconds of 'own' time, family time, time for work, for play, for eating and sleeping?

Human consciousness has ensured we have always felt the passing of time—whether it's the rise and fall of the sun, the gentle passing of the seasons or the changing patterns of behaviour in animals and plants that goes with it. All living things are dominated by time. But the human experience of time is not limited to nature's clocks and rhythms. We also live very much under the tyranny of the man-made clock. A social 'invention' that's interpreted differently in cultures across the globe, the clock's power is sweeping.

We are at what must be the peak of an obsession with time. The world seems to be speeding up: more accurate clocks, faster internet connections, chickens that fatten faster and microwaves that cook them in less time. In quiet rebellion, the 'slow movement', with its emphasis on seizing control of time rather than being dictated by it, and taking time out to enjoy the simple pleasures of life, is gaining support, with the slow food movement gently leading the way.

FARMING AND TIME

We live in the most clock-dominated society that's ever existed. But the beginnings of our relationship with time go back far beyond the invention of timekeepers. 'Time-knowing enabled our ancestors to become farmers,' state authors Foster and Kreitzman in their book *Rhythms of Life*. We had to learn about the rhythms of the seasons in order to anticipate them. The Greek poet, Hesiod (c. 700 BC) captured the oral calendar of his time in a poem called 'Works and Days'. He says, when 'House-on-Back, the snail crawls from the ground up the plants', it's time to sharpen the sickles. And when Orion and Sirius are in the middle of the sky, it is time to cut the grapes from the vine.

RELIGION AND TIME

Fundamental to man's desire to divide time and 'tell' it—whether which hour or which day—is control. This is particularly true in religions. The controversy surrounding the correction of the calendar from the 1200s onwards was the shocking suggestion that saints' days were being celebrated on the wrong days. In the later Middle Ages, the Book of Hours described short services and prayers to be said at a certain time, for example, at sunrise or midday. According to the Koran, time is sacred, and much ritual and daily life is spelled out in the holy book. Days begin at sunrise, while prayer times are prescribed at daybreak, midday, mid-afternoon, sunset and nightfall.

A HISTORY OF TIME

He appointed the moon for seasons: the sun knoweth his going down.
PSALM 104:19

Our attempts to understand, measure and control time have a long history.
- Religion. Christianity, Judaism and Islam take a linear view of creation and the progression of time, depicted in the opening paragraphs of Genesis, while the Navajo of North America believed in a more cyclical, continuous nature of time. Navajo healing ceremonies, also called 'ways', use song, dance, chanting and sand painting to enact and re-tell creation stories. The Hindu god, Vishnu, is at once the creator and destroyer of the universe, 'Know I am Time, that makes the worlds to perish when ripe, and comes to bring them on destruction,' he says in the Bhagavad-Gita.
- The sun. It divides night and day, measures what we call a year and causes the seasons. Sun worship appears in almost every culture at some time in history. In China, the sun was husband and yang principle to his wife, moon, with her yin nature.
- The moon. The moon gives us months, even if they don't quite match our own calendar now. Our seven-day week very likely comes from the attempt to divide moon months into four.
- Cro-Magnon bone carving. A bone carving with a series of notches is thought to date to 28,000 BC. Found in France, it may be a lunar calendar

carved by Cro-Magnon man. They looked to the moon, it seems, for their rhythms. This was a practice which—because during the course of a single year the moon's cycle is not in harmony with the sun's—would mean a year ran 11 days fast. Over a time period of just 16 years, winter and summer dates would be reversed, resulting in a useless guide to planting and harvesting.

- The hours. In ancient times days were sometimes divided into twelve parts—regardless of how long the hours of daylight—resulting in unequal hours across the year. They were also measured by means of a water clock or by observing the rotating heavens, dividing into equal hours like our own. Sometimes these two methods coexisted.

- The sundial. These were invented around 5000 years ago in Mesopotamia and at first consisted of a stick pushed into the sand, allowing a plotting of the sun's shadow as the Earth rotated around it. The playwright, Plautus (254–184 BC), created a character who cursed the introduction of sundials because they 'cut and hack my days so wretchedly/Into small pieces!'
David S Landes in his book *Revolution in Time*, notes the sundial is the most natural of clocks, 'for it simply registers the movement of nature's prime timepiece'. Miniature versions, such as pocket sundials, like the 10th century portable sundial found in Canterbury Cathedral in England (the oldest in the English-speaking world), allowed people to tell time on the move.

- Water clocks. Vessels were filled with water at the beginning of each day. A steady flow of water would flow through a pierced hole and would empty by the end of the day. The first known water clock dates to 1500 BC and was found in the tomb of the pharaoh, Amenhotep. Small water clocks were found in Ancient Greece to limit the time a lawyer could present his case in court. These were called *clepsydras*, meaning 'water thieves'.

- The nocturnal. This instrument was used between the 16th and 19th centuries to tell the time from the stars. It was used in the northern hemisphere only, as it depended on being able to see the Pole Star. The nocturnal involved setting a midnight mark against the date, then moving a pointer to the guard stars in either the Plough (Big Dipper) or Ursa Major (the Great Bear) constellations.

- The hourglass. Although it seems a simple device, the so-called hourglass, with its softly falling grains of sand, made a relatively late appearance on the history timeline. The hourglass could be designed to measure any length of time over a minute. Hourglasses may have been first used to time Roman night watches, and were also later used to time debates and jousts in the time of Queen Elizabeth I.
- Mechanical clocks. Quite when the first mechanical clocks appeared is unclear. Geared mechanisms were used from the 3rd century BC onwards. Usually water powered, they were primarily used to give astronomical information. Mentions appear again around the year 1000, in documents relating to monks who needed to know what time to pray. From the 1300s, hundreds of bills survive to witness the cost of repairing and using mechanical clocks in towers, monasteries and churches. Foster and Kreitzman comment that since then, 'we have been steadily losing a battle with time. Instead of controlling our modern clocks, they control us.'
- Pendulums and quartz. Galileo first suggested the pendulum as a timekeeper in 1656, but it was Christiaan Huygens (1629–1695), a Dutch mathematician and physicist, who put the pendulum into a clock and is credited as the inventor of the pendulum clock—'arguably the most important horological invention ever made', according to Kristen Lippincott's *The Story of Time*. Before pendulums, clocks were accurate within 15 minutes a day, at best. Their invention introduced a far greater accuracy of 10 seconds.

  Quartz clocks triggered a new era of even greater accuracy. First created in the US in the late 1920s, it was not until the 1970s that battery-operated quartz clocks were compact, inexpensive and reliable enough to enter our homes and largely replace synchronous clocks. The quartz clock installed in Greenwich in 1939 has an accuracy of two-thousandths of a second in a day.
- Metric clocks. French revolutionaries divided the day into 10 hours, each with 100 minutes of 100 seconds. This was part of a greater design—the calendar of reason—to simplify timekeeping. Despite trying, for two years, to convert the nation, it never caught on and was officially dropped when Napoleon reinstated the Gregorian calendar in 1806.

Roger Bacon (1214–1294)

Although not a household name, the English friar Roger Bacon nonetheless predicted the invention of the telescope, eyeglasses, aeroplanes, high-speed engines and self-propelled ships two centuries before Leonardo da Vinci. In addition, he sought to correct the calendar of his day (the Julian calendar, initiated by Julius Caesar in 45 BC), which he estimated was out by nine days, having drifted one day every 125 years. His contention was hotly controversial as it drew into question the timing of the Church's holy days, including Easter. Bacon's arguments were not welcomed by the Church, and he was denounced by his own order in 1277, charged with espousing 'suspected novelties' and sent to prison. He died in obscurity, his last essay unpublished and ignored. Yet centuries later his ideas were admired for their modernity, and another three centuries later, in 1582, Pope Gregory XIII (1502–1585) finally heeded Bacon's call and 'fixed' the calendar.

The missing 10 days

As the day that had been called 4 October 1582 drew to a close, bells chimed across Europe, heralding midnight. The calendar then jumped 10 days, and these days were lost forever. The order had come from 80-year-old Pope Gregory XIII in the guise of a reform that saw the end of the Julian calendar, with its estimation of a year lasting 365 days and six hours, to one which is still used today, which puts the year at 365 days, 5 hours, 49 minutes and 12 seconds. An angry mob rioted in Frankfurt against the theft of the days; while others feared the saints would be upset. Sailors, weavers and kings worried about other matters: taxes not collected, wages not earned, deadlines looming early. To confuse matters, not all the countries in Europe enacted the reform. Over the course of the next few hundred years, other countries gradually changed calendars, with Bavaria and Austria, for example, converting in 1583, but England not until 1752.

- Standard time. In 1884, at the International Meridian Conference in Washington, it was resolved that Greenwich Mean Time be adopted as the primary world reference, with Greenwich being given longitude zero degrees at the Greenwich Meridian. Previously, even within one country, times were out of sync. In 1800 in England, for example, people in Dover, on the south coast, saw 'midday' half an hour earlier than those in Penzance in the west.

- Political control. Both Joseph Stalin and Pol Pot tried to abolish the seven-day week. The Khmer Rouge leader tried to instil work camp weeks, with a day of rest every 10 days; while Stalin tore up the Soviet calendar and abolished the day of rest altogether. Both, it should be noted, eventually failed. All work and no play never has been a recipe for success.

- Atomic time. Since 1967 the international unit of time has been recognized as relating to the frequency of oscillation of the caesium atom. More precisely, a second is now defined as exactly 9,192,631,770 oscillations or cycles of its resonant, or natural, frequency. Previously, a second was defined in relation to the rotation of the Earth. Clocks based on this are accurate to the degree of about 30-billionths of a second per year!

  'Much of modern life has come to depend on precise time,' says the National Institute of Standards and Technology (NIST) in the US: transportation, communication, financial transactions and electric power to name just a few. But even that's not accurate enough, it seems. 'Scientific research and the demands of modern technology continue to drive our search for ever more accurate clocks.'

Queen Elizabeth I (1533–1603)

Money can't buy you more time, however rich and famous you are. The so-called protestant virgin queen, who once did time in the Tower of London, led a full and eventful life. Crowned Queen at the age of 25, she survived plots against her life, an attempted Spanish invasion and numerous court romances. On her deathbed, her last words were: 'All my possessions for a moment of time.'

VOX POP: Has the sense of time changed your life?

The older you get, the faster time passes! AS

As a child, time was endless and there was no sense of urgency. Time became much more precious in high school with the demands of school, sports activities and friends. University was pure bliss: time to learn, to wander, think, play, work part-time for pocket money, go on holidays—romance without adult responsibilities.

Adult life was a major change. Work was exhausting. Management of personal affairs was a responsibility. I married young and there were the responsibilities of married life.

The major change was children. That's when life hit the fan: the management of a relationship with my husband, two children with their total dependency, work, family obligations, and I also faced a major illness to boot. Even without illness, that's when life became chaotic. Divorce was even more time challenging. The custody issues, dealing with the crisis of sole parenting and children in crisis. Time was cracking. The next decade was the dramatic one as I juggled everything. Only now has time emerged as a possibility. My time. Phew! I don't want to waste it. SG

As a child there was much more freedom associated with time. It seemed to stretch out ahead of me but at the same time was more immediately enveloping. There was no need to try and live in the moment, because as a child, you're already there. At the same time, your responsibilities are limited to your own—at least mine were: homework, tidying my room and helping around the house. So there wasn't the feeling of others taking up my time. Now that I have my own children I realize what an enormous amount of spare time I had before. You have no idea how much time is going to go on your children. AH

When I was young I thought I was busy. Uni, friends, work … little did I know! SE

I no longer feel time is this infinite resource, but that is only recent. I've come to accept there will be bad days to endure, but that the good times will return. Being sick, or having a sick child has got to be the worst way to spend time. But it makes those healthy, good times so much more appreciated and enjoyable. ML

My mother had cancer and died when she was only 65. That's given me a sense of time being something we should cherish and enjoy. She spent her whole life rushing and making sacrifices for others until in the end it was too late for her. I don't want to make the same mistake and so I consciously enjoy every minute I can. CL

WHAT IS TIME?

I can see Time as a huge slowly journeying animal emerging from each century as from an ocean, shaking the yeardrops and weeds from its armor, lumbering toward the eternal coast, through ravines of rock which tear and crush even the last persistent limpets of moment, and the traces of weed-entanglement, even those one or two sea-flowers so beautiful in color that no man could ever describe them; see how the petals are crushed and torn; nothing remains but the beast itself.

JANET FRAME, *THE ADAPTABLE MAN*, 1965

The 4th century monk, St Augustine of Hippo (354–430), said of time: 'What, then, is time? If no one asks me, I know. If I wish to explain it to one that asketh, I know not.'

We know what time is when we glance at a watch and realize we're late for a train, and we're even more certain when we miss it. Augustine also put his finger neatly on the problem of defining time when he said, 'If the past is over, and the future has not yet come, all that exists is now: so how long does now last?'

The 11th century Islamic scientist and philosopher Avicenna (980–1037) argued that time exists only in our minds, as memories and anticipations. Isaac Newton said it was a substance. Princeton University physicist, John Wheeler, said that time was nature's way of keeping everything from happening at once. According to John Langone in *The Mystery of Time*, time 'brings order to chaos, and structure, meaning and continuity to our lives'.

Some of the major time thinkers have been:

- Pythagoras (582–507 BC). The Greek scientist from Samos was aware of different orbital times of the planets, and the fact that the Earth travelled in a regular fashion around the sun.
- Ptolemy (90–168). An astronomer, mathematician and geographer who applied mathematics to the construction of sundials. He also devised a system of longitude and latitude.
- Isaac Newton (1643–1727). He argued that time was absolute—that the duration of the time between two events would always be the same whoever measured it (he was later proved wrong). His work with acceleration defined the relationship between time and motion.
- Albert Einstein (1879–1955). A theoretical physicist, Einstein made the observation that the speed of light is the same for all observers, no matter how fast they are moving. In turn, this led him to state that time was not absolute, but was personal and relative.
- Isidor Isaac Rabi (1898–1988). The atomic clock that our technological world now rests on was a practical application of his Nobel Prize-winning work on the resonance method of measuring the magnetic properties of atoms and molecules.
- Stephen Hawking (1942–). His theoretical universe has no beginning or end in time. Time is a relative concept, he claims, and to someone high up, it would appear that events down below were taking longer.

We seek to be masters of time—with our urges to hide the signs and symptoms of ageing, our constant juggling with appointments and tasks and the desire to 'get things done'. We want desperately to be efficient (largely a clock-driven quality) and yet we also want to be able to slow down and enjoy the good things in life. Is it possible to have our time pie and eat it?

MONEY

*Up and down the City Road,
In and out the Eagle,
That's the way the money goes,
Pop! goes the weasel.*

W R MANDALE, 19TH CENTURY

The chart topping hit from the Philadelphia soul group, The O'Jays, 'For the Love of Money', says it all: for the love of money people will steal from their mother, rob their brother, they will cheat and sell their bodies. The '70s hit is on the airwaves again as the theme music to billionaire Donald Trump's reality TV programme, *The Apprentice*—in which people show what they are prepared to do to secure the winning prize of a year's job with a six-figure salary.

Love it or hate it, money affects everything we do and it's almost impossible to live without it. Attempts to do so usually end with individuals desperately begging for money. Money transforms lives and is itself transformed into the comforts of daily life, basic necessities and, depending how much you have of it, outrageous luxuries.

About AUS$40 a month will sponsor a family through World Vision and help provide clean drinking water, seeds for crops, vaccinations, and repair for shelters. Just over AUS$100 will buy 50 ml of Chanel No 5 perfume. About AUS$85,000 is the cost of a guided climb of Mount Everest. During the American Civil War, men who were conscripted didn't have to turn up to fight in person if they could pay for someone to go in their place.

As the *Encyclopaedia Britannica* explains, 'The subject of money has fascinated wise men from the time of Aristotle to the present day because it is so full of mystery and paradox.' Social convention it might be, but, continues the Encyclopeadia, money is 'a convention of uncommon strength that people will abide by even under extreme provocation'.

Or, as Jim McKnight, Australian psychologist and author of *A Procrastinator's Guide to Simple Living*, sees it: 'All of the beauty and splendour of money as a concept rests in its usefulness, and more importantly in the confidence we all place in the game we play with each other called *money is valuable*.'

In a nutshell, money allows buying to be separated from selling, so that if you have a clutch of hens and want a sofa, you don't have to find someone with a sofa whose heart is set on egg layers before making a deal (a situation known as 'double coincidence of barter').

The power of money breaks down at times, giving way either to barter or the appearance of other 'currencies'. Cigarettes and coffee were the medium of exchange in post-war Germany; bottled beer was a common currency in war-torn Angola. And throughout history, numerous goods have taken the place money now occupies—cows, pigs, shells and beads among them.

An uneasiness surrounds money, stemming from the earliest philosophers, as well as religious texts. For example, Aristotle believed that wealth accumulated for itself, rather than to provide for the household, was unnatural. While greed is generally frowned upon in society, snobs sneer at 'new money' while talking about money can be considered vulgar in the wrong circumstances. And yet, for all this, money can still salvage pitiable situations.

Folklore has it both ways: the riches that come to the good man (and perhaps his wife) are just rewards for a life well led; the ruthless destroyer who does everything and anything for money, finds that once he has amassed wealth that its promises amount to nothing.

'You have to be a bastard to make it, man. That's a fact … ' John Lennon told *Rolling Stone* magazine in 1970.

What's in a word? Money

The word 'money' owes its origins to the temple erected to the Roman goddess, Juno Moneta. This temple was attached to the first Roman mint.

The word 'pecuniary', meaning 'of money', reflects a time and place when cattle was the common currency, as the Latin 'pecus' means cattle.

Mammon

The love of money is the root of all evil.

TIMOTHY 6:10

Mammon is the evil face of money: sometimes referred to as a demon of riches, sometimes a god. Mammon comes from the Syrian word for money. It features in the Bible when Jesus warns against serving two masters: 'You cannot serve God and Mammon.' Mammon also features in John Milton's *Paradise Lost*. *Brewer's Dictionary of Phrase and Fable* defines Mammon more broadly as the god of this world, noting that the English poets Milton and Spenser portrayed Mammon as the personification of the evils of wealth and miserliness.

PERSONALITY AND THE MONEY GAME

Thomas Wiseman's 1970s classic, *The Money Motive*, described a series of stock characters defined by their relationship and dealings with money. His descriptions give a clear insight to the complex ways that different people deal with money matters. Apologies to women— Wiseman's characters are mostly male. There's a bit of each character in all of us, he warns.

- The romantic. Idealistic, the romantic overestimates his beloved object, which in this case is money, deriving from it the kind of joy that others draw from children or art. Wiseman gives as an example the German industrialist, Alfred Krupp (1812–1887), who built a home for his wife in the centre of the steelworks he owned. This meant he could see workers coming in through the factory gates and also that oily grit and soot soon spoiled his wife's trousseau. Romantic myths lend even the most mundane businesses a glamourous gloss. In his quest for the El Dorado the romantic is prone to becoming the 'mad millionaire', incurring the envy of the gods as well as paranoia.
- The company man: aka the 'gnomes of Zurich'. These money counters deny the power of money to inflame the senses, often

working as actuaries or fund administrators and making money for others. While they claim not to be interested in money per se, they are often rich. Deep personal inhibitions about money mean sheltering behind the facade of the company. They might be quite happy signing a hefty company cheque, but reticent about picking up a restaurant bill. Wiseman suggests the company man is the kind of person who finds money deeply troubling and so turns it all into numbers. Meanwhile, the aim of the company system is to make the employee lose his own identity in the corporate image. The danger for the company man is the possibility of ruthless moneymaking and sinking to mob mentality within the company.

- The collector. The collector loves to see the zeros amass at the end of the figures and watch money reproduce itself in a series of 'immaculate financial conceptions'. Collectors are unobtrusively rich, sailing small yachts, driving old but well-maintained cars and sporting expensive clothes. Their interest in money is in its possession. Wiseman's example is founder of Standard Oil, John Rockefeller, who while dining out one night, is supposed to have demanded the plates back from the kitchen when he felt sure his table had only consumed one chicken yet paid for two—he then set about reconstructing the chicken bones, so the story goes, to prove his point. Collectors are usually considered mean, but might once in a while have a generous splurge. They are interested in using their money to establish control over things and are famous as order and efficiency maniacs. Decisions are reduced to a question of cost-effectiveness, without regard for the people they affect.

- The hustler. The hustler is in the race to make money by beating others. He's a realist, knows the statistics, knows there's not enough to go around, but wants his (or more than his) share. He's a go-getter; wheeling and dealing and moving quickly to secure his advantage, he can be likened to the developer who is supposed to have said to his agent after a night of heavy bombing in World War II, 'Did you hear the bombs last night? There must be some bargains around this morning.'

At his or her best, the hustler takes advantage of a set of circumstances and does something we all feel we could do given the chance. At worst, the hustler is a trickster. He admits that the finer things in life can't be bought, but one day, as soon as he has made enough, he will spend more time with his family, he will travel, ease up, educate himself, listen to music. But he never arrives somehow and even if he makes his pile of money, he can't quite bring himself to quit the race.

- The gambler. The gambler doesn't just entertain the dream of the big win, he has a real expectation. His 'delusional sense of knowing is confirmed by chance', says Wiseman. When hunches are confirmed, the gambler eventually feels he can't lose. He craves the sense that life odds (fate) are in his favour. Psychotherapist Albert Lauterbach proposed that gambling exists where rational action appears to offer little hope. Wiseman suggests that some addictive gamblers may have an unconscious desire to lose, while Freud suggests compulsive gamblers turn a burden of guilt into a burden of debt.
- The double-dealer or the respectable thief. The respectable thief is much like the Godfather, with a discreetly expansive and assured manner that communicates a position in the world. Diners who don't

Fyodor Dostoevsky (1821–1881)

The Moscow born novelist is most famous for the masterpiece, *Crime and Punishment*. Having been ordered to death by firing squad, he narrowly escaped when the order was transmuted to hard labour in Siberia. He and others were charged with anti-government activities and got their reprieve at the very last minute, having already been dressed in white execution shirts and blindfolded. For most of his life Dostoevsky barely escaped poverty. He was a passionate gambler who stayed at the gambling tables until he'd lost everything and was 'totally ruined'. He was even said to have stolen his wife's wedding ring and used the money to gamble rather than spend it on much-needed food and clothing. His 1864 work, *The Gambler*, explored the mind of the pathological gambler, offering insights that are still relevant today.

pay their bills fall into this category and debts may mount alarmingly. Epitomized by the Sir Walter Raleigh dictum that 'taking millions is never regarded as crime', the double-dealer is the thief in us all, with the 'I don't know what came over me' syndrome. Sometimes this character commits white-collar crime for the thrill of breaking out of the suppression of his desires; other 'respectable thefts' occur in the grey area of ambiguity, when, says Wiseman, celebrities cash in on their fame in advertising contracts or when free trips and meals win the influence and good opinion of a journalist.

- The criminal. The criminal chases money and will do anything—even kill—to get it, with no remorse. The criminal employs methods such as kidnapping, murder, extortion, blackmail and violent robbery. Psychologically, says Wiseman, he steals for a show of power, and respect, which is a form of love. Money buys criminals power, standing of a sort, position and fame—all the things that money is supposed to get you anyway. But where the successful businessman will say money is the symbol of his success, the criminal has lost sight of what money symbolizes, so that it is meaningless—more akin to the totems of primitive tribes. These people's lives exude excitement and a touch of glamour. They nurse a grievance or lack something, he claims, that fuels a belief in entitlement. They cannot bear for someone to have something they don't have.

- The loser. The loser literally loses money—whether by losing a handbag or wallet or through bad judgment. They invest in dud companies or buy just as the market begins to fall, or sell before the market rises. Some make their name, lose their position and are left without reserves, despite years of success. Sometimes the loser has a deep-rooted suspicion and resentment of money and power, but being down does not destroy him. Playing at the game of survival doesn't seem to fully explain the loser's motivation. Losing is a way of attacking loved ones, says Wiseman, and sometimes it centres on a fear of winning. One benefit of being a loser is that you don't arouse attacks of envy in others.

- The non-player. Non-players refuse to play the money game, whether because of what used to be called dropping out, sympathizing with non-mainstream culture, taking a vow of poverty,

Jean-Paul Sartre (1905–1980)

The French existentialist philosopher and writer refused the Nobel Prize for Literature in 1964, because he said it went against his principles—it paid US$100,000. He continued to live in a one-room apartment in Montparnasse, a bohemian quarter of Paris, with books for possessions. He was a classic non-player, giving away much of his money to struggling left-wing writers and the leftist press.

or not believing in possessions. Some non-players live by higher moral values (Jesus Christ, Jean-Paul Sartre, Albert Schweitzer, Mother Teresa and St Francis of Assisi, for example). But there are few people who are genuinely indifferent to money. Those that are usually have a greater passion that occupies them.

Wiseman gives the example of Albert Einstein, who was offered a post at the Institute of Advanced Study at Princeton, New Jersey, just before World War II. Einstein asked only for a salary of US$3000, which even then was considered a paltry wage. The Institute made no comment and paid him US$16,000 instead. 'Such people are rare, but they do exist. They have no need of monetary riches because their lives are so rich in other respects,' concludes Wiseman.

A SHORT HISTORY OF MONEY: COWS, COINS AND COMPUTERS

As Glyn Davies, author of A History of Money, said at a conference on digital money in London in 1997: money 'is synonymous with power and shapes history in every generation'. We're now at a stage of electronic money, but there have been many steps along the way.

- Silver ingots. Money emerged as a more convenient alternative to straight barter as cattle were a cumbersome means of exchange and difficult to standardize. Countries around the Mediterranean were the first to start exchanging metals, such as gold, silver and copper in trading transactions.

The Assyrians of Cappadocia used embossed silver ingots from 2100 BC and may have been the earliest people to use metal money, although miniature tool money mouldings were guaranteed by the government in China as far back as 2000 BC.

- Electrum. By the 11th century BC bars of gold and electrum— a naturally occurring blend of gold and silver—were being used by merchants. These were marked to enable identification and weighed to give a value. Eventually, smaller pieces were made that were easier to handle.

  A few hundred years later, in 700 BC, possibly the first coins were made by the Lydians of Asia Minor, with the head of a lion on one side and nail marks on the other. Eventually this stamp came to imply a guarantee as to the coin's weight and quality. In 1995, Sotheby's of England auctioned a single coin that had been minted in 460 BC. It sold for £132,000.

- Ming Dynasty. China printed money during the Ming Dynasty (1368–1644). Paper money most likely developed from the practice of a gold or silversmith giving a receipt when they held precious metals for safekeeping. Eventually this receipt became an acceptable payment of a debt, despite having no intrinsic value of its own.

- Goldsmiths. The first bankers were goldsmiths who kept in reserve only some of the gold deposited with them and invested the rest. The promissory note came into use in the 1700s and was at first illegal. Promissory notes emerge from time to time and are usually cracked down on as they are seen as an alternative currency. Cheques evolved as a legal form of promissory note.

- Convertible paper. In Britain, up until World War I, bank notes were called convertible paper because they could be exchanged for gold. They're now inconvertible.

- E-money. Money is no longer backed by gold of the same value. Nor is it necessary to stand in a bank queue to withdraw cash from your account. We can use ATMs, charge our credit card over the internet and make transfers of money across the globe from one account to another. These forms of money are referred to by a number of terms such as electronic cash, electronic currency or digital money.

In Africa, according to a *Guardian* newspaper report, a common way of transferring money—including bribes—is by sending mobile phone scratchcard numbers by text to the recipient. The payer buys a scratchcard then transfers its value to the payee. What's the currency in use? Money or pre-paid call time?

VOX POP: Do you worry about money?

I think about money when I have none, as then I need to think about how I am going to eat and get to work! I don't like opening bank statements but I know what is in most of them. I get bored with money conversations and although I worry when I have spent it, I know it won't be long till I have some more. I am also lucky, as I know that if I ever really needed help I have good friends who will always offer to lend a hand. This helps me not worry so much, which in turn means that I have not had to ask. AE

It's never really been a problem in the past, so I don't worry about it and place faith in having enough to get by, or better. My work has taken a long time to evolve, and I'm now at a point where I know that I can potentially earn a high salary. I just need the confidence and determination to do it. ML

I have a philosophy that money comes. I don't get into debt or even have lay-bys. If I don't have the money to buy things outright then I reason I can't afford it. I'm neither fascinated nor bored by money. It's just that I like order in my life and abhor chaos. EWB

Sometimes I worry about finances, especially since business can be hard, taxes high, demands and stresses occur. I believe I have to manage money. SG

Money bores me. I don't want to know. As long as we have enough to get by ... SE

I tend not to worry about money too much as I believe that I can sort out any problem as it arises. I am pretty careful about money, however, and don't spend profligately. AH

I like to think it will arrive when needed! However, I am lucky enough to have a husband who's far better at doing the budget than me. AS

I used not to care about money at all. Pre-kids I was earning a lot of money, while my husband (working in the community sector) wasn't, but we had minimal rent and no other debts. We spent money like water. I think it was a reaction to having working-class parents and a mother who was determined to get ahead. She shopped for clothes at op-shops and never went out. I thought that was no way to live—all work and no play—so I went too far the other way. Every time we got a chunk of money together we just travelled overseas. It was wonderful and I don't regret it, but I wish we'd forgone just one of those trips and put a deposit on a flat or a house instead. HF

I enjoy figures and I enjoy working with money—scheming and budgeting are things my partner and I share in. We like to speculate about where we will be in 10 years and what we will be doing. We are running our own business all the time and it is totally interwoven with our lives. This is something we sometimes worry about, but really it's better than plying someone else's business for them. LB

HAPPINESS

Being happy is better than being king.

WEST AFRICAN SAYING

Happiness is important and it's no trivial matter to seek it. Philosophers have explored the issue since Aristotle (384–322 BC) and before. He believed happiness lay in virtuous activity, while perfect happiness lay in what he considered the best activity—contemplation. Supreme happiness, which Aristotle called *eudemonia*, also translated as 'the good life', and occurred with the exercise of reason.

Economists such as 18th century social reformer Jeremy Bentham (whose preserved and clothed body sits in a wooden cabinet at University College at London University) and his 19th century disciple, Englishman John Stuart Mill, had lots to say about happiness. The theory they supported has become known as the 'Greatest Happiness Principle' and is based on the idea that good is what brings about the greatest happiness to the greatest number of people.

The medical profession, from the likes of Freud and Jung, through to today's psychologists, have traditionally focused their work more on understanding why people experience a lack of happiness and what causes it. But new strands of thought, known as positive psychology and the science of wellbeing, are addressing that imbalance. And we're beginning to learn just what a happy brain looks like compared to an unhappy one. (The left side of the forebrain is activated by positive emotions; whereas the right side is more active when a person experiences negative emotions.) Scientists are also examining the depths of the brains of Buddhist monks so they can measure the benefits of a calm demeanour, much aided, they believe, by the simple act of meditation.

Why is it important to be happy? Apart from making life pleasant, seeking out the things that make us happy also gives us better survival odds. We need good things—like friendship, a loving family, enough food and fulfilling work—for protection and growth as well as to feel nice. Bad things, such as pain and isolation, are better avoided, both for the individual and the human race.

POSITIVE PSYCHOLOGY

While you'd be forgiven for thinking that pleasure may equate to happiness, Martin Seligman, the leading US positive psychology protagonist, claims they are quite different, and someone who seeks happiness through pleasure alone will eventually be disappointed. A hedonist seeks as many good moments as possible and as few bad ones as possible. Simple hedonic theory says the quality of life can be measured by the quantity of good moments, minus the quantity of bad moments. However, Seligman believes this is a flawed measure and has written a book, *Authentic Happiness*, to explain the new positive psychology and help people realize their potential for lasting fulfilment. You can have good feelings for any number of reasons, he says, but when it comes to deeper feelings of happiness, it's not so much the feeling itself that counts, but how and why you've achieved it. When positive emotions result from 'short cuts' like chocolate, shopping or watching TV, they will produce emptiness. But when happiness comes about because you are using your strengths and virtues, it is an authentic happiness, he claims.

POSITIVE EMOTIONS

Barbara Fredrickson won the US Templeton Positive Psychology Prize in 2000 for her work on the function of positive emotions. She believes that while momentary happiness may not have a deep effect, moments of positive emotion have a profound effect long after their experience is passed. The University of Michigan professor has developed a theory she calls the 'Broaden-and-Build Model of Positive Emotions'. In a paper called 'What Good are Positive Emotions?' that was published in the 1998 *Review of General Psychology*, she wrote that feelings such as joy, interest, contentment and love are 'central to human nature and contribute richly to the quality of people's lives'.

The crux of her theory is that when people experience certain positive emotions they discard automatic everyday behavioural 'scripts' and instead, pursue novel and creative thoughts and actions. Many of the positive emotions she describes and studies are usually experienced in a safe environment, sometimes a familiar one, sometimes in a situation requiring effort. Some of the positive emotions are listed forthwith.

What's in a word? Happiness

Some mornings I walked out into the courtyard and every living thing there, the seagulls and wagtails, the small trees, and even the stray blades of grass seemed to smile and shine in the sun.

NELSON MANDELA, *LONG WALK TO FREEDOM*, 1994

In the past 'happy' meant fortuitous, having good 'hap' or fortune, was the same as being lucky or blessed. Now we use the word 'happy' to describe a feeling like 'gladness'.

- Joy A high-arousal state often called happiness, and overlapping the concept of amusement, exhilaration and mirth. Joy often creates the urge to play—whether socially, physically, intellectually or artistically. And play, the theory goes, promotes the development of skills, which can be drawn on later.
- Interest. Used interchangeably with curiosity, intrigue, excitement and wonder, it is also conceptually similar to challenge, intrinsic motivation and a state called 'flow', where the mind is totally absorbed by the activity in hand. Interest arises, says Fredrickson, in 'contexts appraised as safe and as offering novelty, change and a sense of possibility'. Interest gives us the sense of wanting to investigate, to become involved, be extended or expand the self. From an evolutionary point of view, interest encouraged our ancestors to explore and seek out new information, which could later be invaluable for finding water, food, escape routes or hiding places.
- Contentment. According to Fredrickson, contentment is a low-arousal positive emotion, like tranquillity and serenity. We feel it in a safe and certain environment, with a low degree of effort. When feeling content, we savour the good things in our lives and feel more 'oneness' with the world at large. Contentment is not simple passivity, but, according to Fredrickson, 'a mindful broadening of a person's self-views and world views'.

- Love. The variety of feelings we call love form experiences made up of many positive emotions, such as joy, contentment and interest, for example. Over time, the feelings build and strengthen social bonds and attachments, which while satisfying in themselves, are also a resource to be drawn on later in times when you need social support.
- Seeing the forest and the trees. While people experiencing emotions such as anxiety and fear tend to 'miss the forest for the trees', another benefit of positive emotions is the ability to be able to see both. Or, if you prefer jargon, you're more likely to experience an 'expansion of attentional focus'.
- Actions speak louder. Not only does positive emotion change your thinking, it can also change your doing. And, significantly, while enjoying positive feelings in a safe and good moment, you build skills and resources that you might need to draw on in rougher emotional times.

The happy nuns of Notre Dame

An unhappy life might seem longer, but does being happy in fact prolong life? Nuns from the order of Notre Dame in the US have inadvertently helped psychologists try to discover the answer. In 1930, 180 nuns who were about to take their final vows were asked to write a short autobiographical sketch. Six decades later these handwritten autobiographies were found in the archives of the order and analyzed by psychologists for emotion: positive, negative and neutral. Each sketch was coded by researchers and the results compared to the longevity of each nun. Phrases and words like 'eager joy' and 'inestimable value' were coded 'high', while simple factual statements of life events rated 'low'.

Of the nuns alive in 1991, only 21 per cent of the most cheerful quarter died in the following nine years, compared with over half (55 per cent) of those in the least cheerful quarter.

Eleanor Hodgman Porter (1868–1920)

Eleanor Hodgman Porter made a career of singing in concerts and at private functions following her study at the New England Conservatory of Music in the US, but by the early 1900s had turned to writing. She is remembered as the author of *Pollyanna*, the story of the 'glad girl' who is determined to stay cheerful and optimistic in the face of hardship. Pollyanna is sent to live with a grim spinster aunt and melts the heart of everyone she meets. Published in 1913, *Pollyanna* was Porter's fourth book and became an immediate success. It sold one million copies in its first year of publication. The word 'Pollyanna' has since been used to describe someone who is cheerfully optimistic, or somewhat cynically, to describe someone who is foolishly or blindly optimistic.

VOX POP: What does happiness mean to you?

I think it's odd, but I attach the idea of happiness to people as much as places or events. Some people make me happy—even just thinking of them, liking that I know them and being able to include them in stories I tell others. Places can do this too. Of course, I have special times I remember, which I call my glory days—times filled with joy. These would include the lusty early weeks with my partner of many years, or the passionate and intense hard work involved in organizing festivals and other art events. LB

Happy is being with my family, enjoying the safety of my home, writing, making it as an author. SG

Being happy seems to me to be a matter of choice, or attitude, or philosophy. It's appreciating the good fortune you have, and not feeling victimized by what you don't have. FH

Happiness comes in many forms: a warm honey-coloured glow inside when the world feels right and I feel one with it, and I am content with my lot for that instant. It's also a spark of enthusiasm and freshness, feeling great about the world, looking forward to something, interested and so on. There's also the less exciting feeling deeper down of being generally happy, like a swell on the ocean, although winds can produce surface waves of irritation or unease. AH

Being happy to me means being healthy, productive, sharing laughter and tears with other human beings, being part of a beautiful world and having the ability to see, hear and touch it. It also means being at peace with myself, accepting and tolerant of my own human frailties and those of others. It means being able to let go of the past and live in the present, and is also about having hope for the future. CL

Happiness to me means freedom from, or a lull in, crises. Leisure makes a big difference. Having the time to read, listen to other people, time to help or console them and rejoice with them. EWB

It means being relaxed, well nourished, both physically and mentally—time with other people and time alone. ML

Happy is being close to my family. Spending time with my friends and being able to have fun with them. Laughing is important. If you can laugh at yourself and others then life never seems as bad. AE

Health and happiness

Quite apart from it being a preferable state of mind, happiness brings about better health. In particular it creates:

- a more robust immune system
- lower levels of the stress hormone, cortisol
- better recovery from major surgery
- less likelihood of catching the flu if exposed to the virus.

You don't find happiness outside of yourself. You don't get happiness in a box with the packages from a shop. You can't really get it from friends and loved ones, nor in a pay cheque. You can enjoy these things but they are outside yourself. It's your own thoughts and experiences that create happiness. Even when you're down, you can find the good in what is happening and focus on that. If you have faith in your work and in yourself, you can be happy—it's your own consciousness that counts, your own viewpoint. It's easy to be fearful and find something bad in any experience, but you can find happiness in it as well—if only you would look. JS

WHAT DOES HAPPY MEAN ANYWAY?

Shakespeare said in *As You Like It*, 'He who wants money, means and content is without three good things.' Seeking all three, money, the means of time and happiness, feels like a modern concern. But is it? As our standard of living has improved—with more money—have we become happier? We appear to feel rushed and and to never have enough time. Lots of people struggle to stay within their budgets. While it's nice to be able to pay the bills and buy new shoes, does that make us any happier? And what does 'happy' mean anyway?

TAKING STOCK

Do you have more money than time? Or are you time rich but money poor? Take a pencil and paper and jot down your thoughts on where time, money and happiness fit into your life. Your answers might reveal paradoxes or underlying attitudes you've not explored.

BEING HAPPY

1. What does being happy mean to you?
2. What do you believe makes a difference? (personality? luck? meditation? religious faith?)
3. What makes you happy?
4. In what ways do you seek happiness in your life?
5. When you think back over your life what types of experiences do you remember as happy ones?

LIVING WITH TIME

1. How timetabled is your life?
2. Do you yearn for a less scheduled existence or do you like the way your life runs?
3. Is there lots of blank space in your diary or do you like to book up every evening and weekend? How does this affect your enjoyment of life?
4. Has your sense of the quality of time changed over time?

MONEY IN YOUR LIFE

1. How do you feel about money?
2. Are you financially phobic (hate opening bank statements and dealing with tax, for example) or pragmatic?
3. Does money bore you or fascinate you?
4. Do you worry about money or believe it will arrive when needed?
5. Is money ever a source of tension in your relationships?

Oh my ears and whiskers, how late it is getting!

THE WHITE RABBIT, *ALICE'S ADVENTURES IN WONDERLAND*, LEWIS CARROLL, 1865

2. TIME

TIME IS ELUSIVE. WE FEEL ITS PRESENCE, BUT CAN'T TOUCH IT. WE KNOW ITS POWER, BUT CAN'T CHANGE IT. WE HAVE LEARNT TO MEASURE IT, DIVIDE IT AND TRACK IT. BUT IN OUR ATTEMPT TO MASTER TIME, WE'VE GIVEN IT EVEN MORE MASTERY OVER OURSELVES.

PRESSED FOR TIME

We live in rushed times. Anxiety about time is a core issue of modern life and as technology speeds up around us, we are in danger of seeking to save time above everything else, often by multitasking and hastening everything we do. But instead of feeling that we gain time we often end up feeling even more pressed for time. Doctors are no exception. An article in the *Medical Journal of Australia* in 2005 titled, 'What GPs want: time and time again', reports that what GPs around the world want most of all is health care reforms that will allow them to give more time to their patients. What they don't want is a 'hamster' health care system that relies on everyone running faster on the treadmill.

According to the article the trend for doctors in the UK, the US and Australia, over the past decade, has been to give patients longer consultations. And yet this is not enough. Patients' needs are also greater and expectations are higher on all fronts. While everyone in our society wants more time, 'few other professionals attempt to undertake complex tasks in 20- or even 40-minute spurts'.

It's not just the medical profession who are noticing the speeding up of time. In the days of snail mail, people generally expected a response in about a week. Now, using email, a response somewhere between 24 and 48 hours is expected, particularly in the world of business. 'So we've really upped the ante,' Juliet Bourke, director of consultancy, WORK + LIFE Strategies told ABC programme, *The World Today*. Not surprisingly, a survey by the Australian Psychological Society in 2003 found 70 per cent of managers felt stressed by the number of emails they received each day and the speed with which they were expected to deal with them.

THE RUSHED STATE

Rushing takes a toll on our bodies and minds. A little rushing may add a welcome shot of adrenalin into life—running for the holiday plane or running for shelter in a storm—and it can also give us a sense of belonging and busy importance. But the trouble with a constant state of feeling hurried is that it leaves little time between events. It removes creative and restful gaps and also means there's little time for reflection and feelings. *Timeshifting* author, Stephan Rechtschaffen, believes some people feel more comfortable when life's a mindless rush. 'Painful feelings are difficult to face, and we'd rather not feel them if at all possible. So we get busy. We speed up. We substitute action for contemplation,' he writes.

VIRTUAL LIVES

Living a rushed life is no better for children than it is for adults. Australian-based clinical psychologist and family therapist, Andrew Fuller, believes a busy life comes at a great cost to our children. If parents spend less time with their children, less reading time and longer hours working, the result is: 'the hurried child interacts with the hassled adult ... and parenting is restricted to an odd combination of bribery, fear and distance.' In his counselling practice Fuller observes kids who live what he calls 'virtual lives', meaning they are 'information rich but experience poor. Rushed from activity to activity.'

A speedy pace can also mean instant gratification and no chance to slow down and reach a state of deep enjoyment in activities. The result is a child with reduced resilience (a term used to describe the ability to bounce back from disappointments and difficulties) and can spell depression later in life.

For older students, a real danger of trying to do too much can mean they aren't doing anything with a degree of excellence. The student who's also working a 40-hour paid week is unlikely to have sufficient time for focused study or the in-depth exploration and application that a degree course demands. As a result, students may feel disappointed with their academic experience, especially as student debt mounts, and also as they may not necessarily accumulate the qualifications they assumed they would.

HURRY SICKNESS

The resultant 'dis-ease' associated with pressure of time in our lives is often referred to as 'hurry sickness'. Californian cardiologists, Dr Meyer Friedman and Dr Ray Rosenman, were the first to coin the term in 1959. They noticed that many of their patients seemed to be suffering a deeply ingrained and continuous struggle against both real and imaginary events in their lives, including other people and time. Impatient, competitive, easily irritated, quick to anger, suspicious and hostile, often highly successful in their careers but dissatisfied with themselves; the battle against time seemed so pervasive to these people that doctors labelled their behaviour pattern as 'hurry sickness', although they later called it 'Type A' behaviour.

Friedman and Rosenman's theories are well known and suggest that Type As are twice as likely to experience heart disease than Type Bs (who show none of the stressed characteristics).

More recently, a study by the Women's Health Australia Project, showed a direct link between feelings of being rushed and perceptions of health. The more rushed or pressured for time someone felt, the greater likelihood they would perceive their health as poor.

Beating hurry sickness

Are you impatient at traffic lights or in a restaurant when the service is not automatic? Do you fume when people are late? Is 'hanging out' a waste of time? If you are in danger of becoming obsessed with speeding up, try:

- Time without clocks. Plan windows of time in the day or the week when you can switch off clock time. JE has what she calls a shut-off time zone between 8.30 pm and 8.30 am when she doesn't answer the phone or look at emails.
- Take off your watch when you don't really need to know the time—perhaps in the evening or a weekend without commitments. Live dangerously: remove your watch!
- Plan nothing. Allow for time in your diary for doing nothing.
- Silence is golden. Bring some silence into your life and let it soothe that rushed feeling.

VOX POP: Do you feel rushed?

We never have enough time in our lives to do the things we wish to. But I never rush to catch up, as rushing causes stress and things don't get done properly anyway. LN

I feel rushed all the time and it's starting to wear thin, I can tell you. I'm in the middle of a court case over a development in the village, and I just want it to be over. We live from minute to minute, 'putting out bushfires' all the time—getting documents for the barristers, complying with court orders, responding to demands as they come in. AL

I find I am very easily sidetracked, and some jobs seem to take longer than originally planned, so a lot of domestic jobs get rushed. Food preparation is sometimes left until the last minute. AS

I feel rushed when the phone is ringing, my daughter is speaking to me, I want to write and I know I have to cook dinner—normal family life. SG

Once I was so rushed I had to eat my lunch in the shower! EWB

I try to never feel rushed because I hate it, but inevitably it happens. Usually when I'm tempted (or coerced) into taking on too much at once. I've got this thing about being punctual, which has been challenged since having a child. I hate turning up late to anything. I used to believe I could do two things at once and used to double-book myself quite frequently. Maybe it was because I found it almost impossible to say 'no' to invitations. ML

I feel rushed when people expect me to know what I'm doing on the weekend if it's only the beginning of the week. Or perhaps when I have a week of meetings at work and then have to catch up on deadlines. AE

I feel rushed leaving for work in the morning and leaving work, too. If I haven't walked out of the office by 5.15 pm, I risk not getting to childcare in time. If there are no traffic problems the trip takes 25 minutes. But on those odd and unpredictable occasions when something goes wrong, I can scrape in only just before the 6 pm closing time. Those times, while infrequent, are very stressful. FH

Getting my youngest out of the door in the morning can be ghastly. I'm okay with the packed lunches, breakfast, finding uniforms and shoes most days. But determined folded arms or last minute tantrums test even my best-laid plans. I feel rushed and hassled when I'm trying to meet a tight work deadline and am bombarded by requests on all sides. Sometimes it's nice to have things to rush to: planes to catch, places to be, but not with young children in tow. AH

I have made a conscious decision not to rush. I find it makes everyone flustered and go even slower. The school run is the one exception. For this I grab sleeping children from their beds at the last minute and make the dash. Nightmare. SE

ARE WE TIME-STARVED?

Most industrial societies have exhibited a complicated trend towards increased free time, while at the same time believing themselves to be subject to greater time pressure.
MICHAEL BITTMAN, 'THE LAND OF THE LOST LONG WEEKEND? TRENDS IN FREE TIME AMONG WORKING AGE AUSTRALIANS, 1974–1992'

Do we rush because there really isn't as much time as we physically need to live life in the 21st century? Are we really time poor, or are we using our time poorly? Is modern life too demanding, or have we become obsessed with time? Are we as time-starved as we think we are?

The answer is not straightforward, nor one that experts agree on. Researchers such as Juliet B Schor, author of several bestselling books, including *The Overworked American*, argues that working hours have eaten into free time, with unhappy consequences.

In recent history, it looked as though our free time had increased, not decreased. A survey in the UK released in 2004 by Mintel caused a stir when it reported that 79 per cent of respondents felt they had enough time, and only 5 per cent said they had no free time at all. 'The British are not really as pushed for time as we would have everyone believe. Constant claims that "there are not enough hours in the day" do not ring true,' stated the report.

The research revealed the following information.

- More money was being spent on time-saving products such as convenience foods.
- The internet saved time on research, banking and shopping.
- Three out of ten people were 'time rich'. These people either did not work or were retired.
- Less than one in 10 people were 'time poor'.
- Those people with the least time to spare fell into the age group 25–44, and were from London or the South-East of England.

Similarly, research by John Robinson and Geoffrey Godbey reported in their book, *Time for Life: the surprising ways Americans use their time*, published in 1997, showed that Americans were enjoying more free time but paradoxically feeling more time pressure and stress. Some free time emerged as people put off marrying and having children until later. Others have cut back work time and time doing housework. Feeling you have less free time is not in itself a bad thing, they point out. If people fill their time with productive activities that they feel good about, there's no problem.

Whether or not the trappings of modern life have freed our time in a real sense is still up for debate. Most research seems to indicate that people in modern society are feeling more anxious about time and believe their leisure time is shrinking. So, why do people feel so pressed for time?

PEOPLE GET BUSIER ACROSS THE SPAN OF THEIR LIVES

Jonathan Gershuny of the Institute for Social and Economic Research in the UK argues that people perceive they are getting busier because throughout their lives they do get busier, but that their lives as a whole may still be less busy than people in previous generations experienced.

BLURRING OF THE BOUNDARIES

The distinction between work time and 'own' time is becoming fuzzier. Technology has made it easier to erode the division. Examples are easy to find: the manager who switches the laptop on after dinner; the self-employed worker who checks for urgent emails over the weekend; the executive who answers overseas calls on their mobile while visiting friends. Modern technology makes boundaries more permeable, particularly for the self-employed who have that uneasy feeling of being 'on call' almost permanently.

CHANGING WORK HOURS

The spread of work into unsociable hours, for example, with early starts or late shifts, also increases the feeling of blurred boundaries between work and private life. And in some cases, people definitely are working longer hours. On an average day in Australia, 35 per cent of working males are putting in an 11-hour work day.

THE DECLINE OF THE FAMILY WAGE

In Australia in 1907, the First Commonwealth Court of Conciliation and Arbitration established a 'fair and reasonable wage' that was to be sufficient for a man to support himself, his wife and his children in 'frugal comfort'.

Over time, as women entered the paid workforce, the idea of the family wage faltered, with ramifications for time use. Women have taken on part of the breadwinning responsibility, but men have not taken up the slack in domestic duties. Family expectations have also changed: or, as Professor Michael Bittman of the University of New England in Australia, points out, if we demand liberty and equality in society in general, it's hardly surprising that we don't think it should stop at the front door of a family home. What this means for the average family is both partners are likely to be working, at least part-time, with less time for housework and looking after children. And while in previous generations, women may, happily or not, have taken on longer hours doing housework, the expectation of equality within the home means more pressure on the male spouse to pull his weight. The overall result is a time squeeze.

THE HARRIED CONSUMER

A more productive economy creates more goods and services and more means to enjoy them, the argument goes. But, enjoying—or consuming—takes time. If you get stuck in the work-to-spend rut, then leisure time can seem to shrink before your eyes.

DOING TOO MUCH AT ONCE

Feeling rushed might also result from the sheer volume of separate activities we undertake, rather than from their total duration. When you're frequently changing what you're doing, undertaking a rapid succession of short tasks, this can result in feeling time-pressured. Modern technology allows us just that: listening to the news on the radio while checking emails, boiling the kettle and making microwave popcorn while keeping an eye on children and answering the phone.

BOOM AND BUST

Economic boom times can reinforce the time squeeze: employers can expect longer hours and more people find themselves working to fill the labour gap.

LEISURE IN THE POST-INDUSTRIAL SOCIETY

Industrial capitalism, some say, has organized, planned and fragmented our time; while industrialization has ensured work is planned for, leisure has been left behind. Yet we need leisure to recover from the pressures of work, to strengthen our friendships and the bonds with our families. Professor Peter Brown, of the Griffith

Business School at Griffith University in Australia argues that we need leisure time, 'to reflect on life's direction and meaning'.

MONEY WEALTH BRINGS TIME POVERTY

That's a conclusion of a paper by Daniel Hamermesh and Jungmin Lee, 'Stressed Out on Four Continents: Time crunch or Yuppie Kvetch?' ('Kvetch' comes from the Yiddish word, 'kvetshn' to squeeze or complain, and now means to habitually complain.)

These researchers looked at data from Australia, Canada, Germany, Korea and the US. They consistently found that the higher the household income, the greater the perceived time stress. Time stress is like poverty, say the authors, 'both reflect the scarcity of resources'. But while the poverty, or 'goods constraint', will relax over time in a growing economy, the time constraint cannot. Their theory seems sweepingly simple: 'any group, regardless of its hours of work, will perceive itself under increasing time stress as its ability to purchase market goods increases.'

PERFECTIONISM

Expectations and aspirations have risen, and the pull to live a perfect life is greater. Part of this manifests itself in what we aspire to in our homes: we have more labour-saving domestic devices, but instead of saving time, we up the stakes, for example, our great grandfather changed his collar and cuff each day, now they don't come off and the whole shirt is washed.

PERFECT PARENTING

Another area where expectations have soared is parenting. Michael Bittman calls it the psychologizing of parenting. 'People are having fewer kids, but spending far more hours with each child.' Today's parenting maxim is 'be there'. The ramifications are manifold. The schedule stiffens. Where a parent might have taught a child to swim (or not), now he takes a child to a swimming lesson. Homework used to be light on, especially in primary school, now even six year olds are likely to have home readers nightly as well as other tasks. Lots of parents drive their children when it was the norm to walk or cycle to school, probably with a band of kids making their way there together.

Time deepening

Robinson and Godbey's research in *Time for Life* indicated a modern trend of people to pack more into their time. They called this 'time deepening' and defined it in the following ways.

- Attempting to speed up a task, for example, loading the dishwasher faster.
- Substituting a longer activity for one that could have been done more quickly, for example, having a three-course dinner party rather than friends over for a bowl of soup.
- Doing more than one thing at a time, for example, answering emails while having a conversation on the telephone.
- Paying more attention to time when undertaking an activity, for example, going for a walk in the knowledge that you will be back in half an hour to meet a delivery.

THE TYRANNY OF TECHNOLOGY.

Recurring, or relentless, deadlines, unfinished tasks, multitasking and information overload are common complaints in modern society. Contemporary communication and technology tends to be more fragmented, resulting in increasing interruptions and a rhythm of life that leads to stress and dissatisfaction. It also has a self-perpetuating effect of acceleration: a web page that takes too long to load has us feeling impatient so we completely overlook the 'miracle' benefits of the internet that was discovered less than a decade ago.

On multitasking: 'To do two things at once is to do neither'.
PUBLILIUS SYRUS (100 BC)

THE SCARCEST RESOURCE

Hold fast the time! Guard it, watch over it, every hour, every minute! Unregarded it slips away, like a lizard, smooth, slippery, faithless ...

THOMAS MANN, *LOTTE IN WEIMAR: THE BELOVED RETURNS*, 1940

The gadgetry's different and the home has more mod cons, but fundamentally, some would say, we're not that different from baboons in the way we use time. They spend about one-third of their life asleep, much like us. When awake, baboons divide their time between travelling, finding food and eating it. Free time is filled with interacting with the group in one way or another—quite a bit goes on picking lice out of each other's fur and grooming. (Ask any mother about head lice spreading in schools and she'll likely sigh in empathy.) According to the historian Emmanuel Le Roy Ladurie, in 13th century villages in France, picking out lice was the most common 'leisure' pursuit. 'Now of course, we have television,' comments psychologist Mihaly Csikszentmihalyi, in *Finding Flow: The psychology of engagement with everyday life*.

One of the first accounts of how people spend the hours and minutes at their disposal was in Maud Pember Reeves' 1913 book, *Round About a Pound a Week*. She was one of several members of the Fabian Women's Group who, for four years before World War I, recorded the lives playing out in 30 houses in Lambeth, London.

Reeves paints a colourful picture of life for the wives of painters, plumbers, builders, handymen, dustmen's mates, printers and potters who were eking out a living on 20 shillings a week. There was a broad range of women living in different circumstances. One was a 20 year old whose day started at 6 am when she would get up and light the fire. At 6.15 am she would wake her husband and get his breakfast. Her day was filled with nursing the baby, carrying dirty water and bringing up fresh water from the yard, blacking the grate, making clothes and repairing her husbands.' When he returned from work at 5 pm, she helped him clean himself in warm water. Noting that he is 'not strong and likes to go to bed early' he would retire by 6 pm. She went to bed at 9 pm. 'As Lambeth mothers' days go, hers is a very easy one,' writes Reeves.

In contrast, Mrs B had eight children under the age of 13. She nursed her baby at 6.45 am, lit the fire at 7 am and started the rounds of breakfast. At 9.30 am her husband, a printer's labourer, came back from his night shift. She cooked him haddock and tidied their room, making the bed so he could sleep. Her day was then occupied by a constant stream of washing children's hands and faces, preparing meals and making beds. The fact that Mr B worked at night allowed them to manage with only two beds: Mrs B and five children slept in one bed at night while Mr B used it in the day; the other three children slept in a single bed.

Maud Pember Reeves (1865–1953)

Born in Mudgee in New South Wales, Australia, Maud moved to New Zealand when her father took a position as bank manager in Christchurch. As a girl she enjoyed balls, garden parties and race meetings. She married the political journalist William Pember Reeves when she was 19 years old and soon became interested in social problems. After the birth of a second daughter she enrolled at Canterbury College for a Bachelor of Arts. She was a key figure in winning the vote for women in New Zealand, and with her companions, worked on her embroidery in the parliament gallery to counter claims that suffragists were losing their femininity.

In 1896 the family moved to London and was welcomed by members of the Fabian Society, who at that time included George Bernard Shaw and H G Wells. In 1907 Reeves formed the Fabian Women's Group who worked for equal opportunity and economic independence for women. To compile her book Round About A Pound A Week, she and sister Effie visited 30 families twice a week for nearly four years. Her detailed account of domestic life of working-class women was reprinted in 1979. 'Maud Pember Reeves did not presume to teach poor women how to run their homes; she wanted to learn about their daily lives from their own lips,' states the publisher's introduction.

TIME USE

Time use analysis can reveal a number of social issues, such as changes in leisure time across age groups, quality of leisure time for men and women, or how working women adapt their days when using childcare. Quite what a picture it paints depends on how the information is gathered; for example, whether only one activity is recorded, or whether secondary activities are also noted.

For instance, Australian research shows that for every hour of childcare that is considered a primary (or main) activity, there are four hours of childcare 'in the background'. (European data shows a slightly different picture—of an extra 24 minutes in the background.) A possible explanation is that parents in surveys in Australia count their time 'on call', for example, when they are asleep, so it is noted as a secondary (or background) activity.

Researchers into time use tend to divide time into a number of categories, such as:

- Necessary time: activities for personal survival such as eating, sleeping and personal hygiene. Necessary time accounts for 46 per cent of time according to Australian data from the National Time Use Survey.
- Contracted time: activities like paid work and regular education in which there are controlled periods of time when an activity must be performed. Contracted time makes up for 15 per cent of most people's time.
- Committed time: where social and community interactions mean a commitment to giving time, such as performing voluntary work, housework, childcare and shopping. About 16 per cent of time is committed time.
- Free time: is what's left after necessary, contract and committed time; usually averaging about 22 per cent of our overall time.

HOW HAS LIFE CHANGED OVER THE PAST CENTURY?

We know that daily life has changed over the past decades, which can be viewed in a whole range of different ways, but how does this manifest itself in the way we use time?

- Sleeping. We sleep slightly less than we did 100 years ago. Sleep experts such as William C Dement have traced our decline in sleeping hours and its resultant 'pandemic of fatigue' to a range of cultural, economic and technological influences that began long before Thomas Edison invented the electrical light bulb. Many of the extra hours for work or commuting are carved out of sleep time.

- Eating. We spend less time eating and a different type of time eating. Home-baked food has been substituted for more convenient, quicker shop-bought foods that are more likely to be eaten away from the family dinner table, if there still is one in the house.

- Laundry. The weekly washing burden takes a lot less time than it did 100 years ago, but hasn't changed much since the 1950s. While most households have a washing machine, in general people now like to keep their clothes cleaner.

- Work. Over the past 25 years many researchers say we're working longer hours. The average figure has budged little, if at all. But if you remove from the equation those who are not working, the people who are working full-time and part-time are putting longer hours into work, says Michael Bittman, expert in the collection and analysis of time use statistics.

- The television. The world spends a lot of its time watching television. Before television was invented, that time went to different leisure pursuits and to civic activities.

- Travelling time. 'The death of the local shopping strips and regional hubs, plus the time it can now take to park, means that we spend more time travelling,' believes Bittman. Additionally if you have children the chances are you spend more time chauffeuring them around when they reach school age.

- Food production. In the 19th century most households grew at least some of their own food and spent time performing various tasks associated with weeding, planting, collecting eggs or making preserves. In the 1920s and 1930s, bottles and tins became much more prevalent and some of the processing that used to take place in the kitchen moved over to commerce.

THE GENDER DIVIDE

Man for the field and woman for the hearth:
Man for the sword and for the needle she.
ALFRED LORD TENNYSON, *THE PRINCESS*, 1847

A difference between how men and women spend their time persists in modern society whether we approve or not. Data from time use surveys show numerous ways that social trends or commitments affect the day-to-day lives of men and women.

- In New Zealand, women spend longer, when you add together paid and unpaid work, working.
- Women in Australia spend three times longer in childcare than fathers.
- When it comes to time spent with children, Australian fathers spend a lot of it playing, are less likely to be alone with their children, and give up less of their own leisure time than mothers.
- In Australia, children add more to the workload of women than men and this acts to deepen the division of labour between the sexes: men add more to their workload on becoming fathers but do not necessarily contribute more domestic labour.
- In Europe, time allocation becomes markedly different between genders once a child enters the household, especially when the children are below seven years of age.
- In Europe, the total working time for women is greater than for men when there are small children in the house, particularly in Estonia, Slovenia and Hungary where it's an hour more.
- In Europe, men's time is spent bringing home the bacon and winning the bread. They do more paid work, but less domestic labour, and at the end of the day enjoy more free time than women.
- Women spend more of their time at home than men, and men spend more of their time in a workplace than women.
- Cooking and dishwashing remain largely the jobs of women. When men do cook, they spend less time on it. In Sweden, Norway and the UK, men do more food preparation than in other European countries.

- Females spend 10 minutes more on washing and dressing than males on average. At age 19 the difference is much greater; in the UK 19-year-old girls spend 40 minutes more than their male counterparts.

In their paper, 'All Else Confusion: What time use surveys show about changes in gender equity', Michael Bittman and George Matheson discuss theories such as a 'stalled revolution' and 'lagged adaptation'. The paper suggests that women entering the workforce have merely taken on a second shift of work. They work outside the home and continue to put the same or similar hours into the housework as well. Have men adapted to the change by taking on more housework? If they haven't taken up the slack, is this only because there's a lag in their adaptation?

It's a common sticking point, as mother of four, SE, explains: 'I still routinely get pissed off at the division of labour thing. It gets better for a while and then back to square one—time to spit the dummy again. And so it goes! I take comfort in the fact that I am not the only one dancing around this issue—ask any woman.'

Part of the problem may be that the way we perceive how labour should be divided is something we learn from our own parents. So any adaptation can potentially take more than one person's lifetime. But, as Bittman and Matheson point out, '... the "stalled revolution" is nowhere more evident than in the failure of younger men, raised in "post-feminist" households, to increase their contribution to cooking.'

Participants in a 2006 seminar in Sydney organized by the Office of Women and the Social Policy Research Centre on Time Use and Gender, were left bemused by a fact that was evident in batch after batch of time use statistics: that men put the same number of hours into housework despite what is happening in the household, that is, whether their spouse works outside the home, works full-time or part-time, has a new child or several children. The only exception is when they live alone. If there's a woman in the house, you can pretty safely bet that she'll be doing more than feminists consider is her fair share. Perhaps someone will get to the bottom of it one day, but certainly at the seminar, none of the many experts present could usefully explain the figures.

Put another way, the price of equality in the workforce has been time bickering. Quite simply, there is less time to go around with the result that a common family grumble is: who's going to be the one to take the children to the doctor/go to the school concert/pick up the kids from the music lesson/ take the children to the movies so the other can catch up on a report? The theme is picked up in Richard Layard's *Happiness: Lessons from a New Science*. The effect of women going out of the home to work meant roles inside the family changed: women ended up working longer and men 'felt they got less attention than before from their wives'. Says Layard, 'In many families the problem is simply a lack of time.'

FAMILY LIFE

Mothers' time is fast and fragmented but productive.
DAY AFTER, TIME USE SURVEY, MOTHERS & MORE

We knew it anyway, but it's interesting to see the figures in black and white.

- On average, couples in the UK spend two and a half hours together a day, with a much lower figure during the week than on the weekends (two hours compared to three and a half). Retired couples spend more time together, and couples where both work full-time spend less together. Cohabiting couples spend half an hour less time together than married couples.
- People with children work harder than those without them. That goes for total hours of paid and unpaid work. In Australia, parents are more likely to be doing more than one thing at a time—usually this involves keeping an eye on children at the same time as trying to complete another task.
- Women who stay in the home, work as many hours as women who go out to work and are more often doing more than one thing. Anecdotally, many women find time at work in a paid job less pressured than time at home.
- Mothers multitask all day long. The degree of multitasking drops substantially once children are in bed, between 9 pm and midnight.

time, money, happiness

AGE

- In Europe, young people spend most time outside the home and spend gradually more time at home as they get older. Retirement means on average an extra five to six hours more in the home than that spent by the youngest adults.

- In the UK, eight year olds spend about 11 hours a night sleeping. By age 13 they spend under 10 hours and by the time they are 20 they spend less than nine hours asleep. When people are in their 60s they start to increase sleep again to over nine hours a night.

- The over-65 age group in the UK spend more time watching television, reading, listening to the radio and resting. They watch television for an average of three hours 45 minutes a day, compared to three hours a day for the 50–64 age group.

- Contact with neighbours decreases with age, but the majority of people have weekly contact with their neighbours.

- In Japan, an elderly person (over 65) who lives alone, spends on average 20 hours and 36 minutes alone each day.

WORK

- Being employed or self-employed means you sleep less (somewhere between 10 and 30 minutes less per day); and spend less time on domestic tasks, including childcare. There's also less time for meals, personal care and free time—the work hours have to come from somewhere.

- In New Zealand, paid workers spend 44 minutes a day travelling to and from work: 61 minutes on average if using public transport and 41 minutes if using private transport, or 28 minutes if on foot or bicycle. Workers on high incomes travel for longer.

- In Australia, part-time work does not reduce a woman's work hours—they have the highest total workload and spend the most time in secondary activities. Mothers who work full-time have longer work days during the week, but taken with the weekend, it's part-time working mothers whose burden is greatest.

- Women redirect time spent in paid work to unpaid work following the birth of a child. And they redirect sleep and leisure time to cope with extra domestic duties and direct childcare time.

54

- One in five workers in the US works from home on any given day.
- Work makes time more 'masculine': employed women do less secondary activity than non-employed women, although still more than men.
- In the UK, people get up later on the weekend, work less but do more housework, and spend more time on travel and leisure activities. On the weekend, eating is a more relaxed affair and people spend more time on personal care too. Bedtime tends to be an hour later than during the week.
- In Japan, almost a third of the population do some kind of voluntary work. The group with the highest rate of participation (40 per cent) is females in their late thirties and early forties. The smaller the population of a town the greater the participation rate, so that more people in a town or village carry out voluntary work than in a city. But those who help out in a city, or a place with a bigger population, do so for more days on average.
- In Europe, volunteer work through an organization is more common in men than women. Informal help to other households is more common than formal voluntary work.

HOUSEWORK

- In the UK, most housework occurs when the youngest member of the household is aged between five and nine years old. It falls when the youngest child reaches 16, dropping by 44 minutes for a woman, compared to having a 10- or 15-year-old in the house.
- In Europe, the amount of housework that people do peaks at different times of the day, mainly around mealtimes, with peaks between 10 and 11.30 am, and around 5 pm.
- Women in the UK do the majority of household chores, 'despite increased participation in the labour market'—three hours a day on average compared to one hour 40 minutes for men. (Men do paid work or study for two hours a day more than women.) Japanese figures are more marked: men do on average 33 minutes a day housework, compared to 3 hours 45 minutes by women.
- In the UK, 84 per cent of men do DIY repair, compared to 50 per cent of women.

Ironing men are exceptional!

More than 1000 men the world over participate in a sport known as Extreme Ironing, and around 80 competed in the World Championships in Munich in 2002. The sport involves taking an ironing board to a remote location and ironing a few items of clothing! Locations have included the Rivelin Needle near Sheffield, England, ironing in a canoe, ironing while skiing and ironing underwater.

Rare eccentrics no doubt, these men buck the trend, certainly across Europe if not the world, that, 'ironing men are exceptional'. 'Men iron very seldom,' reports the 2004 edition of *How Europeans spend their time—everyday life of women and men*. Between one and five in every 100 men will have picked up an iron during the day. In contrast, in countries where ironing is more common—Belgium, Slovenia, France and the UK—about one in four women iron on any given day, and half that number in other European countries.

CULTURAL DIFFERENCES

- Americans work more paid hours than Germans and other Europeans, but Germans invest more work time in the household. This has not always been the case. In the 1970s, for example, the average German adult spent 13 per cent longer hours in employment than the average American. But by the mid-1990s the German workload had fallen by 25 per cent and the Americans had lengthened their workload by 20 per cent, bringing the gap to a 43 per cent difference, with Americans working more. The Institute for the US Study of Labor suggested the difference came down to which was more attractive—going out to work (which they called 'market work') and purchasing many of your needs ('market provision') compared to housework and 'self-provision'.

- Slovenians and Hungarians work the longest and Belgian and Finnish the least. The variance is one hour a day when you take into account holidays and weekends. They sleep for longer on average in France—more than nine hours every 24 (although, this discrepancy could arise because of a different way of capturing the data, and coding 'rest' the same as 'sleep'). In all countries, women sleep for longer, except for Estonia where men and women sleep for equal lengths of time.

- People in Norway and Finland have more free time and time to socialize than people in France and Hungary. Free time ranges between four and a half and six hours a day across Europe: 40 per cent of that free time is spent watching TV. It's more than 50 per cent in Hungary, and falls below 40 per cent in Norway and Sweden.

Time and television

Television has transformed the way we use our time. In Britain, the average person watches three and a half hours of television every day, adding up to 25 hours a week. Figures from the US are similar, while across Europe the averages are lower, but mostly above two hours a day. In Australia, four out of every five minutes of free time are spent watching television, adding up to around two hours a day—a bit more for men, a bit less for women.

Television has been blamed for all sorts of social evils: violence in young adults, obesity in children, passive thinking and reduced socializing, to name a few. 'Nothing men and women have done so far during the millions of years of evolution has been as passive, as addictive in the ease with which it attracts attention and keeps hold of it ...' says Mihaly Csikszentmihalyi in *Finding Flow*.

Professor Michael Bittman believes people have turned TV time into family time. The mealtime used to be family time, now the symbol of family togetherness—not unlike the *Simpsons* sofa line-up—is watching TV together.

If you are not comfortable with the amount of time you or your family spends in front of the TV or you're not sure about whether your television set should be like an extra member of the family, there's always the 'off' button!

REGULAR AS CLOCKWORK

Humans seem remarkably regular when you look at large sections of the population and the time they rise, eat and so on: something you notice in small rural towns when you find yourself wanting lunch at 3 pm!

- In Europe, most people are awake by 7 am and at work by 10 am.
- In the UK, more than three-quarters of the population are up by 8 am.
- In the UK the main mealtimes are between 8.30 am and 9.30 am, at 1 pm and between 5 and 9 pm. Across Europe, most people eat their lunch between 12 and 1 pm.
- In Europe men's working days mostly end between 5 and 5.30 pm, but women's working days vary more than men's.
- By midnight in the UK 81 per cent of adults are asleep, while 12 per cent are awake or at leisure and 4 per cent are working or travelling.

VOX POP: Do you have enough time?

Right now we're fighting a huge development in our village, I'm graduating in environmental science and am responsible for compiling an annual report for a research organization. I coordinate a volunteer bush care group and we're having a planting festival next Saturday—a million things to organize. We have a garden infested with weeds and right now is the window of opportunity to spray it— yet we can't because of these other commitments. We're doing as much as we can but have to accept that we'll have to leave at least half of it undone. AL

If I had more unallocated time I could certainly get more things done. But wishing for that kind of extra time is somewhat of an endlessly expanding honey trap. I don't know at what point 'more time' would be 'enough time', so 24 hours in the day it will just have to be. I never feel that I have enough spare time to do what 'should' be done, so I live with compromise. In my case that means letting the housework slide and not getting as much exercise as I really should. So while I do feel harried at some point most days, in general I spend lots of time with my family, which is the most important time for me. FH

I frequently feel frustrated by the boundaries of time, yet I know that in some ways it's a pointless way to feel and I should feel thankful for the time I have and make the most of it. Family life means I am far from being a free agent and responsibilities bring with them interruptions, changes in plans and demands. There are so many little tasks to be done making up the great muddle of my life that it's easy for a day—or days—to go by and not feel I've achieved anything of note. The basics take a lot of time unless I focus very tightly, some days I don't do much else. And for instance, with a child home sick from school, that can be hard to do.

I'm often in a frustrated mood as far as creativity is concerned. My mind is full of ideas and possibilities, but I have little time to do anything about them. AH

The meaning of free time is different for everyone. I am sure some people think my life is a nightmare. From the time I wake up until the kids go to bed at 7.30 pm, I have pretty much no 'me' time. I have time to type the odd email, ring my sister and make cookies. I make the children have quiet time each day and relish the hour of child-free peace. Woe betide anyone that messes with nap time! I am happy with the way it is. I don't feel I am particularly lacking in time, but I am busy. While there are not enough hours in the day, I am resigned to the fact that things will never be perfect. SE

Sometimes I feel there are too many people in the world and they all want something from me. At my time of life (I'm retired) I do, however, feel I have enough spare time and I relish it. EWB

Rather than a daily feeling, I feel sometimes I don't have enough time over the longterm. There are so many ways of being drawn into being busy, even if you consciously resist it. Occasionally I make a decision to stay at home with my son all day with no plans, rather than rush out and do activities. It's quite a challenge. A lot of people distract themselves by filling up their days. It can be hard to say no to invitations. People don't take kindly to the explanation, 'I just don't want to make any plans'. ML

Time has always been an issue. I have been torn by conflicting demands between being a sole parent of two children, carer of my ageing mother, running a business, being an author, committing to an extended family and working at uniting a step-family as well as major surgeries and health problems. I haven't achieved what I've wanted to, but have gone part way there. I am a busy person, but recently I feel that I have more time. I'm entering a new stage of life. My mother, sadly, is in a nursing home, I have survived my last bout of cancer, my children are independent, my ex-husband is less of a disturbance and my family life is happy. SG

TAMING THE TIME TIGER

Time is the substance I am made of. Time is a river that sweeps me along, but I am the river; it is a tiger that rips me apart, but I am the tiger; it is a fire that consumes me, but I am the fire.

JORGE LUIS BORGES (1899–1986), *BORGES: SELECTED NON-FICTIONS*

Living under the shadow of the clock, we have, cleverly, we think, managed to shred our lives into ever-smaller units. The more we try to manage it and pack more into it, the more exasperated we feel about time. But as psychologist and author Thomas Moore says, we have a choice: 'Like anything else, time can be imagined in a wide variety of ways, and not all of them serve the humane life.'

We are all limited by the 24 hours in a day. We have our senses and our individuality and philosophy of life to make what we will of the time we have. Even in the harshest of environments people make choices about what they will do with their lives—even if they only have the smallest room to manoeuvre. We can't choose everything in our lives, some might argue we can't choose much—where we're born and into what social class and era, are beyond our control. But we do have some say in how we use our time. It's our scarcest resource and one we must treasure.

TAKING STOCK: THINKING ABOUT TIME

Understanding the complex ways you deal with time can be the first step to mastering it. Take a pencil and paper and jot down some ideas based on these questions, you may be surprised at what you uncover.

1. Attitude to time

The following statements are based on the Bortner Type A Rating Scale, which was devised in 1969. They represent opposite poles of a range of attitudes and behaviours associated with time. Which describes you most accurately in each statement?

(a) Are you never late ... or are you casual about appointments?
(b) Are you always rushed ... or do you never feel rushed, even under pressure?
(c) Are you impatient when waiting ... or can you wait patiently?
(d) Do you try to do many things at once and are you constantly thinking about what you are going to do next ... or do you take things one at a time?
(e) Are you a fast eater/walker/talker ... or are you slow?

2. Rushing around?

How fast is your life in the following areas? Are you setting a frantic pace, are you fast, calm, sluggish or just right?

(a) In your work life?
(b) In your home life?
(c) In your social life?
(d) In yours or your children's school lives?
(e) In the community where you live?
(f) In your life in general?

3. Values and time

When you think long and hard, what matters to you most? Family, keeping healthy, having a creative outlet, your career? Is this reflected in how you distribute your time?

4. Do you have enough time to do the things that you value as well as you'd like?

(a) Study and learning?

(b) Contributing to your community?

(c) Helping your children with school work?

(d) Looking after your house and garden?

(e) Creative pursuits such as art and music?

(f) Caring for the environment?

(g) Staying fit and healthy?

5. Are you investing your time wisely?

Think about where your time goes, what you'd like to do but feel you don't have any time for, and whether you are really giving the time to things they deserve. Are there areas of your life where you could trim time to let another interest blossom? For example, switching off the television a couple of nights a week might give you the extra time you need to paint, play an instrument or finish assignments on time. Giving up a part-time job you could do without might give you the focus you need to do well in your studies. Taking up meditation can increase both your sense of calm and your powers of concentration.

6. The time budget

(a) If you find the riddle of where your time goes an impossible one to fathom, try keeping a time diary. Have a think about how detailed you would like to make it. As a minimum you might want to be able to capture:

- Work. For example, time spent in a job or looking for a job (plus associated time such as travel)
- Food preparation
- Housework
- Car care
- Childcare
- Shopping
- Reading

- Exercising
- Sleeping
- Personal care
- Entertainment
- Education
- Interests and hobbies
- Television
- Administration and paperwork
- Volunteer work

Once you have your list, give each a numerical or alphabetical code to simplify the process of recording.

(b) There are a number of different ways you can record your activities. One is to write down what you are doing every 15 minutes. You may choose to record your main activity, or a number of simultaneous tasks.

Another option is to make a note every time you change activity. To get an accurate picture, record your activities during a weekday and then a day over the weekend (if your days differ along those lines). If you don't find it too burdensome, try recording several days, perhaps making sure they are different days of the week to ensure you get an accurate picture, as different days may involve different patterns.

(c) Analyze the pattern of your time. Where is your time going and is that a surprise? Are you happy with where your time is going?

The day, water, sun, moon, night—I do not have to purchase these things with money.

3. MONEY

HUMAN DESIRE KNOWS NO END. WE LAND ON THE MOON, WE WANT TO GET TO MARS. HAVING ACQUIRED A BICYCLE, WE WANT A CAR. AT FIRST WE WERE THRILLED WITH OUR TWO-BEDROOM HOUSE, NOW A THREE-BEDROOM HOUSE IS NOT ENOUGH, FOUR WOULD BE BETTER. ARE WE EVER SATISFIED?

THE LOVE OF SPENDING

Our needs are few but our wants are great. There are plenty of theories to explain the contemporary manifestations of our desire for material goods. That the current market economy awakens and creates desires is one. But scholars have written on the subject for centuries. The Jewish medieval philosopher, Moses Maimonides (1135–1204) said in *The Guide for the Perplexed*: 'The desire is without a limit, whilst things which are necessary are few in number and restricted within certain limits; but what is superfluous is without end.' In other words, if you have silver vessels, you might start thinking perhaps golden ones would be better, or even ones made with emeralds and rubies.

The resultant suffering that Maimonides describes—'constantly in trouble and pain'—does not sound unlike the more recently described scenario of the 'hedonic treadmill'. This term was coined by two researchers working in the 1970s, Philip Brickman and Donald Campbell. They proposed that man was condemned to seek new levels of stimulation to stay in the same spot as far as happiness is concerned. This is because we adapt to circumstances whether good or bad. The term, 'hedonic treadmill', is often referred to as an explanation for why as our income rises, we don't get correspondingly happier. Luxuries like elaborate heating, more expensive food and better clothes become the norm, where once we were happy to put on an old jumper and call out for a pizza. Economist and philosopher, Adam Smith (1723–1790), was talking about the same effect in *An Inquiry into the Nature and Causes of Wealth of Nations* when he said, 'even a creditable day labourer would be ashamed to appear in publick without a linen shirt.'

Thomas Wiseman took a slightly different take in *The Money Motive*. 'We want more than we are entitled to. We could, and sometimes do, resolve our problem by reducing our desires, as Zen Buddhism urges. But this is the hard way in our society, which does not readily allow us to want less.'

To this scenario, add all-time high debt. In the UK, of people earning less than £8730 in one year (2000), one-third had debts and these came in at an average of £3337, excluding mortgages. In the US in 2003, consumer debt, that is credit card and car loan debt (excluding mortgages), was approximately US$18,700 per household. Australia's capital territory, the ACT, announced in 2005 it was launching a pilot study to teach people how to recover from large personal and household debt. An estimated 13,000 Canberra residents were in extreme financial stress, according to the ABC. It quoted a politician commenting that because of higher income in the ACT, people were more prone to reckless spending.

Quite apart from the fact we can adapt and get used to both good and bad circumstances, a number of explanations have been put forward to explain our love affair with spending.

APPLES AND ORANGES

We can't help comparing ourselves, our homes, our holidays and our cars to what other people have. This in itself is not a problem if you stick to comparing apples with apples, but when it's apples with oranges, you can run into trouble. Juliet Schor, in *The Overspent American*, says that instead of comparing themselves with their neighbours whose earnings are in 'the same ballpark', Americans compare themselves with a totally different reference group. This might be a group with earnings between three and five times greater than their own and can include people like co-workers, colleagues or what she calls 'media friends'—TV families, celebrities and other public figures.

If our peer group is appropriate and supportive we feel okay. If it's out of sync, it does not help to know that we're rich compared to the average third-world resident. Comments Wiseman, writing in the '70s, 'One can, in practice, be quite wealthy, and feel poor. This is the common experience of those who live above their means. They are desperately hard up on US$20,000 a year, and it is not an act: they are. In the milieu in which they move, what they earn is not enough to pay for what they have come to regard as their needs.'

VISIBLE STATUS SYMBOLS

You could argue that having time could be seen as a symbol of having enough and of having 'made it': if you've got time, maybe you don't need to work like a slave. But traditionally that's not how people compare their status. In seeking status people lean towards earning money rather than enjoying leisure. What appears to be of most concern to people are commodities such as cars, clothing or holiday homes. And while the competition remains oriented towards this visible, or conspicuous, consumption, people are continually driven towards income rather than time off. This picture doesn't apply to everyone, however, with downshifters—people who seek to earn less to achieve a better work/life balance—among the exceptions.

Martin Seligman, psychologist and leader of the positive psychology movement, is among those who believe this is changing. He believes money is losing its power, heralding a change from a money economy to a satisfaction economy, in which time is the greater currency. He points to New York law firms that are spending more on retention than on recruitment since young associates are leaving for jobs that give them more satisfaction.

Keeping up with the Joneses

The phrase, 'keeping up with the Joneses' entered the English language soon after the cartoon strip of the same name was launched in 1913. Arthur R 'Pop' Momand was the creator of the strip that ran in American newspapers for 28 years. Now the phrase describes a desire to be seen to be as good as your neighbours—the original title referred to the McGinis family who were often striving not to be outdone by their next-door neighbours, the Jones family.

Momand wrote the strip while renting a cheap apartment in Manhattan, drawing on his experiences in the wealthy suburb of Cedarhurst. More recently, notes the online encyclopedia, Wikipedia, the phrase 'Keeping up with the Gateses' has appeared—referring to the mostly insatiable desire to live and spend like the richest people seen on television and in magazines.

RETAIL THERAPY: THE THRILL OF THE PURCHASE

As anyone who's watched children buy things for the first time, a purchase itself can be exciting, and the act of spending has great appeal, particularly to people who were deprived when growing up. One of the legacies of the Great Depression says Schor, 'was a long-lasting emphasis on finding security in the form of material success'. To others, spending can be thrilling, almost an aphrodisiac, with people flashing money much like spreading peacock feathers. Compulsive consumption is also seen as a coping mechanism where material goods compensate for lack of emotional warmth.

BECAUSE YOU CAN: SPENDING IS EASY

Personal loans are relatively easy to get, if you buy a car, the dealer may also be able to arrange finance, or debt, that will enable you to drive the car away and call it your own; it's not unusual to own more than one credit card and be offered a higher limit regularly. Modern banking and purchasing systems make it very easy to spend money, especially with hire purchase, store cards and internet shopping.

Hey big spender! What sort of buyer are you?

When it comes to shopping, does money burn in your pocket or are you reluctant to pull out your wallet? Are you any of the following?

- The avoider: resists situations of temptation by avoiding shopping malls or window shopping.
- The aware buyer: rarely tempted to buy what they don't need.
- The compulsive buyer: must have the latest gadget, reads the glossy ads as avidly as the news pages.
- Impulse buyer: flashes the credit card with little forethought, only to regret it later.
- The conscientious buyer: put themselves beyond the reach of marketers by making a firm decision to carefully control their money rather than feel controlled by it.

BECAUSE COMPANIES SPEND A LOT OF MONEY TO PERSUADE YOU TO SPEND A LOT OF MONEY

Otherwise known as advertising and marketing, this persuasion is a powerful force in modern society. Are advertising and marketing unavoidable evils of contemporary living, or just the facts of business life?

- Anxiety. In his book, *Ways of Seeing*, John Berger says: 'All publicity works upon anxiety. The sum of everything is money; to get money is to overcome anxiety. Alternatively the anxiety on which publicity plays is the fear that having nothing you will be nothing.'

- Brand identity. Spending is not a simple matter of buying possessions to display wealth and hence gain status, but a way of 'creating the self through association with certain products and brands'. Advertising feeds this process. We don't want to keep up with the Joneses, but trump them by differentiating ourselves from them, say Clive Hamilton and Richard Denniss, authors of *Affluenza*.

- A lubricant of the consumer society. Advertising, made easier by television, was the necessary element to make late 20th century society function smoothly says E Royle, author of *Modern Britain: a Social History 1750–1985*.

- Product placement. In a trend away from 'in your face' advertising, showing a commercial item in a film is a more subtle way of publicizing it—with an assumed stamp of approval too. *The Truman Show*, directed by Peter Weir, parodied this idea by depicting an entirely false world that was shown 24 hours a day and funded by product placement. The James Bond movie, *Die Another Day* was labelled as one giant advert, for hauling in a record-breaking US$70 million in product placement fees for vodka, cars and watches.

Personal bankruptcies

In 2003–2004, 21,000 Australians filed for personal bankruptcy. The most common age of the people who filed was between 22 and 44 years. Interestingly, households in the lowest income group (who earn less than AUS$20,000 a year) have the lowest debts and are much more likely than high-income households to have no debts.

Affluenza

Dissatisfied, stressed, overworked and up to our ears in debt, some people call this unease, 'affluenza', a term used as the title of a US television show, and since taken up by a number of authors and the media in general. The key definition is:

Af-flu-en-za (n). 1. The bloated, sluggish and unfulfilled feeling that results from efforts to keep up with the Joneses. 2. An epidemic of stress, overwork, waste and indebtedness caused by the dogged pursuit of the [American/Australian/other country's] dream. 3. An unsustainable addiction to economic growth.

SEEKING STATUS

'How am I doing?' is the niggling question that people who worry about status are asking themselves. As Alain de Botton points out in *Status Anxiety*, different societies have awarded status to different groups. Since 1776, he says, status has been increasingly associated with financial achievement. But in previous times, people with high status have been hunters or fighters, or those with ancient lineage, such as knights and priests. Botton believes that today's money-centred anxiety about status is due to, among other causes, recession, redundancy, promotions, retirement, conversations with industry colleagues, as well as increased media profiles of the prominent and successful.

Commenting on the drive by already very wealthy people to accumulate even more money he writes: 'Their endeavours are peculiar only if we insist on a strictly financial rationale behind wealth creation. As much as money, they seek the respect that stands to be derived from the process of gathering it.'

But, he claims, much like the content associated with the material gains on the hedonic treadmill; status is not something to be gained once and for all. It's a precarious trip and with rising wealth comes a greater anxiety about status. The peer group and how they are doing is, again, key: 'We will take ourselves to be fortunate only when we have as much as, or a little more than the people we grow up with, work alongside, have as friends and identify with in the public realm,' says de Botton. Or as JN said, facing the litmus test of the 25-year school reunion, 'I've only got six weeks to make a success of my life'.

For much of human history, low expectations and inequality has been standard. Peasants may have been miserable, but on the whole, as far as we know, they knew their place. Peasants' revolts notwithstanding, no-one aspired to live like a lord. Today, we have democracy, mass media and a whole new arena of aspirations, expectations and possibilities. In a capitalist world, the playing field might not be level, but it's flat enough for all to see the game. The winners earn respect as well as dollars; earning money and holding down a job is seen to require a degree of energy, intelligence and discipline. On the other hand is the populist mistrust of anyone who's made it 'too' good. Sudden, unexplained, or undeserved wealth arouses suspicion about how it was amassed: whether it was by honest means, or by quite what sacrifices.

Hetty Green (1834–1916)

Businesswoman Hetty Green was born into a family of American Quakers who owned a large whaling fleet. She read financial papers at the age of six, and by 13 was the family book-keeper. She inherited US$7.5 million on her father's death and invested much of this in civil bonds. Her suitor, Edward, had to renounce all rights to her money before their wedding in 1867. She quickly developed a winning investment strategy: conservative investments, substantial cash reserves and a cool head.

She is remembered as a miser who never turned on the heating or used hot water. She wore one old black dress, changed her undergarments only when they had worn out, did not wash her hands and travelled in an old carriage. Her son's leg was amputated after it turned gangrenous, a result of her not wanting to pay the hospital bills. In her old age she refused an operation for a hernia because it would cost US$150. She lent money, invested in the railroad and real estate and was known as the Witch of Wall Street. When she died aged 81, she was worth up to US$200 million.

VOX POP: Do you have enough money?

Yes, I do have enough money. But lack of funds still prevents me from doing what I dream of because I have big dreams. The trouble is I have to be responsible first and that doesn't leave much for the dreams. SG

More money would be great. I'd love to win the lottery, buy a home for us, buy my mum a better home and a trip, help my sister out and support some good causes. FH

More money is always useful. But I can get by on what I have. When I was a kid I wanted to travel the world, have adventures, meet people, find an interesting way to make a living—and learn a bit about myself in the process. I've found those things. Life would probably be pretty much the same whatever my income. PN

We have pretty much what we need, though we have fantasies about building an extension; 10 per cent more than we earn now would make a big difference. AL

I definitely don't have enough money! But then I am also trying to clear student debts and want to live somewhere nice and have fun. If I had more it would all still go, as I tend to spend how much I have. AE

On a world scale I'm incredibly rich. Compared to my friends, I have to juggle just like them—I think you do whatever your income is. Being self-employed can make it hard to save for the future and for tax. I guess a lot more money would mean less angst on the tax side of things. A bit more money could mean a bigger house, probably being able to go up a storey, which would have a big impact on the way we live. On the other hand, we could have gone for a bigger house in a cheaper suburb, but we chose the modest house in a fantastic area—which has an even greater impact on our lives. AH

We would all like more money. I buy the occasional Lotto ticket and routinely win nothing. These days I have money to do what I want, not necessarily what I need. I like having enough to buy what I want, do some recreational shopping, drink lots of cappuccinos. But at various times of my life I've had to go without. I remember once I didn't have a pair of shoes to wear to go and buy a pair of shoes. I resolved not to let that happen again. EB

I have enough money, but lack of funds still prevents me from doing some of the things I'd like—holidays in far away places are expensive and have to be saved for. CL

I feel lucky to have what I have compared to some. I never have to worry about where my next meal is coming from or a roof over my head, or whether I'll be warm enough in winter, and I can afford to buy good organic food. However, if we won a large amount of money I would buy an organic farm—and give away money to charities dear to our hearts. AS

Imelda Marcos (1929–)

Imelda Marcos spent her early years as a beauty queen and married politician Ferdinand Marcos in 1954 after an 11-day romance. She instituted a number of social welfare programmes during the Marcos regime, including houses for the poor and a 'Green Revolution' that increased rice production. After her husband died in exile in Hawaii in 1989, Imelda won a seat in the House of Representatives.

She was arrested for charges of corruption and extortion in 2001, over a sum of US$684 million that allegedly disappeared from the Filipino treasury during her husband's reign. However, it's her shoe collection she will be remembered for. 'I did not have three thousand pairs of shoes, I had one thousand and sixty,' she once defended herself. She also collected lingerie: 500 bras, including a bulletproof bra, and 200 girdles. The Marikina City Footwear Museum, which she opened in 2001, houses hundreds of her shoes that were found in the presidential palace when she and Ferdinand fled the Philippines in 1986.

DEPRIVED OR DISENCHANTED?

According to an Australian Newspoll survey, a large proportion of Australians believe they do not have enough money. Almost half of the top-earning households say they can't afford to buy everything they really need. At the same time, they believe that society places too much emphasis on money and material goods. Authors of *Affluenza*, Clive Hamilton and Richard Denniss, argue that this suggests disjunction—a separation or disconnection—between how people assess their own financial position (self-focused and income driven) and their recognition that society in general is too materialistic. We are a society surrounded by affluence they say, but we indulge in the illusion that we are deprived.

But the apparent contradiction is not necessarily hard to understand. Theoretically, as wealth rises, so too does the concept of what is 'necessary'. How you think about your personal situation can be different to how you view society. On the one hand is the small picture, how people manage to feed their own money monsters: mortgages, phone bills, children's piano lessons. On the other, is the ability to step back and see yourself as part of something bigger— something you may or may not be comfortable with.

WAR ON WASTE

The wealthier a household is, the more it can afford to waste and the more, according to research, it does waste. We throw away food, we buy clothes and shoes that do nothing but gather dust, CDs that we don't listen to, books we don't read, exercise bikes that we don't pedal after the first month, cosmetics get trashed and blenders and other kitchen appliances sit in a cupboard, unused.

In Australia, $1226 is spent on average per household every year (a total of $10.5 billion) on goods that are wasted. Most of that is on uneaten food, including fresh fruit and vegetables, takeaway food and home-cooked leftovers. For many households, the figure's much higher. Every year, one in seven households throw away food to the value of $2500.

WHERE DOES THE MONEY GO?

This is a game for all you Big Spenders out there. I will give you a sum of money and all you have to do is spend as much of it as you can. Aren't I generous?! Your aim is to get as many items as you can and be left with the least amount of change.

CHANNEL 4 ONLINE CHILDREN'S GAME, 2006

If you've ever seriously been mystified as to where your money goes and sat down and worked it out, you would find that it goes on providing the basics for survival: housing and food, plus, depending on your stage of life or the circumstances you find yourself in, more.

But it's the 'more' that makes all the difference and defines the expectations of life in a Western country. The more cash flowing through your day-to-day life, the less proportionately goes to the basics, and the more there is to spend on the 'better things in life', whether you consider them to be your children's soccer boots, opera tickets, a shiny car, a tent for holidays or education.

It's a pattern repeated worldwide: the poorer you are, the more of your income goes to the necessities like food, clothing and shelter. Spending on goods increases with wealth, services and discretionary items account for more of our expenditure as income rises.

Engel's Law states that the greater the level of affluence, the less proportion of income goes on food. It's not very difficult to work out why—there's only a certain amount of food a person can eat and as long as they're not having caviar and truffles at every meal, there's only so much you can spend on food.

Figures vary, but, for instance, according to the American Farm Bureau in the US, spending on food has fallen from almost 25 per cent of household income in 1930 to 10 per cent today. In Australia, on average, 17 per cent of household income goes on food and beverages.

Engel's Law, named by Ernst Engel (1821–1896), a German statistician, also applies to goods as a whole, such as food, clothing and shelter. The more affluent a person is, the less money goes on basic necessities and the more goes on luxury or discretionary items.

THE NEW ECONOMY

Survival in 21st century society is as much about communication as it is about adequate food, clothing and shelter. Even the discussion of poverty centres on 'participation'—in leisure pursuits, the workforce and society in general—rather than meeting basic physical needs.

The so-called 'new economy' reflects these changes. Mobile phones, internet connection fees, home computing costs and other communication and technological devices, have made growing inroads into our household budgets. The latest figures on spending in Australia, for example, show that compared to the previous five years, spending on mobile phone calls was up by 183 per cent. Dr Alistair Greig, senior lecturer in sociology at the Australian National University says we're paying more on services to compensate for increasing workloads. He says our time is becoming more complex, people have less time and more people in the family unit are going out to work. To compensate, they're buying technology and services as a coping mechanism.

In the US in 1947, according to the State of Indiana and Indiana University Partnership for Economic Development, less than one-third of consumer spending went on services, but by 2000 services represented over half (58 per cent) of a household budget. The price of non-durable goods has fallen relatively over the same period, so they account for 30 per cent of spending, compared to 56 per cent in 1947. The proportion of spending on durable goods has seen a shift. Spending on furniture and household equipment has fallen, but there has been a rise in spending on computers, boats and 'assets of affluence'. Spending on some services has doubled, including the barber, beautician, nail decorator, veterinarian and mini-storage facilities.

HOUSEHOLD EXPENDITURE

In Australia, according to the results of the 2003–04 Household Expenditure Survey, around half of the average household's budget goes on food, transport and housing. These figures represent the largest broad categories of expenditure. The remainder is made up of a range of categories including personal care, alcohol and household services and operation.

Food (including non-alcoholic beverages)—17 per cent

Transport—16 per cent

Housing—15 per cent

Recreation—13 per cent

In the US, according to the Consumer Expenditure Survey it goes on:
Housing—31 per cent
Transportation—19 per cent
Food—13 per cent
Insurance/Pension—10 per cent
Utilities—6 per cent
Apparel and services—5 per cent
Health care—5 per cent
Entertainment—5 per cent
Cash Contributions—3 per cent

Averages can hide a range of situations. In Australia, for example, in the highest income bracket, food accounts for 16 per cent of spending, whereas in the lowest, it's 20 per cent. Similarly, 23 per cent of spending is on housing in lowest income brackets, compared to only 11 per cent in the highest. High housing costs are associated with renting or with interest payments on large mortgages. There's also a disparity in spending on medical care and health expenses. It's two and a half times greater in high earning sectors than the lowest— although this could reflect an age difference.

Earning your bread

The Speenhamland allowance scale enacted in England in 1795 set a minimum wage for labourers according to the price of bread. When a gallon loaf cost one shilling, the labourer's wage was set at a minimum of three shillings. The scale allowed for £3.72 of bread per day for a single labourer, amounting to 4100 calories a day. A family man was not to earn less than 7 shillings 6 pence, equivalent to 2.33 pounds of bread per day for a family of four. These figures represent an absolute minimum wage for survival. An agricultural labourer in 1450 England could buy almost 23 pounds of bread a day; a handloom weaver in 1798 could buy nearly 28 pounds of bread a day, but by 1831, fortunes had changed with the power loom and his wage represented only 4.5 pounds of bread a day.

SAVING

When your outgo exceeds your income, your upkeep will be your downfall.

POPULAR SAYING

It's a simple calculation but one that is all too easy to get wrong. Spending 110 per cent of your income is common, instead of trimming spending to within earnings, as Mr Micawber of Charles Dickens' *David Copperfield* recommends: 'Annual income twenty pounds, annual expenditure nineteen nineteen and six, result happiness. Annual income twenty pounds, annual expenditure twenty pounds ought and six, result misery.'

While the iron-willed savers among us may be proud of their affairs, less-disciplined savers are often tripped up by one or more of the following money traps.

- Ignorance but not bliss. Not having a handle on how much you've really got coming in and what your outgoings are can make planning very hard and getting ahead impossible. Complexity can hide the bottom line: numerous credit cards, accounts and schemes make it harder for some people to organize and devise good savings habits

- Easy loans. 'Waiting is boring' said a recent high street banking campaign on its ATM screen, 'apply for a personal loan now'.

- Easy credit. Buy now, pay later schemes and credit cards with increasing limits have balances that can creep up. Paying off debt eats into your earnings, as well as costing you more in added interest if you don't pay off the balance. If you have a bad credit rating and want to borrow more, there are companies that offer to secure loans for you—usually at very high cost with sky-high interest.

- Flexible banking products. The line of credit mortgage facility, for instance, offers flexibility and control, but at the price of forgoing seeing the balance decrease as you would with a traditional mortgage that requires a monthly or weekly payment.

- Direct debits. These painless payments for anything from subscriptions, union fees, cable TV and phone bills, are convenient but their 'under the radar' nature means less awareness about their size and frequency.

● Culture change. With ideas like negative gearing and 'buy now, pay later', as well as the rise and rise of the credit card, carrying debt does not have the stigma it used to. People are relaxed about borrowing and owing money.

Oniomania

Is a little retail therapy good for you? Or is 'shop until you drop' a disorder worthy of therapy itself? In the US, an estimated 15 million people have little control over their spending habits. Apparently, people 'overshop' to boost their low self-esteem in the euphoric moment of the purchase. The American Psychiatric Association defines compulsive shopping or oniomania as an obsessive–compulsive disorder. The symptoms include:

● Buying more than you need: buying three new business suits, for example, when one would do, or setting out to buy one or two items and returning with shopping bags of irresistible items.

● Spending more than you can afford: the new dinner service looks great, for example, but you're not sure how you're going to pay the power bill.

● Building up debt to reach a crisis point: until you hit the red light, you're not concerned about credit card debt or loans as long as the cash keeps flowing. Sufferers may also have problems with gambling, drug dependency and eating disorders, such as anorexia.

If shopping habits spin out of control, some tactics to try to help yourself include:

● Don't carry credit cards without previous planning for a particular purchase.

● Only carry a limited amount of ready cash.

● Avoid window shopping.

● Turn a blind eye to advertising.

● Stop trying to justify purchases.

● Stay away from shopping areas except for necessities.

● Call a debtors' helpline if you need support or professional help.

VOX POP: Are you good at managing money and saving?

Pretty good, but it wasn't always this way. During the early part of our marriage, about 25 years ago, we got into debt and lived beyond our means to a certain extent. When we managed to pay this off (because I was invalided out of work due to rheumatoid arthritis and received a lump sum) we were determined never to get into debt again, despite the fact that it wasn't a large amount of money by today's standards. We then kept a closer eye on our spending and I wrote down all the household expenditure. With computers this has all become a lot easier. We like the feeling of being in control by knowing where every penny is and where it is spent—hopefully without becoming too obsessed by it! AS

Can't budget to save my life. We muddle through. We are not extravagant but the end of the month can be interesting. You just have to laugh. SE

I don't like ignoring money and letting problems build up into an overwhelming mess. Sometimes that happens, but so far things usually work out okay. KD

I'm pragmatic when it comes to working out the best options, but on the whole, I don't like dealing with money issues. I've recently confronted our family finances 'head-on', trying to get a system rolling that allows us—a totally freelance household—to have more of a handle on what we're earning, spending and what we can regard as 'extra' income to be spent more extravagantly. I'm fed up of living with a partner who's in almost constant panic about money. AH

I've become good at it. I could squeeze more, but I don't want to. I want financial security and am working towards it, but not at the cost of the kids not being able to go to swimming classes, or being able to buy them a milkshake, or a bicycle or whatever. FH

I am definitely phobic about money. I loathe the anxiety of working out my tax and the time it takes. I wish the government would just charge a flat tax to everyone—anything to make it easier. I've never enjoyed mathematics or been much good at it, and the boring exigencies of finance fall into the same bracket—morbid drudgery. PN

I have always managed whatever income I've had no matter how tiny. I always save. I learned thrift from my mother who is still, in retirement, a great model of how to prosper and enjoy yourself. She showed me how important it is, particularly for women, to be the master of their own income and to run their own financial affairs. My mother also combined her thrift with spending well—not only investing, but also enjoying regular, well-earned holidays. On the other hand, my father (they are long divorced) always tried to keep money in the bank, which is a flawed approach and does not bring contentment. LB

Guilty or saint?

The Australia Institute has come up with four categories of people according to their attitude to waste. Where do you fit?

- Guilty wasters. These account for around 14 per cent of the Australian population. They feel guilty when they buy things they don't use, but buy them—and waste them—nonetheless.
- Who cares? wasters. These people aren't bothered about spending money on goods and services they don't use. They account for 14 per cent of the population. They are particularly unconcerned about the effect of their spending habits on the environment.
- In denial wasters. In fact they waste a lot, but they say they hardly ever buy things that aren't used. They account for 15 per cent of the population.
- Saints. Accounting for around 40 per cent of the population, these Australians waste little and think carefully about how much they will use something before they buy it. If they do waste something, they feel guilty.

Money habits

Understanding how you deal with money can help you get on top of your financial affairs. Which of these money characters do you resemble?

- The champagne set. Visible wealth and status signs are popular—supported by big mortgages and deep debt if necessary—with new, fashionable car models and designer label clothing. Beware champagne tastes on a beer budget.

- Squirrels. They don't like debt and are cautious investors with little taste for risk. They'll shop around for the best prices and switch off light bulbs around the house. Security is a top concern. They worry about the future and like to have money on hand for emergencies.

- Penny wise, pound foolish. They make good day-to-day spending decisions, for example, at the supermarket or scrimping to make work lunches. But when it comes to more costly purchases they are 'pound foolish' and don't get ahead like they feel they should.

- Bargain hunters. They enjoy shopping, especially when on the trail of a good deal. But desires can be without regard to need and purchases can be fuelled by a reliance on retail therapy.

- Wheelers and dealers. Their reckless attitude to money means they're usually either rich or poor—but rarely in between. They love a deal and aren't put off by failure, often jumping into the next venture without hesitation.

- Illiterates. These people don't know what they earn or what they spend; they don't know how much debt they have or what it's costing them in interest and fees. They often experience financial difficulty, often because their outgoings exceed their income. They frequently have high credit card balances.

- Helpless me's. These people are in a similar situation to illiterates but feel helpless too. They see themselves as victims of their circumstances and dream of someone else coming along to help.

- Whizzes. They have it all under control. They know what they spend and earn and have a plan to minimize expenses. They have financial freedom from investment income and may borrow, but only to invest.

Nikola Tesla (1856–1943)

The Serbian born physicist and electrical engineer is remembered for discovering the rotating magnetic field, the basis of most alternating current machinery and the Tesla coil used in radio technology. He worked for Thomas Edison, redesigning direct current generators, but left when Edison refused to pay him a promised US$50,000 for successful redesign that brought the company increased profits.

Tesla worked on many ideas, and to feed himself and fund his inventions, worked as a labourer in New York for a time. He invented the 'polyphase alternating system', which could carry 1000 times more electricity. While Edison couldn't see any benefit from the alternating current, George Westinghouse could. He offered Tesla a million dollars for the patent rights. Tesla agreed and later agreed to forgo royalties. Among his friends were writers Robert Underwood Johnson and Mark Twain. 'He was quite impractical in financial matters and an eccentric, driven by compulsions and a progressive phobia', says the *Encyclopaedia Britannica*. He died broke and in debt.

On debt: it 'allows us to act on the desires created for us by the marketers, free of the banal constraint imposed by our incomes.
CLIVE HAMILTON AND RICHARD DENNISS, *AFFLUENZA*, 2005

The love of zeros

A money forger made a greedy mistake when producing counterfeit US dollar bills and smuggling them from South Korea to the US in 2006. The bills were expertly stained and aged, with authentic serial numbers and would have passed unnoticed but for one thing: the forger didn't realise there was no such thing as a one billion dollar bill. 'If he'd printed $100 bills of this quality, he might have got away with it,' a secret service agent told the *San Francisco Chronicle*. 'Greed is a terrible thing.'

Fighting over the purse strings

Even within well-off households, women in the past have not always had access to money and been forced to resort to devious strategies when extracting it from their husbands. In the US, Joseph Schulz was taken to the Buffalo police court in 1905 by his wife, who'd found a rat trap rather than small change in his left trouser pocket. The court upheld Mr Schulz's right to protect his small change from his wife.

EARMARKING MONEY

In economic theory, money is colourless, faceless and impersonal. A dollar is a dollar. But social researchers such as Viviana A Zelizer, author of *The Social Meaning of Money*, argues it is anything but. Money ain't money: it comes tainted with a history.

She refers to a study of prostitutes in Oslo in the 1980s, which found that the women carefully budgeted 'straight' money that came from welfare payments, health benefits or other legal income. They used this money to pay for rent and bills. Money earned from prostitution was quickly squandered on going out, buying drugs, alcohol and clothes.

Zelizer cites a Philadelphia gangster who'll give 25 cents from his mother to the church, because it is honest, hard-earned money, but he won't donate from his gang takings because it is not honest money and therefore couldn't be offered to God.

Sometimes money is separated into different currencies for different uses. In the small traditional community of Rossel Island in the Pacific, separate coins of low value were for women's use exclusively. Whereas in Yap, in the Caroline Islands, women's money consisted of mussel shells hanging on a string, while men's money was larger stones. (Stone money is still legal tender on the islands of Yap.) The Kenya Luo people in East Africa regard some money as 'bitter' if it comes from commodities such as land, gold, tobacco or the homestead rooster. The community believes that if this bitter money (for example, money from a sale of land) is spent on livestock, the animals will die.

Budgeting has always involved an element of earmarking to divide up the pie astutely. Tin-can accounting keeps money separate according to what it's for—whether for rent, entertainment or clothes. An article, by Alice Bradley in a 1923 edition of *Woman's Home Companion*, entitled 'Fifty Family Budgets' gives several examples of how families differentiated their money to cater for their needs:

- One father put aside every coin that bore the birth date of his child, for that child's education.
- A mother built a nest egg by saving the difference between the regular price and the bargain price of her purchases.
- Immigrants sent some of their earnings back home to their villages.
- One lady collected eight cans and pasted categories onto them—groceries, car fare, gas, laundry, rent, tithe, savings, miscellaneous.
- Other stashing strategies involved stockings under the mattress, envelopes, china pitchers and boxes under the floorboards.

Raimond Gaita (1946–)

In his book, *Romulus, My Father*, philosopher Raimond Gaita describes the poverty of his childhood in a tiny settlement called Frogmore, near Baringhup in Victoria, Australia. When Raimond was four years old, his family emigrated from Germany where he noted people often stayed indoors, 'for there was little food to buy and no fuel to burn'. The tiny farmhouse in Australia had no electricity or running water—'a single kerosene lamp served us well'.

Gaita writes: 'The winters were sharp … the water froze in the tap in the tank, so we filled basins the night before. In the morning, stripped to the waist, we broke the ice and washed ourselves.' Life at Frogmore was certainly spartan. But Gaita never felt that they were poor. His father's childhood was poorer still and this, says Gaita, 'informed my sense of poverty'.

'We were in need of nothing,' he writes. In fact, being adequately clothed and fed, and having each week almost limitless fruit, thanks to his father's weekly rides to town for trays of peaches and oranges, he felt rich in what he enjoyed.

NEEDS AND WANTS

The influential British economist, John Maynard Keynes, put needs into two classes: 'absolute' needs are defined as those we feel regardless of our peers; and 'relative' needs are ones which make us feel superior to our fellows.

Thinking about what are real 'needs'—whether material or spiritual—and what are merely 'wants' can be a powerful way of reviewing the role money has in your life, whether it's the time and stress involved in earning it, or just what that hard-earned 'life energy' is spent on.

Money is not a rational beast. As AN explains, 'I can feel many different things about money. I can negotiate a good price on a house, and be objective, yet, I'd like to think, fair. But when it comes to more personal dealings, I feel less easy about taking money from people—I'll give more than strictly necessary when buying books at the school book stall but when it's my turn to be stall holder, I'd rather give people a bargain.'

Gertrude Stein said, 'money is money and that is all there is to it'. It is a convenient means of exchange, which because of its infinite transformability, and its power to transform, is imbued with deep feelings about security, love, esteem, envy and greed. But it's only one value system and we operate in many more. So many things in life are priceless and are not measured in money. 'The best things in life are free,' says the proverb. And many, many worthwhile things in life simply have no value within the financial realm, but are nonetheless precious. Clearly, it's a mistake to put a money value on the very best in life: spontaneous music, friendship, love, companionship, beauty in nature and art, family, *joie de vivre* and curiosity. 'Give to Caesar what is Caesar's,' said Jesus. Money in the money realm—but don't forget the rest.

TAKING STOCK

THE HOUSEHOLD BUDGET

Are you mystified as to where your money goes? Prepare a household budget or keep a spending diary for a week and you'll quickly gain an insight into your spending habits.

The household budget is the basic financial planning tool at its simplest—a list of where all your money goes, from the mortgage and meals to underwear and union fees. Looking at annual spending on say, cable TV fees, supermarket bills or wine can be a sobering experience. Don't forget things like internet costs, direct debit payments, weekly payments, takeaway coffees, petrol and banking fees.

1. Money and values

(a) Do you spend money on what you value?

(b) Where do you put your dollar? Does it go mainly on the basics, such as housing? How much goes on transport? How much on what some might call status symbols, such as top-model cars?

(c) When you look at where your money goes, are you disturbed by the implicit value you give certain domains?

2. Needs and wants

List all the items that you spent money on in the past week or month.

(a) Now divide those items into 'needs' and 'wants'.

(b) Look at the list. Were there any conflicts or tricky areas where you weren't sure how much was spent?

(c) Are you happy with where your money goes?

The blossom is out in full now ... it looks like apple blossom but it's white and looking at it ... I see it is the whitest, frothiest, blossomest blossom that there ever could be ... Things are both more trivial than they ever were, and more important than they ever were, and the difference between the trivial and the important doesn't seem to matter. But the nowness of everything is absolutely wondrous.

DENNIS POTTER, *SEEING THE BLOSSOM*, 1994

4. HAPPINESS

HAPPINESS IS AN EMOTION AND A WAY OF LIFE. IT IS QUIET, SERENE CONTENTMENT AND EXHILARATING EXCITING JOY. IT CAN BE THE RESULT OF A WELL-ORDERED LIFE OR AN ATTITUDE OF LIGHT DETACHMENT. HAPPINESS ENCOMPASSES PLEASURE BUT DOES NOT EQUATE WITH IT. THE EXPRESSIONS OF HAPPINESS ARE INFINITE AND TAILORING IT TO ONE DEFINITION RISKS SQUEEZING OUT THE BLISS.

WHAT'S IN A SMILE?

The strongest signal of happiness in the moment is a smile. But can you tell the difference between a true smile and a fake one? You probably instinctively can, but do you know what makes the difference?

The 'Pan American' smile, named after the flight attendants in television ads for the now defunct airline, is one you make consciously when you want to appear polite. It's considered insincere at best, fake at worst and is sometimes called a 'professional smile' because it is an expected part of customer service. While the Pan American smile uses only the muscle called the zygomaticus major (the one that lifts the corners of the mouth) the Duchenne smile (named after the 19th century doctor who first described it) also uses the orbicularis oculi muscle around the eyes. The Duchenne smile is considered to be a more heartfelt smile (when you're smiling on the inside) and if you do it enough, you'll eventually develop telltale 'crow's feet' around your eyes.

Psychologists, Dacher Keltner and LeeAnne Harker, of the University of California in the US, studied the smiles of 141 students' photographs from a 1960 yearbook and published their findings in 2001. Of the 138 smilers, half were Duchenne (genuine) smilers. All were contacted again at the ages of 27, 43 and 52. Genuine smilers turned out to be more likely to be married, stay married and experience greater wellbeing.

Between the Pan American and the Duchenne smiles lie a myriad of subtle and rich differences, as Angus Trumble wrote in *New Statesman* on 6 September 2004: 'Mouths wide open: the smile was once full of meaning—exchanged between lovers, deployed strategically in conversation, even used to provoke and enrage. By contrast, the default-position broad grin that flourishes in our time seems little more than a forced expression of politeness.'

But whether they originate from pure politeness or sheer joy, smiles are an important social currency. And the consequences are unhappy when we're deprived of them. Take, for example, the facial paralysis which occurs as part of Moebius syndrome, a disorder which prevents people from being able to smile. People with Moebius syndrome react to humour and happiness with a deadpan expression and as a consequence, can have difficulty keeping even casual friends.

Guillaume Duchenne (1806–1875)

French neurologist Guillaume Duchenne is remembered for his mapping of the muscles of the body. The son of seafarers, he started his medical career treating fishermen and their families in Boulogne, France. He was prone to depression and almost gave up medicine after a particularly bad episode in his 20s. But he was revitalized by a growing interest in science, specifically how when electricity was applied to the skin it caused muscles to contract. His 1862 work, *The Mechanisms of Human Facial Expression* featured 'The Old Man', a photographic subject with almost total facial anaesthesia who was fitted with electrodes to stimulate different muscle groups in his face. Duchenne mapped 100 facial muscles and pointed out that while false smiles use only the muscles of the mouth, true ones that express the 'sweet emotions of the soul' activate also the orbicularis oculi muscles around the eyes: hence the expression, Duchenne smile.

THE HAPPY BRAIN

Brains show they are happy too. When people report feeling good, their brains show lots of neural activity in a part of the brain called the left prefrontal cortex. This area is generally more active in optimists than people with predominantly pessimistic styles of thinking. Some studies show that people prone to pathological crying or depression tend to have damage on the left side of the brain. Differences between people can be picked out very early in a person's life—even babies demonstrate a variety of levels of brain activities, suggesting we're born with a certain level of happiness.

The other physical change that occurs with a positive mood is in the brain's chemistry. When we experience pleasure, a number of chemicals are released into the brain, each affecting our moods in different ways.

- Dopamine. Released in the nucleus accumbens and the frontal cortex when food gives us pleasure or we enjoy sex. Dopamine floods neurons that are involved in memory and emotion, the more dopamine, the more neurons are activated and feelings of joy are reinforced.

- Endorphins. These are chemically similar to morphine, they produce a high and at the same time reduce feelings of pain. Physical exertion, such as long runs, cause endorphin release—hence the possibility of becoming addicted to 'runners' high'.
- Drugs. Artificial highs imitate the natural ones above—narcotics mimic opioids like endorphins; cocaine triggers the release of dopamine; alcohol and nicotine influence both the endorphin and dopamine circuits.
- Serotonin. Released in a number of brain centres when stimulated by the hypothalamus, serotonin makes you feel more alert, in a better mood and more sociable.

So, what is the happiness that these changes map? It's almost impossible to find a precise meaning for what we call 'happiness', whether we're looking for a definition in the fields of psychology, philosophy or poetry. So it's perhaps no surprise to find that it's hard to pinpoint a meaning from the spheres of biology and physiology. But clearly, there's an association between what we call happiness and the cluster of good moods, positive emotions and outward, engaging demeanour that these chemicals induce.

Time magazine quotes Richard Davidson (Professor of Psychology and Psychiatry at the University of Wisconsin in the US) defining happiness as a 'kind of placeholder for a constellation of positive emotional states'. Happiness is a state, he goes on, that people aren't motivated to change, 'associated with an active embracing of the world, but the precise characteristics and boundaries have really yet to be seriously characterized in scientific research'.

VOX POP: When you look back, what experiences are happy ones?

Every day brings happy moments, from the little stuff to the 'postcard' moments. Today it might be a funny or sweet thing one of my children does; past ones include looking out over Venice from a private terrace in an inexpensive hotel. FH

Mixtures of sensual and emotional experiences: cycling back from a happy, chatty night with friends in a sleeveless T-shirt, the cool wind on my arms; swimming with new prescription goggles in the rock pool and the joy of seeing fish; lying in bed peacefully with a relaxed, calm five-year-old son asleep next to me; walking home from primary school with friends; exotic experiences like horse riding near the pyramids of Egypt or riding in a taxi in Cairo with teenage friends; the timeless feeling of creating art, whether pottery or printmaking. Happy times are when the senses are filled, I'm content, tuned in and there are no excessive demands on me. AH

Getting married, having children, celebrating their achievements, revelling in their concern when I'm unwell. Being a widow can be happy too. No longer concerned with other people's wants or needs, your time is your own. EWB

The happiest day of my life would have to be when my son was born. Others include days travelling when it all felt easy and fantastic, or camping in some remote and beautiful place, such as near Lake Atlin in British Columbia or in the Himalayas. Being in those places brought a special kind of happiness that equates with 'being at one with the universe'. In fact, when I look back over the past 20 years or so, the happiest experiences are the simplest ones, and involve the beautiful wilderness places I've been lucky enough to visit. ML

Travel has always been a great enjoyment and still is. The experiences I have had and the people I have met while travelling have enriched my life. LN

My happiest experiences are holding my babies, celebrating my books, resting against my husband's shoulder and talking over cappuccino with my beloved father. SG

Happy experiences have been holidays, watching dolphins off the Welsh coast and riding on the back of a scooter in the Italian sunshine. CL

PHILOSOPHY AND HAPPINESS

Philosophers' concrete advice about how to be happy isn't any better (in fact, it's probably worse) than that of the average person. They generally don't know enough of the relevant facts, and they don't have the right temperament.

NICHOLAS WHITE, *A BRIEF HISTORY OF HAPPINESS*, 2006

Being happy is one thing. Thinking about it is entirely another. In *A Brief History of Happiness* Nicholas White, Professor of Philosophy at the University of California in the US, articulates the problems eloquently. The trouble with the idea of happiness can be summed up in one word: plurality. White says happiness makes a claim 'to take into account all considerations about what's desirable and worthwhile'. Or, put another way, happiness is 'the expression of a firm but undeniable hope for some kind of coherence of aims'.

DESIRE

Success is getting what you want. Happiness is wanting what you get.

DALE CARNEGIE (1888–1955)

At a childish level, happiness might seem to be quite simply having our desires fulfilled. Thomas Hobbes (1588–1679) defined his concept of 'felicity', as 'continual success in obtaining those things which a man from time to time desireth, that is to say, continual prospering ...'.

But even a child soon learns that short-term wants don't always lead to long-term needs. At the most basic level, desires bring conflict—if only because we can't do everything at once. And not all desires are equal—as Plato pointed out. We don't even want to claim all our desires: consider the smoker who simultaneously desires a cigarette and wants to give up smoking. In White's view, the concept of happiness is about figuring out how to take into consideration all our different aims and apply to those aims the same type of planning we apply to shorter periods with less aims, like an afternoon at home.

OUR GREATEST GOOD

But do we really *know* what we want—or know what we *really* want? Immanuel Kant (1724–1804) said it was impossible for anyone to frame 'a determinate concept of what it is that he really wants'. We can't say with certainty what will make us happy, because to be able to do that would require omniscience—an infinite knowledge and understanding. Even if we did have the certainty of knowing that one action could lead to a particular scenario, the possible scenarios in the way our lives roll out are so endlessly varied, that the real impossibility is being able to weigh up which circumstances make us the most happy.

A more Eastern perspective, as Howard Cutler puts it in *The Art of Happiness* (written in consultation with the Dalai Lama), is to see happiness as 'not to have what we want but rather to want and appreciate what we have'. Instead of keeping your eye on the horizon on the road to happiness, stop and look around.

HAPPINESS AS OUR GUIDE

If you want happiness for an hour, take a nap.
If you want happiness for a day, go fishing.
If you want happiness for a month, get married.
If you want happiness for a year, inherit a fortune.
If you want happiness for a lifetime, help someone else.

OLD CHINESE PROVERB

The answer to the question, 'What is it to be happy?' might give us a guide to managing our lives and how to deal with the various aims and conflicts we encounter in life. Philosophers as a group have not agreed on an answer. Alternatively, we can look to happiness as what philosophers call a 'regulative concept'—a concept that guides our conduct, even though we know it may not be true.

Immanuel Kant believed that to look for a system of knowledge that was coherent and complete was a rational thing to do—even if we have no guarantee that such a system exists. In the case of happiness, this could consist of searching for a viewpoint from which we can coordinate all our desires and aims.

But this leaves us with the problem of coordinating them. Plato plumps for harmonization. He believes in organizing our many desires in such a way as to prevent them conflicting. For him, a soul or psyche can be divided into parts that have different motivations and desires. For example, hunger ensures we obtain food for health, the spirit defends a person, while our reason directs and coordinates overall.

Aristotle on the other hand, saw no need for total harmony and did not believe that a better society is always a unified one. But he did value the organizing force of having a focus in life through which to filter and integrate aims. Nietzsche believed that incompatible aims were not necessarily a bad thing. He believed that the best life did not make a harmonious pattern, or to paraphrase, a little poison can be a beneficial thing.

YOUR OWN CONCEPT: ARISTOTLE VERSUS PLATO

In *A Brief History of Happiness* White says that the view that we don't need a general concept of happiness goes back to Aristotle. The idea, says White, 'cuts against the grain of tradition—which is chiefly a Platonic one'. The tradition is that we deal with our plurality of aims by referring to a general concept of happiness, or a grasp of what a satisfactory condition would be. Plato says to avoid conflict and frustration, we need to articulate a harmony of aims, and that harmony is happiness; without the guidance of harmony, we can't effectively improve our condition.

But Aristotle thought it was possible to come up with a satisfactory human condition without defining 'the good'. He criticized Plato for trying to use a general definition of 'the good' for guidance. Aristotle's notion of happiness takes our aims—actual ones that we have in the here and now and not ones that we 'should' have according to a general concept of happiness. Aristotle's description of happiness comes from his observation of humans and their aims. His view is that, simply, we have particular aims, some specific, some more general, and we use these as our starting point to build our own concept of happiness.

THINKING HEADS

With apologies to scholars, just some of the most influential thinkers on happiness are:

Plato (427–347 BC)

The 'completely good man' puts himself in order, is his own friend, and harmonizes ... the parts of himself like ... limiting notes in a musical chord.

A student of Socrates, Plato was the first philosopher to attempt to deal with happiness systematically. For him, happiness was harmony of aims. To Plato, inconsistent aims spell frustration and demonstrate that reason has not successfully governed the personality by organizing its desires. The happy man is unified and self-controlled, in contrast to the 'democratic' man who is fragmented and pulled this way and that by his desires. Plato recommends a neutral judge in deciding between aims—like the traditional concept of prudence.

Aristotle (384–322 BC)

Happiness lies in virtuous activity and perfect happiness lies in the best activity, which is contemplative. Contemplation is preferable to war or politics or any other practical career, because it allows leisure, and leisure is essential to happiness ... The supreme happiness is in the exercise of reason ...

The Greek philosopher, scientist and naturalist was a student in Plato's Academy, and later tutored Alexander the Great. Happiness is simply the human good, Aristotle believed, the result of an active life governed by reason. Such a good life is gratifying because it is meaningful, achievable and, with effort and discipline, sustainable.

But presumably, not everyone was destined to savour happiness—certainly not slaves, who he described as 'living tools'. The best in life was due only to the few, and husbands and fathers had superiority over wives and children.

Immanuel Kant (1724–1804)

Men cannot form any definite and certain concept of the sum of satisfaction of all inclinations that is called happiness.

The Prussian philosopher lectured on mathematics, physics, anthropology, geography and philosophy. Kant led a regimented existence, but was known for his brilliant conversation. Although he believed that you couldn't grasp the concept of happiness by reason, he was prepared to say it was a reward for virtue.

Virtue and happiness walk arm in arm with morality, which Kant described in *Critique of Practical Reason*, as 'the worth of a person and his worthiness to be happy'.

John Stuart Mill (1806–1873)

If by happiness be meant a continuity of highly pleasurable excitement, it is evident enough that this is impossible. A state of exalted pleasure lasts only moments, or in some cases, and with some intermissions, hours or days, and is the occasional brilliant flash of enjoyment, not its permanent and steady flame.

An enduring supporter of women's rights, Mill is associated with the concept of utilitarianism, in conjunction with other philosophers such as Jeremy Bentham and Henry Sidgwick. In a departure from religious and conventional traditions, utilitarianism proposes that happiness is the ultimate aim towards which all human actions are directed: actions are right in proportion to how much they promote happiness.

Bentham used the words happiness and pleasure synonymously, Mill also equates happiness with pleasure, and the absence of pain. Mill argues that higher pleasures—pleasures of the intellect, the feelings, the imagination and moral sentiments—not lower ones, will make us happy. He claims that a string of unrelated pleasures won't do, but that to experience true happiness we need an ordered whole—knowledge, artistic and cultural activity, and moral goodness.

A foundation of happiness comes with realistic expectations: 'not to expect more from life than it is capable of bestowing.' This phrase from his autobiography is often quoted: 'Ask yourself whether you are happy, and you cease to be so.' Its fuller context shows a realization for Mill that minds 'fixed on some other object' are more likely to find happiness—the happiness of others, the improvements of mankind, art or pursuit. 'Aiming thus at something else, they find happiness by the way.'

Friedrich Nietzsche (1844–1900)

That tension of the soul in unhappiness which cultivates its strength … its inventiveness and courage in enduring, persevering, interpreting, and exploiting suffering, and whatever has been granted to it of profundity, secret, mask, spirit, cunning, greatness—was it not granted to it through … the discipline of great suffering?

This German philosopher was sceptical about the entire idea of happiness and also of morality. He thought clashes of desire could be desirable when they were a source of exhilaration and grand impressive accomplishment—preventing life from settling into humdrum routine. It is only weak human beings that want the happiness that is like a tranquilliser and a rest, he believed. Waging war against oneself can result in 'magical, incomprehensible and unfathomable ones' who arise, 'predestined for victory and seduction'. He liked the idea of striving for something difficult, for extending yourself in challenge and even in frustration.

While he is often associated with nihilism, this is misplaced according to *The Oxford Companion to Philosophy*, which describes him as a 'profoundly positive thinker' and sums up his message thus: '… we must find a new and more viable way to the affirmation of life than those that have been based on fictions, illusions, impossible dreams, and leaps of faith.'

Charles Dickens (1812–1870)

For Dickens ... the pursuit of happiness embraced a fragile belief in the power of human desire to recreate the world while facing life's baffling inequities, accidents and defeats.

ANNETTE FEDERICO, 'DAVID COPPERFIELD AND THE PURSUIT OF
HAPPINESS' VICTORIAN STUDIES, 2003

The celebrated English novelist who wrote classics such as *Oliver Twist* and *Great Expectations* had an unsettled childhood and a restless adulthood. When his father was imprisoned for debt, the 12-year-old Dickens was put to work in Warren's blacking factory for several months, an experience he found humiliating and spoke little of. He fell in love in 1829 when he met Maria Beadnell. He was by then working as an office boy in a company of attorneys. But as her parents disapproved, the association ended after four difficult years. Dickens married Catherine Thompson Hogarth in 1836, but by 1858 (and 10 children later) they were separated. He loved to travel, was welcomed with enthusiasm in Boston and toured the US. He moved to and lived in Genoa, Italy, also visiting Vesuvius, Rome, Naples, Florence and Venice, before returning to England two years later in 1845.

Despite Dickens' literary success, happiness seemed to elude him. He called the novel, *David Copperfield*, his 'favourite child', but writing it brought back painful memories of a neglected childhood and his unrequited love for Maria. Victorian pursuit of happiness embraced a combination of hedonism (looking for individual happiness) and utilitarianism (a concern for the good society). Throughout *David Copperfield*, while the narrator, David, chases after his own happiness Dickens searches for its truth. Does it come accompanied by passionate friendship, or is it an attitude to be picked up and brushed off each day? Is one person's happiness the same as another's? David's regrets about his past reflect Dickens' fears that happiness is always just out of reach, but no less worth striving for.

Eudemonia: the good life

The word, eudemonia is derived from the Greek term meaning 'to have a happy, good, or true spirit', or, as the *Oxford Companion to Philosophy* defines it, 'having a good guardian spirit,' which sounds a little different, like philosophy's version of a guardian angel.

Aristotle called eudemonia 'the good life', while Augustine called it 'the happy life'. In ancient times, it summed up the view on happiness, which was seen to consist of having a desirable life in objective terms, whereas our more modern version centres on being happy as an individual or having a satisfactory life from a subjective point of view. Just what constitutes 'the good life' was up for grabs then, just as it is now. Aristotle believed external aspects, such as good fortune, were necessary to achieve eudemonia.

Expanding on the idea of happiness in *Rhetoric*, Aristotle lists characteristics of happiness: the prosperity combined with virtue; secure enjoyment of maximum pleasure; and good condition of body and property. The constituents of happiness, on the other hand, are good birth, friends, strength and stature, children and wealth.

Other schools of thought, such as the Stoics, and also Socrates, said virtue alone was sufficient to have a good life. More recently, Martin Seligman likens happiness, or 'gratification', to the accompanying grace of a well-executed dance. He says it's part and parcel of right action, and is had only by action with a noble purpose.

The most common error of men and women is that of looking for happiness somewhere outside of useful work. It has never yet been found when thus sought, and never will be while the world stands.

ROOM AT THE TOP: OR HOW TO REACH SUCCESS, HAPPINESS, FAME AND FORTUNE, A VICTORIAN SELF-HELP BOOK

RELIGION AND HAPPINESS

In religious and spiritual traditions, happiness is seen as a quality of life. 'It's a quality of life that is good, that feels good and that is deeply meaningful, usually something that is sacred,' said Rachael Kohn, radio presenter and doctor in philosophy of religious studies, speaking on Australia's Radio National programme *Life Matters* in 2005. These traditions differ over the details of a meaningful, happy life, but they all emphasize the importance of an internal life and one that is not materialistic.

THE BIBLE

In Western religions, a biblical version of primal happiness is often symbolized in the Garden of Eden where Adam and Eve lived in bliss and union with God. But after Genesis, happiness is something to be earned, and biblically speaking, that's by living a virtuous life. The Sermon on the Mount steers men away from the worldly, setting an inward path to God.

'Happiness is not about things—that really is the nub,' says Kohn. For instance, in Ecclesiastes, you see someone who has everything, a rich man surrounded by all of the accoutrements of wealth but over and over again he complains that his life is nothing—it is meaningless.

The Book of Proverbs describes a programme of how to live— judiciously, carefully, with wisdom, to be obedient. It describes how to live beautifully in the home and also how to treat one's parents and children. Happiness is a consequence of the good life. It is never pursued per se.

'Happiness' is not a word used much in the Bible, the theme is explored more in terms of qualities. In the tradition of the Old Testament, faithfulness is the ultimate expression of happiness, whether it is a person's faithfulness to the covenant or to the values laid down in the Bible.

In Christian mysticism the soul strives for unity with God and while some of the 'rewards' are in this life (that experience of unity sometimes called 'grace'), the main 'goal' is a promise of blessedness in the hereafter.

THE NEW TESTAMENT

Says Kohn, 'Christians believe what happened to Adam and Eve, their original sin is removed by the sacrificial death of Jesus Christ.' Because of that, only true happiness occurs when someone embraces faith in Jesus Christ. The Christian tradition is an invitation to imitate Christ's exemplary life of altruism.

A striking conflict is how Jesus is both a source of joy but also a terrible image of suffering. Explains Kohn: 'Over all religious traditions is the message that joy and happiness never exist without the dark side, without the sacrifice, without the tragedy against which it is measured.'

BUDDHISM

Buddhist concepts of happiness differ greatly to the Biblical tradition. In the Bible, causes of suffering are depicted as our enemies or things outside ourselves. But Buddha said suffering exists because we don't see the world properly, that everything is temporary because even our most wonderful moments of joy disappear. So he evolved a method of viewing the world by removing expectations, an attempt to prevent people to stop clinging to life.

As a Buddhist the essence of happiness can be found when you are freed from the expectation that you can have things forever and they will give you happiness. Once you give up this expectation you are then free to relate to the world more openly, with lightness and compassion. For Buddhists, the notion of joy is known as nirvana, or enlightenment.

The image of the laughing Buddha replaced the skeletal and emaciated Indian Buddha in Chinese tradition. A nation that loved food so much responded better to a round and happy-looking figure.

HINDUISM

Hinduism is a colourful, festive and life-affirming religious tradition with many celebrations. But the apex of Hindu happiness, or bliss, is the yogic tradition, expressed in the path of the religious virtuoso, the Holy Man, who renounces the world for communion with God. Such a way of life excludes that of a householder or any 'normal' expressions of family life. It's a mystical tradition, demonstrating an attempt to connect to the divine, and to be almost indistinguishable from Brahma or God. Ultimately it is meant to lead to a blissful state.

Kahlil Gibran (1883–1931)

Born in Lebanon, Kahlil Gibran arrived in the US with his parents at the age of 11 and lived with them in poverty in Boston. The flamboyant decadent portrait photographer, Fred Holland Day, noticed the slum boy's talent for sketching and took him under his wing, giving him Keats and Shelley to read, and having him model for him.

Gibran met Mary Haskell in 1905 and she soon became his patron, sending him to Paris for several years to study art. Although she declined his proposal to marriage, they remained friends and she was a great support, assisting his English as well as his art. While his works were, and still are, much loved and a source of comfort and inspiration to many (*The Prophet* has sold more than 11 million copies since its publication in 1923) the real facts of his life are less than inspiring. He kept Syrian and American friends apart, because while the former knew the truth about his impoverished background, he told new American friends he came from a wealthy and influential family. He became known as 'the prophet', and created a mystic poet persona full of exotic airs. He pleaded with his sister to send him bottles of arrack (an alcoholic spirit) during the Prohibition, had trouble forming deep relationships and most likely died of alcoholism.

Biographer, Robin Waterfield, believes Gibran's *The Prophet* was modelled on Nietzsche's book *Thus Spake Zarathustra*, but its wider popularity may be due to its optimism, and simple, direct language that goes to the heart. And while Gibran did not practise what he 'preached', he had the ability to channel his own unhappiness into a meaningful body of creative work.

ISLAM

For the medieval Muslim poets and philosophers, considered Sufis, happiness is a beautiful life. It involves complete submission to God and is expressed through beautiful acts, through charity and through love. A life that is wise and beautiful and aesthetic is also the happy life.

NEW AGE

'Take this course, buy this product, and you'll have a happier life,' is a dominant perception at the commercial end of spirituality, says Kohn. But on the other side of New Age theory, she says, is a desire to alleviate the pressures of materialism and the rat race of modern society. It incorporates attraction to beauty, simplicity and appreciation of nature. Kohn believes it attempts to consolidate a romanticism that exists in all traditions.

PSYCHOLOGY AND HAPPINESS

Psychologists offer another perspective on happiness that differs from the various traditional philosophical and religious suggestions. 'Most people know very well what [happiness] is,' says Professor Michael Argyle in *The Psychology of Happiness*. He summarizes happiness as being in a state of joy or other positive emotion, being satisfied with one's life, with the absence of depression, anxiety or other negative emotions.

Freud had a similarly common sense approach when he wrote in *Civilization and its Discontents*: 'What do they demand of life and wish to achieve in it? … They strive after happiness; they want to become happy and to remain so.'

Happiness comes in many different guises. It can be loud, noisy and excited or quiet, calm and sometimes solitary. Psychologists tend to divide happiness up into components, such as self-acceptance, positive relations with others, autonomy, environmental mastery, purpose in life, personal growth, life satisfaction or by weighing up positive effects on one side and depression and anxiety on the other. Argyle offers yet another division: 'Joy is the emotional side of happiness, in contrast to satisfaction—the cognitive side.' Others have used phrases such as 'feeling really alive' and 'peak experiences'. High-profile US clinical psychologist, Martin Seligman categorizes emotions according to their time frame.

- Past—satisfaction, contentment, fulfilment, pride and serenity.
- Present—joy, ecstasy, calm, zest, ebullience, pleasure and flow (for a definition of flow, read below).
- Future—optimism, faith, hope and trust.

FLOW

Caught in the treadmill of social controls, [a thoroughly socialized] person keeps reaching for a prize that always dissolves in his hands.

MIHALY CSIKSZENTMIHALYI,

FLOW: THE PSYCHOLOGY OF OPTIMAL EXPERIENCE, 1991

'If one wants to improve the quality of everyday life, happiness may be the wrong place to start,' says Mihaly Csikszentmihalyi, professor of psychology and education at the University of Chicago. Feeling active and strong is part of feeling happy. Using the mind to its fullest, developing goals that give meaning to life, dreaming dreams and taking risks are also part of Csikszentmihalyi's 'happiness'. Managing your goals is an important part of achieving excellence in everyday life, and the best way is to understand the roots of your motivation and the biases in your desires. And the aim: to create order in your consciousness without costing too much disorder in the social or material world around you.

When what we feel, what we wish and what we think are in harmony, we're almost certainly in what he calls a 'flow' state—that effortless, all-absorbing concentration a musician or an athlete might report when 'in the zone'. In theory, any experience can be a 'flow' one. The characteristics of flow are defined below.

- They allow the person to focus on goals that are clear and compatible, such as performing surgery or weaving a rug.
- They provide immediate feedback; for example, as you climb the cliff face you know how you're doing or when reciting a musical piece you can tell if all the notes are right.

- A person's skills are fully involved in overcoming the challenge— if the challenge is too great, you are frustrated, if it's too easy, it's relaxing and ultimately boring.
- Quite often the sense of time disappears, and we lose our self-consciousness.

These situations provide flashes of intense living in which the attention is ordered and we are totally focused. Csikszentmihalyi says this full involvement is what makes for excellence in life rather than happiness. When we're in flow it's not happiness we feel, but afterwards, when we look back we feel grateful for the experience, and happy in retrospect.

This happiness is an important part of personal growth and what Csikszentmihalyi calls 'complexity'. For him, complexity is the twofold result of a flow experience. On the one hand, overcoming a challenge leaves a person feeling more capable, more skilled, less predictable and more of a unique individual. He calls this first process 'differentiation'. At the same time we experience 'integration'—focusing and bringing together many aspects of a person in the deep concentration that accompanies a flow experience: one feels more 'together'.

Flow activities might be exhilarating ones like rock climbing or surfing, but some people find flow in ostensibly mundane tasks such as factory production lines. People often report flow during their favourite activities, whether gardening or listening to music. It's also reported quite frequently during driving and at work (very little is reported in passive leisure activities such as watching television). But it's not so much about what the activity is that matters; it's what you bring to it.

POSITIVE PSYCHOLOGY

Seligman, is a pioneer of a movement he calls 'positive psychology'— a psychology of rising to the occasion. It sits in contrast to the psychology of mental illness and fixing problems, which has been the realm of most psychology to date. Or, put another way, until recently most psychology has been concerned with going from 'minus five to minus three' on the happiness scale, while positive psychology is trying to help people get from plus two to plus seven.

The movement seeks to overthrow the idea of original sin and the parallel idea that happiness is not a natural state. Freud 'dragged this doctrine into the 20th century defining all civilization ... as just an elaborate defense against basic conflicts over infantile sexuality and aggression,' says Seligman in *Authentic Happiness*. Seligman believes we have evolved both good and bad traits and that real, 'authentic' happiness comes from identifying and cultivating your most fundamental strengths and using them every day in work, love, play and parenting.

'Positive psychology takes seriously the bright hope that if you find yourself stuck in the parking lot of life, with few and only ephemeral pleasures, with minimal gratifications, and without meaning, there is a road out. This road takes you through the countryside of pleasure and gratification, up into the high country of strength and virtue, and finally to the peaks of lasting fulfilment: meaning and purpose.'

Exercising strength and virtue of character is central to the themes in positive psychology. Seligman's approach has three 'pillars': the study of positive emotion; the study of positive traits such as strengths and virtues, and abilities such as intelligence and athleticism; and finally the study of positive institutions (democracy, strong families and free inquiry).

Seligman distinguishes between what he calls the pleasures and the gratifications of life. While the word 'gratification' has more often been used to refer to immediate reward, such as 'instant gratification', Seligman defines it differently. He claims that pleasures are about senses and emotions, while 'gratifications' draw on personal strengths and virtues. He believes that seeking gratification rather than pleasure offers a deeper experience.

Pleasures don't build anything for the future in themselves, but when our minds are engaged we're building psychological capital for the future. Gratifications produce flow, they require skill and effort and present the possibility of failing. The wellbeing (or happiness) that arises from gratifications is different from happiness for the moment and pleasures with raw feelings and immediate sensory delights. These are momentary and fade once the external stimulus disappears, whereas gratifications bring a more 'authentic' happiness that is longer lasting and has a greater knock-on effect.

Seligman proposes enhancing gratifications through developing what he calls signature strengths and virtues (from curiosity and honesty to forgiveness and zest). The good life, he says, that is, a happy one, involves using your signature strengths in daily life. A meaningful life, in addition, uses these strengths to further knowledge, power or goodness.

Short cuts to happiness, such as chocolate, beer, shopping and television, will only give you short-lived happiness. For a deeper, longer lasting feeling about your life, you need to flex your strengths. Seligman chose 24 strengths, which are valued in their own right across almost all cultures and are what he calls 'malleable' or learnable. The core virtues outlined below form the basis of the 24 strengths.

In praise of kindness

Call it philanthropy, call it kindness, but doing a good deed for the day does you a favour as well as your recipient. So believes Seligman, who tested the theory on his students. He writes in *Authentic Happiness*: 'When our philanthropic acts were spontaneous and called upon personal strengths, the whole day went better.'

When you engage in a kind act, you tend to be totally absorbed. Time stops and you lose self-consciousness. Afterwards you feel better about yourself too. Next time you're down or grumpy, try a dose of kindness.

The idea is echoed in Buddhism, where 'metta', usually translated as 'loving kindness', is encouraged. While it encompasses a wide interpretation of desiring the welfare of others, it's also about cultivating kindness in daily life—in the way you interact with colleagues at work, or help about the home.

Six core virtues

Confucius, Aristotle, Aquinas, the Bushido samurai code and the
Bhagavad-Gita share the following core virtues, says Martin Seligman,
and serve as a guide for the positive psychology movement.

These core virtues form the basis of Seligman's strengths and
virtues, representing clusters of related qualities.

- Wisdom and knowledge. These cover strengths such as curiosity,
  love of learning, judgment, originality and social intelligence
- Courage
- Love and humanity, which includes kindness and generosity and
  the capacity to be loved as well as to love others
- Justice
- Temperance
- Spirituality and transcendence.

LUCK

*If it wasn't for bad luck
I wouldn't have any luck at all.*

TRADITIONAL BLUES REFRAIN

What is the secret to a happy and meaningful life? Could it be luck,
asks Dr Richard Wiseman, a research psychologist at the University of
Hertfordshire in the UK, who started out as a magician, and one of the
youngest members of The Magic Circle, a society for magicians.

'Lucky people meet their perfect partners, achieve lifelong
ambitions, find fulfilling careers and live happy and meaningful lives,'
purports Wiseman. But they are not born lucky, he says. They live their
lives to four basic principles, which he explains and explores in his book,
The Luck Factor. Many of Wiseman's examples seem trivial, such as the
luck of winning raffles or competitions, and many concern money, but
the role of luck, and the question over its existence is intriguing.

'Luck is the missing ingredient in a good deal of philosophy,'
claims Robert C Solomon in his book, *The Joy of Philosophy*. Chance

and probability get a mention in science, but not luck, he says, even though we appeal to it frequently: crossing fingers for luck in the lottery, thanking our lucky stars in a near-miss car accident. 'But there is something hollow in our appeal, as if we do not really believe in it, in luck,' says Solomon. We treat good and bad luck very differently, he observes. When we're lucky, we feel we deserved it, but when we're unlucky, it's definitely not deserved.

For Kant, goodwill would manifest itself in unfortunate times, not 'luck', whereas Aristotle counted 'good fortune' as essential for a happy life. And the word 'happiness' echoes its earlier meaning of good luck or chance: happen chance. But to see a life in terms of luck is to see it as meaningful, says Solomon, in contrast to chance, which appears meaningless.

Wiseman's luck, meaningful or not, is, in the end, self-made and can be improved on, he believes. His principles are based on interviews and survey results, where he found that most people say they are consistently 'lucky' or 'unlucky'. The main principles for improving your luck, according to Wiseman, are outlined below.

- Maximize chance opportunities. Being in the right place at the right time has more to do with being in the right frame of mind than anything else. For example, people who win lots of competitions enter even more.

Build your lucky network

Increasing your chances of 'lucky' encounters and events, means making contact with people. Wiseman recommends:

- not trying to chat to people who make you feel uncomfortable.
- capitalizing on naturally occurring events to avoid seeming contrived.
- asking for information you need, preferably in a way that avoids a 'yes' or 'no' answer.
- playing the contact game: each week make contact with someone you haven't been in touch with for a while, whether it's someone from your old job or an old friend who's moved.

- Build and maintain a network. 'Lucky' people tend to be extroverted, and build what Wiseman calls a 'network of luck'. They have a higher likelihood of a chance encounter, because they meet a large number of people and they act as a social magnet, keeping in touch with lots of people. Meeting and talking with people increases the chance that someone you meet will have a positive effect on your life. Lucky people report talking to people in supermarket queues, on trains, they smile more and according to Wiseman's observations, show open body language more than closed (crossing legs and arms).
- A relaxed attitude to life. Lucky people are less neurotic, more relaxed and more likely to notice an opportunity that arises naturally. 'By not trying too hard to look, they end up seeing far more,' Wiseman observes.
- Lucky people also see the bright side of bad luck, says Wiseman. They don't dwell on ill fortune. When lucky people hit bad times, they take constructive steps not to let it happen again.

THE EXPERIENCE OF HAPPINESS

In the end, our experiences tell us what happiness is. Very often what makes most people happy are the same ideas that have engaged philosophers over the centuries: being part of a family, simple pleasures, harmonious times. The things that make us happy echo our wonder with the world, as this account from PN shows:

When I think of happy experiences, I think of being with Mum and Dad when the world was young. Roaming the hills of New Zealand in the area where we lived. Dad telling me amazing bedtime stories that he made up. Family Christmases that came and went, each looked forward to and enjoyed, waiting for the uncles and aunties and cousins who would come to visit. The school holidays seemed to go on forever. Watching the sun rise over the hills as a little boy and listening to the steam trains thunder past in the night. Singing with my grandad while my father played the piano and inventing adventure tales with my brother when we both lay in our beds at night.

Flatting with friends as a young man. Writing poetry. First loves and second loves. Falling in love and realizing, occasionally, that the person you loved, loved you too. Watching a huge thunderstorm in Sydney and running through it for kilometres, getting soaked and enjoying it. Exploring forests and jungles and seeing fireflies at night in South America. Travelling to new continents on ships.

My wedding in an ancient English church, as the bells pealed and the frost sparkled. Eating a punnet of strawberries with my three-year-old son as we sat on some steps and watched the rain fall in great curtains and splash our feet. Walking by myself through quiet lanes in Devon and being astonished by giant rainbows that looked as though they had been made just for me. Whistling.

The ideas explored in philosophy, religion and psychology cover lots of territory, but there's common ground too. It's up to us how much importance we place in our concept of happiness. But if we wish to embrace a rich idea of happiness, it seems we need to look most closely at the quality of our lives in a deep and broad sense: how we treat and relate to others, how we engage with our world, how we frame and mould our desires. And with the comfort of a wide definition of happiness, we can, as some philosophers and psychologists suggest, take an anxious eye off it and get on with the business of life.

TAKING STOCK:
THE QUALITY OF HAPPINESS

Happiness comes in many shades, which ones do you value?

- Peace
- Tranquillity
- Calm
- Serenity
- Harmony
- Challenge
- Exhilaration
- Excitement

- Reaching goals
- Satisfaction
- Contentment
- Fulfilment
- Pride
- Joy
- Ecstasy
- Zest

- Ebullience
- Pleasure
- Optimism
- Faith
- Hope
- Trust

THE GOOD LIFE

Taking a look at the various interpretations of eudemonia, or 'the good life' on page 100, what does it mean for you? Is it the desirable life or the virtuous one? Do you take your cues from philosophy, religion or popular culture?

A large income is the best recipe for happiness I ever heard of. It certainly may secure all the myrtle and turkey part of it.

JANE AUSTEN, *MANSFIELD PARK*, 1814

5. MONEY AND HAPPINESS

IT IS A MYTH TO SAY THAT MONEY CAN'T BUY YOU HAPPINESS, BECAUSE TO A DEGREE IT CAN. BUT ITS INFLUENCE WAXES AND WANES ACCORDING TO CIRCUMSTANCES— PARTICULARLY FINANCIAL ONES. AND AS HAPPINESS HAS SO MANY FACES, MONEY ALONE CANNOT BEGIN TO SATISFY ALL ITS TASTES.

THE PARADOX OF MONEY

An apparent paradox surrounding money and happiness is summed up in these words: 'Most people want more income and strive for it. Yet as Western societies have got richer, their people have become no happier.' These words come from *Happiness: Lessons from a New Science*, by Richard Layard, one of Britain's best known economists.

Our lives 'should' be more comfortable, says Layard, given that average incomes have more than doubled in the past 50 years, even allowing for inflation, and we have more food, more clothes, more cars, bigger houses and more central heating.

Layard refers to Jeremy Bentham's Greatest Happiness Principle— that the best society is the one where citizens are happiest; the best public policy is the one that produces most happiness; and the best private action is where it produces the most happiness in the people it affects. Everyone's happiness counts and what matters in the end is how people feel. But such a principle has been hard to apply, says Layard, because so little has been known about the nature and cause of happiness. Into the vacuum left by religious participation has entered 'the non-philosophy of rampant individualism'. The dominant thinking of Western governments is, says Layard, that national income is a 'proxy' for national happiness, based on elementary economics that reasons that 'perfect markets' will lead to the greatest possible happiness. In Britain, 'happiness has been static since 1975', he claims.

So what are the facts about money and happiness?

● Poverty. When you're in poverty, money makes a difference. When you are in need of basics, such as shelter, food, clothing and basic education, money can do a lot and it does make people happier. How far this relationship stretches depends on interpretation. The exact picture depends on which figures you look at and whether you compare rich countries with poor countries or rich and poor people within a country. For example, there's a weak correlation between a country's income and self-reported happiness. But this may be due to factors other than money, such as political freedom and democracy.

● The middle ground. More money makes little difference to happiness after a certain point. Extra money makes less difference if you are already wealthy, and the wealthier a person is, the less the difference extra money makes. Interestingly, many people classed as 'wealthy' in this context would not use that term to describe themselves. According to a 1993 report in the US, there was little difference in happiness between those earning around US$20,000 and those bringing in around US$60,000 a year.

This characteristic is clumsily referred to as 'the declining marginal utility of money'—the more you have, the less difference getting even more makes. This principle applies in areas outside finance, too. For example, when you are very thirsty it is very satisfying to drink a glass of water, but you wouldn't get as much satisfaction from a second glass, and less again from a third glass.

A 1981–1984 study by Ed Diener, Alumni Professor of Psychology at the University of Illinois in the US found a strong correlation between money and happiness in the poor, levelling off for the more well-off, and a rise again in happiness for the very rich. Until great wealth, there was little increase in happiness beyond US$15,000.

While dire poverty is more likely to make someone unhappy, even then, there's more to life. As Diener says: 'It is easy to forget that poor people can have many strengths in their lives. For example, in Robert Biswas–Diener's study of the slums of Calcutta, even the homeless (who are extraordinarily poor by Western standards) have friends, often have a family back in the countryside, gain positive feelings from their religion, have decent self-esteem, and so forth.'

- The very rich. Diener's paper showed a rise in happiness for the 'very rich'. Other studies have confirmed those findings. One looked at 49 people who earnt more than US$10 million. On average, the group reported being happy 77 per cent of the time, compared to 62 per cent in a control group. Separate studies by Andrew Oswald, Professor of Economics from Warwick University in the UK, found US$1.5 million to be a magic figure that bumped happiness levels from 'fed up' to 'very happy'.

- Affluenza. More money makes you less happy. This is the thrust of the arguments centred on the idea of 'affluenza', a term used to describe the consumerist, desire-centric unfulfilled feeling that people experience from trying to keep up with the Joneses. Wanting more money can be a recipe for unhappiness, ditto materialistic values.

VOX POP: Does money make you happy?

I don't think money makes you happy, but nevertheless it's important to have enough for your immediate needs, for a bit of enjoyment besides and for something to look forward to. Drudgery, toil and poverty are not fun—the grind can shrink your horizons and squash your life. But those who make huge amounts of money often become so obsessed with the lifestyle and power it involves, they finish up being driven more by money and power than by seeking true happiness or satisfaction. When I think back, the best times in my life relate more to what I was doing and who I was with rather than how much money I had. Money comes and money goes, relationships and love are infinitely more important. PN

Happiness has got almost nothing to do with how much money you have or how little. AL

Banal but true: money may not make you happy, but the lack of money certainly makes you unhappy. Money to get decent housing and food and pay the bills, I mean. Not money to buy a plasma screen. Money does not take away from what matters, but it can protect what matters to you—being able to feed and house your kids and buy them a Christmas present, for example. FH

Money can help, but earning it (just for the sake of having money by doing something you hate) can take you further away from what really matters. AS

Money certainly helps, but thinking about money does not. It also depends how the money comes your way: pursuing it for its own sake doesn't seem the way to happiness, but money itself does not necessarily prevent you from being happy. AH

Money ... don't need buckets of it, just some more. It would be nice if it weren't an issue—just so that we didn't have to think about it so much. SE

Not on its own, but I think it can contribute to happiness by allowing us to live more comfortably, to be well nourished and able to have outlets such as movies and travel that broaden our experiences. ML

Money is an aid to happiness, but happiness is more than how much money you have. Much joy can be gained from simple, free things in life. CL

Money doesn't make me necessarily happy, but it makes it easier if I have enough to be able to go out and do something. AE

AVERAGES OR INDIVIDUALS

The money happiness story is different depending on whether you look at averages over time, or if you look at a group of people in one snapshot in time. The situation seems to be that when people get richer compared to others, they feel happier. In any one society, rich people are happier than poor. But when whole societies become wealthier, the overall reported happiness does not increase.

COUNTRY TO COUNTRY

The relationship between money and happiness in individual countries is not so clear-cut. Some research points at money making you happy. In Belgium, a fall in national prosperity was matched with a fall in reported happiness, according to research in 1986. Similar parallels were drawn from falls in prosperity in Japan, Brazil and Ireland.

Falls in income may be a different matter, since they cause frustration. But in general, where there have been substantial increases of income in a country, the same increases have not shown increasing measures of happiness. Japan is often cited as an example. Before 1960, it was a very poor country. In the next two decades its per capita income expanded manyfold, some say five times, putting it amongst the richest in the industrialized world. But happiness levels were no higher in 1987 than 1960. It seems that owning washing machines, cars and cameras does not register on the happiness scale.

SATISFACTION PARADOX

In some cases, people are poor but happy and seem sincerely satisfied with their lot. The so-called 'satisfaction paradox' has been explained by long periods of adaptation and what researchers call 'learned helplessness', a state of apathy and submission. They've become used to their situation, don't expect it to change and don't seem to be too worried about it either way.

WEALTH OR INCOME?

Many studies have focused on income and its link to happiness rather than wealth, or 'net worth'—the sum total of all your assets. But clearly wealth too has the potential to affect how happy you feel. It provides a cushion for bad times and security for the future.

Bruce Headey and Mark Wooden of the Melbourne Institute of Applied Economic and Social Research at the University of Melbourne in Australia, say wealth provides economic security and is at least as important as income to both wellbeing and ill-being. When you stop and think about it, it certainly seems to make sense. A small income against a solid financial background is different to a similar income against a shaky one.

Their paper, 'The Effects of Wealth and Income on Subjective Wellbeing and Ill-Being', drew on data from the 2002 survey, 'Household, Income and Labour Dynamics in Australia'. The authors define wellbeing as comprising life satisfaction and positive feelings such as joy and vitality; ill-being comprises anxiety, depression and other negative feelings. People can experience both simultaneously, they argue.

The sample consisted of 7934 observations drawn from the data of people of prime working age, between the ages of 25 and 59. For each person they constructed a financial stress measure derived from questions about difficulty in paying bills, dealing with financial emergencies (for example, how easily you could raise $2000 in an emergency), needing to pawn possessions, going without meals or heating, and needing help from friends, family or welfare organizations.

One of the reasons research has tended to focus on income rather than wealth is that wealth is harder to measure. People are less willing

King Midas

Midas, according to Greek mythology, was king of Phrygia in Asia Minor and renowned for his wealth—and his skills as a rose gardener. Dionysus, the god of vegetation, wine and ecstasy, thanked Midas for his kindness to Silenus, his tutor. When he offered Midas whatever he wished, the King asked that everything he touched be turned to gold. His wish was granted, and at first Midas was overjoyed. But when his food and drink were also turned to gold on touching his lips, he was horrified. Dionysus took pity and told Midas how to wash away the golden touch by bathing in the River Pactolus. The King, now hating wealth, moved to the country and became a worshipper of Pan, the god of the fields.

to answer all questions in surveys, they under-report their wealth and as the top few per cent of a society owns a vastly disproportionate amount of wealth, these are under-represented in samples. The research used in this paper covered assets such as housing, businesses, investments, vehicles and collectibles, superannuation and bank accounts on the one hand and credit card and other personal debt on the other. Income covered that from labour (wages and salaries); asset income and other income, such as private superannuation.

Researchers compiled several indicators of subjective wellbeing and ill-being, including overall life satisfaction and financial satisfaction. The results showed that women report higher levels of life satisfaction than men. They also score higher in negative emotions, which suggests they are both more up and down than men.

People who moved 'up' the economic ladder, from the lower quarter to the second highest quarter, would gain two percentiles in life satisfaction and nearly nine percentiles on the financial satisfaction scale, and these changes were equally due to changes in disposable income and wealth.

Comparing the benefits of an improved economic situation with other life events, the authors calculated:

- Getting married or being partnered brings twice the increase in life satisfaction as moving up 50 percentiles in the economic ladder.
- Moving 50 percentiles on the economic ladder brings greater financial satisfaction than getting married.
- Getting a job brings greater gains in life satisfaction and financial satisfaction than merely moving up the economic ladder.
- People at different stages of the financial ladder show more difference than between men and women, or between younger and older people, or between tenants and homeowners. In other words, financial 'welfare' has a greater impact on life satisfaction than gender or age or homeownership—although there are some measurable differences in these groups, with women, older people and homeowners being slightly more happy.
- Wealth is more important for wellbeing than income. And when you analyze what aspect of wealth makes the most difference to people's wellbeing, housing and superannuation are most important.
- Researchers found a much stronger relationship between mental health and wealth than between mental health and income. The authors were not really surprised however, as it is long-term factors that make a difference for mental health, while income can vary substantially over the short term. Movements on the financial ladder that improve mental health are wholly due to changes in wealth.
- When you improve your economic circumstances, it has less of an impact on mental health than major life changes, such as getting married or finally securing a job after a period of unemployment.

THE WEAKNESS OF MONEY

We don't need explanations for why money has a positive effect on people's lives, says Michael Argyle, Professor of Psychology at Oxford Brookes University in the UK. It correlates with biological needs, civil rights, protection of the environment, literacy and intellectual achievement. 'What needs explaining is why the effect of money is so weak, within countries at least, and in historical terms,' he says. The explanations are forthcoming.

COMPARISON WITH PEERS

An often-quoted study conducted at Harvard University in the US asked which you'd prefer: US$50,000 a year when others are getting an average of US$25,000 or US$100,000 a year when others get on average US$250,000.

Nearly everyone said they would prefer the first scenario. The world seems rosier when you're reaping more than your neighbours.

BRONZE, SILVER AND GOLD

It's not just the fact of comparison that affects how we feel about the money in our lives, but also the particular way we tend to compare ourselves. One of the explanations of why the rich are indeed happier than the poor is not the extra benefits that money brings, but the way they rate in the comparison stakes. When the richest of the rich compare themselves with their peer group, there's bound to be people less well-off than themselves. When the poorest of the poor compare themselves, they come up against people better off than themselves. Those in the middle tend to look 'upwards' rather than 'downwards' when comparing their financial situation. Who you choose to compare yourself with makes all the difference in satisfaction.

The same goes for bronze and silver medallists in the Olympics: the silver winner wishes he got gold and feels worse off than the first winner, but the bronze medallist compares himself to those who didn't win a medal, and feels good. The 'upwardly mobile' experience a similar situation when they find themselves more wealthy; their 'rise' may bring about dissatisfaction, since in the company of the upper class they are not so well-off.

Quite how far the comparison theory stretches is not clear: one study looked at people on the same income in different parts of the US, both poor and rich areas. But while the theory of comparison would predict that those in poorer areas would feel they were relatively better off than their neighbours, and therefore be happier, this wasn't the case. They were not objectively any happier than the same income earners in richer areas. Maybe there are other explanations; perhaps the 'richer' areas were genuinely 'nicer' places to live.

THE GOAL ACHIEVEMENT GAP

According to the Michigan Model of Life Quality Assessment, proposed by Alex Michalos in 1985, happiness and satisfaction are a function of the 'goal–achievement gap', that is, the size of the gap between what you have and what you want. The bigger the gap, the greater the dissatisfaction. The size of the gap, says the model, is determined by two comparisons: your past life and 'average folk'.

THE LAW OF AVERAGES

Another theory about why happiness doesn't increase at the same rate as wealth, is that the averages hide a multitude of other stories. A society might develop greater material wealth in a way that cancels out any gains in happiness.

Richard Layard, author of *Happiness: Lessons from a New Science* believes relationships have become less harmonious—so a household might have the benefits of extra material comfort, but at the cost of less time. Extra money usually means extra work hours and the time's got to come from somewhere, with the result that couples feel time-pressured and are more likely to bicker about it: who should do what and when? Such time bickering can eat away at an otherwise good relationship.

The free (or cheap) list

You don't have to feel activities with friends are like keeping up with the Joneses. There's plenty to do that's free, or almost:

- Picnics
- Walks, treks, hikes and swimming
- Camping
- Singing and other musical get-togethers
- Working bees
- Pot luck or rotating dinners (no one has to fork out for all the food or do all the cooking)
- Local theatre and film clubs that offer cheap or discount ticket options

At the money altar

Of the character descriptions below that appear in *Affluenza* by Clive Hamilton and Richard Denniss, which best describes your attitude to money?

- Deferrers. These people sacrifice time for money, postponing possible happiness for later. They concentrate on earning money now, giving it lots of time. It's tough—but later on they'll reap the rewards. They hope.
- Gratifiers. These people sacrifice money now for money later. They pinch and skimp and put aside all the money they possibly can so that it will grow over the years, eventually turning into a vast nest egg, providing the comfort and security they deserve.
- Downshifters. These people sacrifice money for time. Downshifters decide to free up some time by putting less time into earning money, to fully appreciate the 'here and now', perhaps sacrificing a little material comfort along the way.

VARIANCE IN EARNINGS

Within a society it's the variance of earnings that matters and affects how happy people feel. A society with great inequality is an unhappy one. Says Clive Hamilton in *Growth Fetish*: 'Increases in average income often conceal widening inequality, and in countries undergoing industrialization large numbers of people are thrown out of rural impoverishment into a worse condition in the informal economies of the cities.' Research by World Database of Happiness director, Ruut Veenhoven, found that average happiness was greater in countries like Switzerland where there is a relatively small variance in earnings.

CHANGING VALUES AND SHIFTING VALUES

As our needs change, our values change and the things we worry about change. For instance, as money needs decline, freedom and friendship become more of a priority and take on more value. With increased income the focus of people's worry shifts from money to other areas of life, such as self-development.

The 'hedonic treadmill' theory says that we're fated to stay put on the treadmill of money and happiness. If our situation changes for the better, other parts of the picture change too, so we don't feel any happier. One way of explaining the limited effect of extra money on our wellbeing is that yes, it does make us happier, but its effect is only temporary as we quickly get used to the idea, adapt to it, and start on the comparison treadmill again.

Similarly, what we perceive as our required income changes as we earn more. Whatever we earn, or whatever money comes our way, we think more would make life easier. The amount that we think would be good—that we think we 'need' is referred to as 'required income'. One study found that for every dollar extra earned, the 'required income' increased by 40 cents. Every time our earnings increase, our notion of what we need also rises, so psychologically, the gain of the extra pay is diminished.

Richard Layard astutely sums it up in *Happiness: Lessons from a New Science*. 'If we do not foresee that we get used to our material possessions, we shall overinvest in acquiring them, at the expense of our leisure. People do underestimate this process of habituation. As a result, our life can get distorted towards working and making money and away from other pursuits.'

MONEY AND WORK

What is the effect of pay on satisfaction? Say Adrian Furnham and Michael Argyle, authors of *The Psychology of Money*, 'the power of money as a motivator is short-lived'. Its power changes with taxation levels (when taxes are high, people prefer 'things', like cars) and with political stability (in an unstable economy, money is valued for its portability). Other similar findings include:

- Relative pay is more important than absolute pay and the more comfortable someone is, the less important it is.
- When it comes to earnings, it's not how much you earn in real terms, but how you perceive your income. A study conducted in Switzerland found that what mattered to people most was the

difference between what you earned and what you aspired to earn. And what you aspire to earn is largely related to what those around you are earning.

- People are prepared to take a pay cut when everyone else does.
- If your sister's husband earns more than your own husband, you are more likely to go out to work, according to Layard.
- Pay increases are more rewarding if you're satisfied with other aspects of the work.

East and West Germany

On 9 November 1989, the Berlin Wall 'fell'. East and West Germany were reunified soon afterwards, ending 28 years of separation. Australian researchers from the Australian National University and the University of Melbourne tracked the levels of satisfaction in East Germany in the 10 years after reunification—a period which saw a real increase in income of 60 per cent. They used data from the German Socio-Economic Panel, which had asked 'How satisfied are you at present with your life, all things considered?'

Responses ranged from completely dissatisfied (0) to completely satisfied (10). The researchers observed a 'border variable', where people didn't improve their satisfaction with life, perhaps because they compared their lot unfavourably with West Germans.

Satisfaction in general rose among East Germans following reunification, with improvements such as greater personal freedom, mobility and better housing and public services. Although life satisfaction in the East remained below the West in the decade following the fall of the wall, there was an improvement in the East, and around a third of this was due to greater household income, the study concluded.

LOVE OF WORK

For some employees, primarily motivated by the love of their work, being paid more makes them less satisfied with their work. Researchers at the University of California, Berkeley, in the US, found that the effect of money depended on your 'orientation' (a term used to describe your outlook on work and how you are motivated to work).

They followed a group of 124 (relatively well paid) graduates between 1986 and 1995, assessing measures of satisfaction, wellbeing and income. For those who had what the researchers called an 'extrinsic orientation' (people who value money) more money made them more happy. But for those with an intrinsic orientation (people who value work because they enjoy it and find it fulfilling) it could have the opposite effect. There are a few possible explanations for this.

- Sometimes a well-paid job has been chosen precisely because of its earning capacity, but for people who deep-down want a job that's intrinsically fulfilling, ignoring their intrinsic values leads to unhappiness.
- Sometimes being paid for something you enjoy takes the fun out of it. 'Your sense of how fulfilling and personally rewarding you find a task is very fragile, and money can shake this delicate sense of enjoyment,' says Ariel Malka, one of the researchers.
- People need to feel that they are not just working for money— and if you're intrinsically motivated, that need is even greater.

THE CONTRIBUTION OF MONEY

So, if money matters, but not entirely, to happiness, is it possible to put a figure on how much it matters? Clive Hamilton of the Australia Institute believes you can. When you look at the many contributions to happiness, he says income and material wealth account for about 10 per cent of them. He points to research that looked at the variations of happiness between individuals and put a figure on the degree to which money, participating in society and other aspects of life seem to affect a person's overall happiness: a bit like giving quantities in the happiness recipe. The figures below relate to the variance between individuals. What accounts for the difference between a really happy person and a very miserable one, for example, and to what degree (expressed in percentages) does money, or other aspects of life, matter? The suggested percentages are drawn from different studies, so these particular figures do not add up to a 100 per cent 'happiness pie'.

- Personal psychological factors account for 30 per cent of an individual's happiness.
- Life events (births, deaths, marriages or end of marriages) make up 25 per cent of their happiness.
- Social participation (voluntary and paid work) account for 10 per cent.
- Income and material wealth make up just 10 per cent of the pie.

CAN MONEY BUY HAPPINESS?

Simply having money doesn't guarantee you happiness—there are many more influences on your wellbeing than the health of your bank balance. But to what extent does money allow you access to other sources of happiness?

- Leisure. If you're satisfied with your leisure time, you're likely to be satisfied with your life overall. Lack of money can limit leisure—but many activities are free, or nearly, such as going to church, walking, the public library, or voluntary work, to name a few. Obviously, some are more expensive: travel, meals out, theatre and opera, and sports, like sailing, horse riding and some hobbies.
- Relationships. Middle-class, richer couples stay married for longer and have a much lower divorce rate, according to authors Furnham and Argyle. This is because they marry later, the bride is less likely to be pregnant at the wedding and they wait longer before having a child. They get an easier start and 'probably choose more carefully'. They tend to have fewer money problems and are more likely to have a place of their own.

    While money can't buy friendships it can make some things easier—in some situations, owning a car makes it easier to see friends and offer lifts, for example. And feeling the pinch can make it harder to join in activities that involve paying for drinks and a meal out. 'However, having the right social skills is even more essential,' say Furnham and Argyle reassuringly.

What's it worth?

Andrew Oswald and colleagues calculated a 'compensating amount' of money that corresponded with various life events and in 2002 reported it in a paper entitled, 'A simple statistical method for measuring how life events affect happiness'.

- Marriage has the same impact as an extra $100,000 per year.
- Having children has no overall impact on happiness.
- Losing a job is like losing $60,000 a year.
- Losing a spouse would take $245,000 a year to offset.
- Poor health (declining from excellent to good) is like losing somewhere between $180,000 and $220,000 a year.
- Poor health (from excellent to fair) would have to be compensated by $600,000–$800,000 a year.

- Health. On average, richer people enjoy better health, not just because they are able to 'buy' better health but because they tend to have a healthier lifestyle. For example, a British study looked at people born in Britain in 1972. Those in social class 'I' (higher) had a life expectancy 7.2 years longer than those in social class 'V' (lower). A lot of the difference was due to risks in childhood, and by age 15, the difference in life expectancy narrowed to 4 years. Working-class death rates are higher because of male child deaths, mental disorders, injuries, infectious diseases, diseases of the respiratory and digestive systems, heart disease and cancer.

  A 1990 study by Mildred Blaxter, called 'Health and Lifestyle' also found great differences in health according to income. Blaxter surmised there were a variety of reasons. In Western cultures, lower socioeconomic groups tend to smoke more, do less exercise, are more often obese and have higher blood pressure and cholesterol levels (due to a culture of poor diet, effects of stress and poor medical education). Groups with more money enjoy better health care, both by making more use of free services and private ones, and by taking more preventative measures. Some studies also found doctors spent more time with people of a 'higher' class.

The study found manual workers often experience bad working conditions, such as heat, dust, and other pollutants, poor heating, damp and dirt, which can all contribute to poor health. Broken marriages, loss of job relations, unemployment, less participation in church and leisure groups, all mean the working class tends to have less close relationships and less social support. They also have weaker immune systems.

In Britain, the poor are over-represented in mental hospitals. Blaxter's study found poorer people experienced much worse mental health, with a reversal for the very rich (that was due to excessive alcohol consumption). This pattern can be explained in part by a downward drift of the mentally ill to lower socioeconomic groups. In addition this group were more likely to experience higher stress levels from unemployment, trouble with the law, drunken partners, or lots of young children at home. Some groups are also more vulnerable to stress because of passive and ineffective ways of coping.

Dale Carnegie (1888–1955)

Dale Carnegie was born into a poor farming family in Missouri in the US. As a teenager, Carnegie got up at 4 am every morning to milk the cows. He went to the State Teachers College and his first job on leaving was selling correspondence courses to ranchers. Later, he sold bacon, soap and lard for Armour & Company and his sales territory was the firm's national leader. He is remembered for self-improvement courses in salesmanship, public speaking and interpersonal skills. His book, *How to Win Friends and Influence People* first published in 1936, has sold 15 million copies and is still popular today. Dale Carnegie Training, founded in 1912, is still going strong, with 2700 instructors in 70 countries and 25 languages. Around seven million people have completed the training, which focuses on improving corporate performance. Presentations based on personal experience still form a large part of the training, as they did when Carnegie himself ran courses. 'Believe that you will succeed, and you will,' was his catchcry.

THE HAPPINESS INDUSTRY

Thomas Wiseman, author of the 1970s book, *The Money Motive*, suggests that questioning your happiness is a symptom of wealth: 'Once the financial constraints have gone, people become very aware of "their happiness". They subject it to regular check-ups,' he says, and constantly ask, as the hypochondriac asks, 'am I really well? Am I really happy?'.

Wiseman believes happiness is an episodic phenomenon, 'arising out of the sudden satisfaction of some long dammed-up instinctual need' (a definition he quotes from Freud). And the rich seek happiness (this, by definition, is an 'episodic' quality) as if it were an attainable permanent condition. In contrast, those without the wherewithal to independently seek happiness, see it as something they can't afford to pursue, so settle for putting up with things as they are.

Money can't buy you love, but can it literally buy happiness? The burgeoning happiness industry would perhaps have you believe it can, with all that's on offer: counselling, psychology, self-help gurus and techniques. At one level, it seems logical that given the consumer society we're said to live in, plus the individualist nature of it, that happiness itself can be dressed up as a commodity within reach of anyone. Religion will tell us it's not possible, but market economics will predict that suppliers of the commodity will multiply and fill the demand. Hence a billion-dollar industry in self-help books, workshops, seminars and courses on how to be happy, not to mention a world of businesses, coaches and counsellors who ask for—and get in some cases—hundreds of dollars an hour.

If a society and its values create depression and anxiety, then the new happiness business is guaranteed a constant supply of needy people willing to part with their earnings for more happiness. To paraphrase *Affluenza* authors, Clive Hamilton and Richard Denniss, 'consumerism creates the problems and presents a cure'.

In *Affluenza* they take the argument a step further, pointing out that part of the way the industry works is to suggest that if you're not happy, it's because there's something wrong with you, rather than a broader problem with society. They point to disease-mongering, 'widening the boundaries of treatable illness in order to expand markets for those who sell and deliver treatments'.

An article in British magazine *New Statesman* in 2004 called, 'The happiness industry' points out the big profits of those who claim to make people happy. Sales of self-help books and CDs promising a better life are soaring; there are more counsellors than GPs in the UK and life coaches outnumber dentists.

They are also in some cases outpaid: '... people seem readier to pay £100 an hour to talk to unqualified strangers about how to transform their lives, relationships and careers, than they are to pay a trained dentist,' points out author Barbara Gunnell. Some will charge even more, up to £300 per hour.

A press release from January 2005 from PR Leap tells of 'international happiness promoter' George Ortega's plans for two new reality television shows centring on happiness. 'He's betting the two shows will spark a new happiness training industry', says the release. In one show, *Happy House*, participants (ambitious sad sacks) compete

Money can't buy you love ...

Or sex, according to researchers, David Blanchflower from Dartmouth College (and the National Bureau of Economic Research) in the US and Andrew Oswald from the University of Warwick in the UK. Using 1990s data from the General Social Survey of the United States, the pair analyzed the relationships between money, sex and happiness. 'Money buys more sexual partners' their paper concludes, 'but not more sex'.

While commuting to and from work creates the lowest levels of happiness, research shows that, when people look back, sex is the activity that produces the largest single amount of happiness. Blanchflower and Oswald studied data from 16,000 Americans. Income buys greater happiness, they said, but does not buy more sex. And men who pay for sex are considerably less happy than other people. (Those who have ever had sex outside their marriage also score lower for happiness.)

Thomas Tusser (1524–1580)

English poet and farmer, Thomas Tusser, is best known for his instructional poem written in rhyming couplets, *Five Hundred Points of Good Husbandry*, published in 1557. Born in Essex, he became a chorister at an early age, moving later to St Paul's Cathedral choir, and from there, Eton college. After studying at Cambridge University, he spent 10 years at court as a musician, then married and settled as a farmer in Suffolk.

Tusser's book was reprinted many times, most recently by Oxford University Press in 1984. It includes instructions and observations about keeping house, living life and farming. Tusser recorded many of the proverbs and terms current in Tudor England, including the still well-known proverb: 'A fool and his money are soon parted.'

to see who can 'make their spirits soar the highest'—with (of course) the help of a professional happiness trainer. The second show, called *Happiness Hero*, enlists the help of a trainer to 'raise the bliss quotient of ... gloomy/grumpy families'.

SELF HELP OR HELPLESS?

Humpty Dumpty sat on a wall
Humpty Dumpty had a great fall
All the king's horses and all the king's men
Couldn't put Humpty together again

NURSERY RHYME

The happiness industry is nowhere more pronounced than in the US. Steve Salerno, investigative journalist and author of 2005 book *SHAM* [Self-Help & Actualization Movement]: *How the Self-Help Movement Made America Helpless*, sees an insidious trend in American society that some call the Humpty Dumpty syndrome: take people apart and they can't put themselves back together again. The gurus and practitioners of the self-help movement are guilty of turning people into victims, he believes, then offering them 'empowerment' through their seminars, books and CDs; a guaranteed repeat business that he estimates is worth at least US$8 billion a year.

'An entire generation of baby boomers searching desperately for the answers to the riddle of midlife has entrusted itself to a select set of dubious healers who are profiting handsomely, if not always sincerely, from that desperation,' writes Salerno.

While the gurus offer no evidence to support their theories, there is plenty of evidence to show they don't work, says Salerno: high divorce rates, obesity and depression, for starters.

At the top end of the happiness industry are speakers who've set up entire industries based around their 'teachings': TV programmes, books, even insurance policies. At the other end of the scale is the proliferation of life coaches, which Salerno describes as wearing multiple hats: '… part consultant, part oracle, part cheerleader, part provider of tough love.'

Money itself has a role to play in happiness. It is hard to be happy in abject poverty—although some people do find ways to be happy in almost any circumstances. But happiness is multifaceted and although you can be happy about 'things', happiness is not about things that money can buy. Money is one aspect of a comfortable life and there is a lot more to happiness beyond the reach of money.

TAKING STOCK

1. To what extent do you believe money makes you happy?
2. If it's true that money only accounts for about 10 per cent of the differences between people's happiness, how does that figure compare to the relative importance you apportion to the pursuit of money?
3. If you're ready to ask some sticky questions about money, try these for starters:

(a) What does money bring into your life?

(b) What good things in your life have nothing to do with money?

(c) What are the downsides of money in your life? (For example, working longer hours, increased stress.)

(d) Do you ever try to 'buy' happiness in any way, whether with retail therapy or self-help products. Are these effective?

(e) When you compare yourself to friends, family or neighbours, how comfortable are you in your financial situation?

Lotto, Daily Play, Thunderball, Lotto HotPicks and Dream Number are closed for the draw, but you can still play EuroMillions and Instant Win Games.

NATIONAL LOTTERY WEBSITE, UK

6. FOR RICHER FOR POORER

JACK FINDS HIS GOLD AT THE TOP OF THE BEANSTALK, J K ROWLING WEAVES THE HARRY POTTER MAGIC AND BECOMES RICHER THAN EVEN THE QUEEN OF ENGLAND. FAIRY TALES ARE THE ULTIMATE IN RAGS TO RICHES TALES, BUT SOME PEOPLE SEEK RICHES IN ANOTHER WAY AND CHOOSE A LESS MONEY-CENTRED WAY OF LIFE IN THE PURSUIT OF HAPPINESS.

FOR RICHER

'There is nothing in biological necessity to account for the drive to get rich,' says author Thomas Wiseman in his 1974 classic, *The Money Motive*. But that doesn't stop people dreaming. Until the Industrial Revolution, around the turn of the 18th century, it was more or less impossible for anyone to get rich quick; by the 20th century things were very different. The dream to acquire wealth comes in many different guises:

- A longing for security, based on the desire to be free from dependency of any kind. Security offers a certain kind of freedom from being at anyone's beck and call.
- A desire to 'show them all' and triumph over others. Particularly when people feel as though they have been slighted or humiliated in some way.
- Omnipotence of money. People dream that having money can help them do anything, even secure love, as though money has magical qualities. Its power is at least convenient: when the Greek ship owner, Stavros Niarchos, was refused the principal suite at the Paris Ritz, on the grounds that it was permanently reserved for Barbara Hutton, he instructed agents to buy the hotel's shares. When he'd bought almost 50 per cent of the shares, the management found out and promptly gave him the room.
- Transforming qualities. 'As Cinderella rose from the ashes and became clean, so shall we, if we have enough money,' explains Wiseman. In new clothes and plush surroundings, a wealthy you will be stronger, less fearful, more charming, wiser and less vulnerable— even, to some degree, immortal (the wealthy often leave behind them foundations and prizes).
- The good life. Opulent houses, extravagant holidays and private jets are all part of the dream.

THE TRULY RICH

A 2004 article in the *US Journal of Accountancy*, reports that the number of 'ultrawealthy' families is growing at a rate of 12 per cent a year.

' … even average Americans need to be millionaires,' says the *Journal*, so it's important that anyone wishing to service the ultrawealthy sector, can differentiate between the 'comfortably wealthy' and the 'ultrawealthy'—or the 'merely rich' and the 'truly rich'. This is defined by a person's net worth (what they're worth once assets have been counted and liabilities, such as loans, deducted) and 'his or her goals' (what they expect to do with their money). The ultrawealthy expect their assets to outlive them and need advice on transferring funds to heirs or charities, while the merely rich expect to spend most of their assets within their lifetime and leave only a modest inheritance. In the US in 2001, most financial planners drew the line for the ultrawealthy at US$25 million. But some merely rich people with net worths of US$5 million or US$10 million 'act like the ultrawealthy', says the *Journal*. Quite how much the ultrawealthy leave behind depends, of course, on the running costs of their lifestyle.

Let's face it, life for the very wealthy has a different texture: helicopter rides to school (James Packer); a nursery consisting of a day room, two bedrooms, a bathroom and a kitchen (Prince Edward); perhaps five or more homes, why not one a 1600 rose brick chateau, a bedroom with mirrored walls and a thirty foot ceiling (Valentino Garavani); round-the-clock medical support on hand, maybe four private rooms permanently reserved for the family at the hospital (David Rockefeller).

Nick the Greek

Nicholas Andreas Dandolas, otherwise known as Nick the Greek, won and lost over $500 million during his life. Born to wealthy parents in Crete in 1883, he was a philosophy graduate, sent to America when he was 18 years old with US$150 a week allowance. After winning US$500,000 on horse racing in Montreal, he moved back to Chicago and lost it all on card and dice games. In 1949 he played a five-month poker marathon with Johnny Moss and lost millions. He claimed to have gone from rags to riches, or vice versa, 75 times. He gave US$20 million to charity over his lifetime and is said not to have respected money. He died broke, but still gambling.

SUDDEN WEALTH SYNDROME

Being rich is not all rosy, we're told, particularly when wealth is amassed quickly. According to the UK's *Financial Times*, many millionaires and billionaires are worried about the effect of new-found wealth on their families. Rapid rises in the wealth stakes can bring problems of what to do with money. For many the first move is to buy a new house and resign from a job. But this can cut ties with workmates and neighbours, without creating a new network. And of course, one of the perils of having lots of money is losing it.

There are plenty of cases of people drinking away the dollars, borrowing even more, and finding themselves bankrupt, as well as battles among relatives and spouses for their share, fair or not. In the US, it's estimated almost a third of state lottery winners become bankrupt. Another source estimates 70 per cent of those who receive a windfall end up losing it. While these figures are hard to verify, there is certainly no shortage of reports of individuals who've run into problems after a big win.

Susan Bradley, founder of an American organization called the Sudden Money Institute, says on its website: 'In our culture, there is a widely held belief that money solves problems. People think if only they had more money, their troubles would be over. Wealthy people are envied for what they have and what they can afford. But when a family receives sudden money, they frequently learn that money can cause as many problems as it solves.'

So what are the symptoms of sudden wealth syndrome, apart from a fatter bank balance? Anxiety and panic attacks, ruminating about money, obsessed thinking, insomnia, irritability, identity confusion and a marked loss of control are just some of the negative outcomes for winners.

LOTTERY WINNERS

Today's economy makes the dream of getting rich a real one, even if not a frequently fulfilled one. And although the odds of winning a big money prize like the lottery are very slim—somewhere in the region of one in 14 million—somewhere, someone has the lucky ticket.

Viv Nicholson (1936–)

Viv Nicholson won £150,000 in 1961 on the football pools in the UK, a figure that would represent around £3,000,000 in today's money. She'd been earning £7 a week working in a cake factory and her husband had been earning the same amount working night shifts. Within four years of winning her money, wild purchases, such as a shocking-pink Cadillac (for a while she bought a new car every six months) reduced her fortune to nothing, and she's now living on the state pension. Her life was recreated on stage in a musical, *Spend Spend Spend*, based on a book that she co-authored. She later said that it was very sad and frustrating to see the performance. Viv found herself distanced from the people she'd lived with and when her husband, Keith, died in a car crash in 1965, she spent her last remaining pounds, until banks and tax creditors deemed her bankrupt. She's been married five times and in 1979 became a Jehovah's Witness.

Does winning the lottery, or similar, make you happier? In general, people's ability to adapt to new circumstances means they get used to the idea of having more money pretty quickly, so although a win is nice, and people are happier for it for a while, soon after they return to the level of satisfaction they experienced before. A 1975 British study looked at 191 winners of the football pools who'd won £160,000 or more. Many said they were a little happier than before the win.

The study, by Stephen Smith and Peter Razzell also revealed the downside of big wins.

- 70 per cent of winners had given up work, and lost out on job satisfaction and the company of their workmates.
- Some winners moved to a bigger house, but found themselves rejected by snobbish neighbours.
- Some winners quarrelled with friends and family who wanted a share of the winnings.
- Some winners experienced an identity problem, and around three-quarters said they didn't know what social class they were in.

But maybe the British have learnt to be more adaptable. Camelot, the operator of the UK National Lottery, commissioned a survey of 249 lottery winners and came up with a more positive picture. They interviewed people who had won £50,000 or more between 1994 and 1999. Of those winners, 111 players had won more than £1 million. Among the study's findings:

- more than half the winners (55 per cent) said they were happier after the win than before. Most of the remaining winners said they were happy before and they were still as happy (43 per cent). Two per cent said they were less happy. The size of the win made no difference.
- of those who said they were happier, most (65 per cent) attributed it to greater financial security and fewer worries. Around a quarter said they could now buy what they wanted and that life was generally easier.
- the vast majority did not experience any kind of negative impact on relationships.
- a bigger win spread the happiness further: the bigger the win, the more that the family, as well as the winner, expressed greater happiness (due to increased security) after the win.
- the greater the win, the more chance family will ask for money. Around a third of those winning £2 million or more, were approached by family for a share in the winnings.
- most winners made increased donations to charity.
- about a fifth of the winners went on a holiday overseas for the first time.
- about 40 per cent of winners moved house; 50 per cent of winners of more than £2 million moved house. Most of these moves were within nine miles of their previous home.
- 10 per cent of winners switched to private medical care and one per cent had plastic surgery.
- around half of the winners who were in regular work before the win were still in the same job. But this dropped with a bigger win: around half of the winners of more than £1 million had given up work altogether.

I'm in the money

UK Lottery company, Camelot, recommends going slow if you find yourself suddenly wealthy. Don't rush into anything and take time to get used to what you have. In addition it makes the following recommendations for people who become suddenly wealthy.

- Consider all your options and plan your future.
- Consult a financial advisor you feel you can trust.
- Make sure you understand exactly what is happening to your money.
- Make a will.

Other research into sudden wealth showed more mixed results. Most research supports the idea that we get a happy buzz after winning a big sum of money—and that buzz can last a few years. But after that, we return to our 'normal' happiness level. The classic 1978 study by Philip Brickman, Dan Coates and Ronnie Janoff-Bulman interviewed a number of people in two very different 'camps'. One group had been involved in a crippling accident, and another had won between US$50,000 and US$1,000,000. Their control group had experienced neither. Comparing the groups, the researchers found that the 'normal' group was just as happy as the lottery winners, and a little happier than paraplegic and quadriplegic people.

Notably, lottery winners took significantly less pleasure from mundane activities like watching television. The findings, published in the *Journal of Personality and Social Psychology*, suggested what the authors called a 'contrast effect': life after the major event, whether 'good' (winning a lot of money) or 'bad' (becoming crippled), was compared to previous episodes in life. In the case of the winners, they compared life with the peak experience of the win—and it fell short. The pleasures of ordinary activities faded. The paraplegics tended to idealize their past life, making their present happiness seem less than it had been: a kind of 'nostalgia effect'. Despite this finding, the accident victims were not as unhappy as predicted. Although they reported lower happiness in general than lottery winners, their happiness levels were well above the middle of the scale.

Another suggestion to explain the dampening of a positive or negative effect is the fact that after a dramatic life-changing event people may find themselves in a newly peopled environment. One author speculates that the lottery winners may find themselves in an environment of greed and jealousy, which feeds on fears of losing their money, reducing the positive quality of everyday life. On the other hand, someone who has suffered a bad accident may find themselves with very caring and supportive people, thus easing the negative impact of the accident.

Another possible explanation is that with a big win, the goal of working hard to earn money is removed—but what should replace it? At least earning money is a reachable goal. Perhaps once that is removed, a lottery winner is struck by all sorts of unsolvable issues of how best to use their time. On the other hand, accident victims could feel some sort of relief at no longer having to join in the rat race. The accident might also be the explanation for anything that goes wrong in their lives. Muses researcher, Pascal Wallisch, 'This could (in my opinion) boost their self-esteem and enjoyment of life—they are relieved of the responsibility to lead a successful life.'

INHERITANCES

In a study of lottery winners and people who received windfalls and inheritances (by Jonathan Gardner and Andrew Oswald of Warwick University in the UK), the researchers measured wellbeing a year after the windfall. Not surprisingly, they found those who'd received an inheritance had better mental health scores than those who hadn't. But the highest level of wellbeing was associated with relatively small inheritances—less than £2500.

Inheritances of more than £10,000 seemed to also bring about stress and unhappiness. As the authors point out, the possible happiness of receiving an inheritance tends to coincide with the sad passing of a close relative or friend. Smaller sums of money might signify a different relationship: grandchild rather than child, for instance. As the inheritance amount increases, the individual is more likely to have a closer tie with the deceased, and feel the weight of grief as well as the potential benefits of extra money. In addition, larger amounts are more likely to be in the form of property, which can bring additional stress when disposing of it. Inheritances are often a mixed blessing, as this person discovered:

After my mother died I inherited half the proceeds of her house. She died at the age of 60 in not the best of circumstances. In the weeks following her death, the fact that my sister and I were now recipients of her estate brought on mixed emotions. I knew it was what my mother wanted, and who can deny that a windfall does not have its benefits. But obviously, I was distressed she'd died, and I felt slightly uncomfortable when I thought about the materialistic side of things.

The consequences of her death were both good and bad for me personally, and this paradox made me uneasy early on. When a relatively small amount arrived in my bank account a few months after she died, it was quite a shock and I found it quite upsetting. It was as if all I'd done to date had been about changes to do with her life: arranging her funeral service, clearing the house, choosing a few keepsakes. But with the money arriving, it was a change in my life and while sad, it enabled us to take a trip to New Zealand we'd had to put off. The rest of the money took well over a year to materialize, and by then I must have got used to the idea, or hardened. I thought I might be upset again, but I wasn't. I felt I wanted to do something good with it, with long-term benefits. It basically went on half a house, much like where it had come from. But I had a little fun too!

Does money make you fat?

Research into British lottery winners revealed that although 14 per cent of winners of more than £50,000 had lost weight since their win, a third reported a weight gain.

Shaking the money tree

The Chinese traditional scene, *yao qian shu*, translated as literally 'shaking the money tree', depicts a tree laden with strings of coins, under which the god of wealth enjoys the ripe abundance of money. Tangerine trees are popular both at home and in business places to bring peace and wealth as the fruit is said to look like gold coins hanging on the branches. The Chinese believe that a gift of a tangerine tree should never be refused as it's like turning away wealth and luck in all things. The fruit is popular at New Year because the word for tangerine, '*ju*' sounds very much like 'auspicious' or 'lucky'.

The Chinese god of wealth comes in a number of varieties, both civil and military. One legend tells of Zhao Gong Ming who lived on a mountain and practised asceticism. He aided his ruler in battle against a general, Jiang Zi Ya, who performed ritual on a straw doll he'd given the name of Zhao Gong Ming, making the real Zhao Gong Ming sick and then die. Later, after the Shang dynasty's defeat, Jiang Zi Ya deified Zhao Gong Ming as the god of wealth because he felt he'd had no choice but to kill him, even though he was a moral and honourable man. The god's duties were to uphold justice and ensure the even distribution of wealth.

In China, the many symbols of wealth include goldfish, the number eight, gold and silver ingots and the 'beckoning cat', which originated in Japan and is often seen at the entrance of a Chinese business, inviting wealth and success. The desire for wealth and success has no negative connotations in China, and people surround themselves with symbols of wealth in the hope it will help their businesses run smoothly and profitably.

VOX POP: Have you ever experienced a dramatic change in the amount of money at your disposal?

I've never come into a great deal of money and I treat it with too much respect to gamble it or squander it. I respect it but I don't treat it with reverence. It's only money. When I arrived in London in the 1970s I lived on canned sardines for weeks because money was so tight. I left London and returned later, obtaining a job that paid five times as much as the amount I was earning before. With money, London turned into a different city. PN

I've been in a position of having to eat potato soup to stay fed, so guarding against the absence of money is important. KD

I studied for a PhD on a shoestring budget for the sake of higher work challenges, not for the money. I experienced a dramatic reduction in money when I retired. Having adjusted by spending less on things like clothing and entertainment, we're not really restricted much. AL

I inherited $10,000 from an uncle and we spent it travelling to the US and Mexico. I've never quite quit a job because it didn't pay enough. In fact, twice I have taken major pay cuts to move fields and try something new. I've also dropped salary for family-friendliness. In one case I dropped about $30,000 and the job was a hell of a lot less interesting and challenging, but had great family-friendly conditions. For me that compromise was definitely worth it. FH

We inherited a modest amount, which was used to pay off the mortgage, which in turn allowed us to move to an area of the country we'd always wanted to live in. AS

I've never lost any large amount of money. I don't have investments nor do I gamble. I have received unexpected inheritances from my English cousins. They were brought up to 'look after poor little E in Australia'. Naturally I am delighted. One cousin left me a sizeable amount in his will. I regard this as family money and use it to help out children and grandchildren when the need arises. Mostly they repay it, and it goes back in the account, ready for another emergency. EWB

I gained enough money to buy a house and the feeling was akin to winning the lottery. It was an incredibly good feeling and it led to increased freedom in how I live my life. It enabled me to feel confident about having a child on my own. In fact, without it, I possibly wouldn't have taken that risk. ML

I have lost a large amount of money. Divorce was financially disastrous. I have had huge financial stress when developing my private hotel. There were huge unexpected losses initially. How did I feel? I couldn't sleep. I experienced stress, but I always knew that with hard work and good management I'd make it out of that crisis. I did. SG

I've been very near the poverty line at times in my life and although I have more money now than I ever did, I don't want to save it for a rainy day. Life is too short and I can't take it with me. CL

I was not interested in pursuing a career in law even though it would have paid well. My husband used to joke that he wished I was a barrister, as we'd have a greater family income. But I'd point out that he'd not see so much of me and I'd be a lot less happy. I tend to adjust my spending according to how much is coming in. I don't like set budgets with allocations for this and that, but I'll take a general tightening approach quite easily: being careful about eating out and buying clothes. When I was a student and ran out of money I got a job—once it was delivering newspapers before lectures started, another time it was a Wednesday afternoon speaking English to a French brother and sister. AH

FOR POORER

Full fathom five thy father lies;
Of his bones are coral made;
Those are pearls that were his eyes:
Nothing of him doth fade
But doth suffer a sea-change
Into something rich and strange.

WILLIAM SHAKESPEARE, *THE TEMPEST*, 1623

For all those who strive for more money, there are some who strive for less. Linda Cockburn is one of those. She persuaded her partner, Trevor, and their six-year-old son, Caleb, to try living for six months without spending a dollar. In 2005 they did just that, living off the food they could grow on their 2000 plus square metre block in Queensland, Australia.

She wrote about their experiences in a book, *Living the Good Life: How one family changed their world from their own backyard*. They survived largely without spending money on a day-to-day basis, although some essentials they agreed up front would have to be paid for. Namely, taxes, rates, mortgage repayments, insurance, medical costs and educational expenses. But the point was not just the money.

Linda explains: 'Our motivations are manifold. We wanted to change our lifestyle to one that, while being easy on the environment, was also easier on us. We were unhappy with how things were; we had no time, for either ourselves or each other. Little peace of mind, often no money, and certainly no real meaning to what we were doing ... To say we were unsatisfied with our cycle of consumer dependence is an understatement.'

Trevor and Linda survived cravings for chocolate and boutique beer, killing chooks and milking the goat, and emerged six and 11 kilograms lighter respectively from the experiment. They bartered—feta cheese for sunflower oil, goats milk for flour—and from about halfway through the experiment, they bartered for money, $20 here, $30 there. It helped buy treats like Vegemite or potatoes for

Caleb, who was finding the more restricted diet unpalatable (and officially ceased to be a full-playing participant after three months).

Lapses did occur: for example, a computer adaptor and hot chips on a hospital visit. But on the whole, the challenges of their life centred on what to make for dinner, how to reduce electricity consumption, so as to only use what the solar panels on the roof produced and what to plant given the lack-of-rain forecast. Said Linda in month five: 'It occurs to me that really all we're doing is changing the perspective on how we live. Sometimes it seems I am obsessed with kWh, protein, energy and time, but really it's only replacing our original obsession: money, the lack of, accruing, spending and sacrificing all else to its warping qualities.'

Reading between the lines, a lack of variety comes through, with a less varied diet and very few outings breaking the routine of home life. But the overall feeling is very positive. It was an extreme position to take, concedes Linda, but they showed it was possible to considerably reduce their ecological footprint and while it was far from being the aim of the 'adventure', they also saved almost half of Trevor's salary.

LIFE WITHOUT MONEY

There are two ways to get enough: one is to continue to accumulate more and more. The other is to desire less.

ATTRIBUTED TO G K CHESTERTON

'Couldn't we live perfectly well without money?' postulated Marxist Albert Langer at a public forum at Melbourne Town Hall in Australia in 2000. He told the forum he believed the answer was 'yes'. In fact, he says he can't imagine a future world organized on money: watch *Star Trek* and it's hard to imagine them going off to pay for their canteen supplies, or being paid to explore the reaches of the final frontier. Look at the software driving the internet, he says, and you'll find it's largely free. It operates without money, on a 'from each according to their ability, to each according to their need basis'. So in his ideal society, how do we get our tomatoes? Those who want to grow tomatoes will, argues Langer. But whether there are enough people willing to grow tomatoes for the sheer joy of it to supply tomato eaters is another question. 'Personally, I would find tomato-growing extremely non-satisfying,' he said.

TRADITIONAL BARTER SYSTEMS

Tibetan nomads and farmers operate barter systems where, for example, a yak is equal to ten sheep, or you might swap flour for dairy products. But if they want something with a money price on it—like batteries for the radio—they need to come up with cash. When people turn their backs on money, it's usually the values wrapped up in the moneyed society they are shunning—whether it's because they want to live with more awareness of religion, spirituality or the environment.

LIVING ON LESS

In our money-focused society, attempts at living without cash are short-lived and rare. Much more common are people who consciously choose to live a less materialistic life that needs less currency to fund. It's not self sufficiency they're after, but a shift in lifestyle and emphasis. Writers and artists have traditionally spurned the material life. But as Laurie Lee, author of *Cider with Rosie* once said: 'The way to exist as a poet is to *enjoy* a low standard of living.'

Earlier in the 20th century perhaps it was easier. D H Lawrence, although always hard up, could live on a £50 advance for *Sons and Lovers* with his wife, Frieda, for seven months or more in a garden apartment on the Lake of Garda in Italy. It had large furnished rooms, a pleasant dining room, kitchen and two bedrooms. Wine, figs and even a cleaner, came cheap.

Once the domain of the bohemian, people outside the world of art and literature are also wanting a less materialistic life. It's a trend, often called downshifting, witnessed in Australia, the UK, the US and Europe.

- In 1997, 1.7 million people in Britain downshifted, but by 2002, the number had risen to 2.6 million.
- From 1990–1996, one-fifth of the American population made a voluntary change in lifestyle that included earning less money. Just over half of these people expected the change to be permanent. Almost all, 85 per cent, were happy about the change.

- A 2002 survey by the Australia Institute showed that 23 per cent of adults in their thirties, forties and fifties had downshifted in the previous 10 years.

'Downshifters', 'sea changers', even 'tree changers' are some of the labels used to describe such people. According to the book, *Affluenza* by Clive Hamilton and Richard Denniss, what defines a downshifter is that they have made a conscious decision to accept a lower income and move toward a lower level of consumption. They choose to earn less and spend less. The motivation is to achieve more balance in their lives and more time with families. While some are real estate refugees—driven out of the city by high housing costs and the pressure to work longer hours to cover them—many do not move house, but change the way they live in it.

WHY DOWNSHIFT?

Today's downshifters are not doing it to live in communes, nor are they necessarily ideologically motivated. The most common reason for downshifting in America according to Juliet Schor, author of *The Overspent American* is wanting more time, less stress and more balance in life. They also want to do something more meaningful with their lives. Slowing down at work might mean 'upshifting' in other areas. Many want to simplify their lives because they are fed up dealing with too many demands on time, too much information and too many choices.

It's a similar picture in Australia. According to Clive Hamilton, director of the Australia Institute, the main motivation for people to downshift is to achieve more balance, more control in their lives, more time with families and more personal fulfilment. Of all the reasons people give, the greatest is to spend more time with families (especially women), and the next most important motive is a healthier lifestyle (particularly important for men). High-income earners are more likely to mention personal fulfilment than low-income earners.

Sometimes downshifting is a conscious rejection of the corporate world and its values. Climbing the corporate ladder, some say, makes them lose sight of what matters. Some talk of giving something back by volunteering, or taking a career change to a more caring type of job.

While the decision appears to hinge on money, it's really about values. Hamilton, author of *Growth Fetish*, comments: 'To make the transition [to downshift], they take a crucial but simple psychological leap: they decide that they will no longer judge their own worth by the amount they earn and consume.'

What sort of reductions in income are we talking about? The average drop in Britain is 40 per cent; drops range between 10 and 100 per cent. An important figure that is usually left out of the equation, however, is the accumulated wealth a downshifter might already have. It's one thing to take a 50 per cent drop in income when your house is paid off and you have savings to fall back on for rainy days and emergencies, but quite another when you're paying rent or a mortgage. And dropping 50 per cent from a six-figure salary still allows for a greater than average income, whereas 10 per cent off an already low wage can make life difficult. With apologies to cliché spotters: it's all relative.

As Michael Quinion notes: 'Ironically, it seems a requirement for remodelling one's life is financial independence; significantly, downshifting has been taken up principally by middle-class professionals who can afford the loss of income.'

The author of an article on the web-based *Irregular Times* was rankled after watching the TV show *Affluenza*, because the people used as examples in the show who were choosing to spend less money were earning AUS$100,000 or more before they made their life-changing decision: 'They don't really speak to me or the hundreds of millions of people across the country like me. I earn AUS$12,000 every year, about one-tenth what the corporate lawyer raked in ... For him, simple living is a choice. For the rest of us, simplicity is a necessity.'

In his book *Affluenza*, Clive Hamilton argues that downshifters are not confined to the wealthy and middle class who can afford the drop in income. In fact, the largest proportion of downshifters in the survey conducted by the Australia Institute were earning below $30,000 a year. But rather unhelpfully, this figure represents income after the change, not before. Hamilton estimates the Australian drop to match the UK average of 40 per cent. Whether or not you would see these people as 'well-off' depends on your perspective. The parameters within which it is possible to lead a reasonably comfortable life are wide.

What's in a word? Downshifting

The word 'downshifting' first appeared in the English language in the 1950s in the context of changing gear in the car. The Trends Research Institute in New York is credited with first using the term in 1994 in the new context of shifting down an income level or two, which it heralded as a 'new Renaissance philosophy'. Notes Michael Quinion on his website, World Wide Words, downshifters 'believe that time is more important than money and that it is better to work less and be happy and fulfilled than be well-paid'. It means cutting out surplus, unnecessary spending, without going as far as 'dropping out' or attempting total self-sufficiency.

SAVING UP FOR DOWNSHIFTING

What do downshifters give up? Where do the savings come from? If the change means no longer turning up to a corporate office, some savings are automatic. Working costs money too—office clothes, transport, childcare and extra food bills, for example. Perhaps even a 'shrink' to deal with the pressure. Although if stepping aside from the rat race means becoming self-employed, there can be extra costs in setting up a home office.

Changes typically reported by downshifters include the following.

- No more impulse buying on clothes or gadgets.
- Upping the money alert—downshifters think more about what they're spending money on before they spend it.
- More budgeting—careful planning means cutting out waste and more economical spending.
- More planning—savings come from choosing where and how to allocate the family budget.
- Less stress—some savings come from redirecting money that was spent coping with the emotional and social consequences of overachievement in work and overspending in general.
- Downshifters eat out less and go to cheaper restaurants when they do.
- Downshifters don't go on expensive overseas holidays any more, choosing cheaper domestic ones instead.

● Opportunity shopping. Appealing brands might be purchased at the op-shop, charity store or a garage sale rather than the high street.

HOW DOES LIFE CHANGE FOR DOWNSHIFTERS?

The crux of downshifting is, say Hamilton and Denniss, a psychological transformation 'in which money and material things are relegated to a much-diminished position on the list of life's priorities'. People talk of rediscovering the joy of living, feeling more relaxed, less stressed and enjoying a slower pace of life.

Some downshifters move out of the city, but many do not move house and in Australia, there are proportionately more downshifters living in cities, so it is by no means a trend associated only with rural living. Many report spending more time outdoors in one physical activity or another. Others struggle with a feeling of loss of status or being embarrassed; for example, if friends suggest a meal that would blow the budget. Many find they spend more time cooking and preparing food; some grow their own vegetables.

When looking at downshifters the Australia Institute found:

● 90 per cent are happy with the changes in their lifestyle
● 38 per cent missed the extra income
● 17 per cent said they were happy with the change but found the loss of income 'very tough'.

THE DOWNSIDE OF DOWNSHIFTING

There is a powerful, indeed overwhelming, assumption that everyone is committed to acquiring the best material lifestyle they reasonably can. It's just how life in Australia is, and bemusement and expressions of derision are typical responses to downshifters' decisions to flout this convention.

CLIVE HAMILTON AND RICHARD DENNISS, *AFFLUENZA*, 2005

Downshifting's not for everyone. Nor is it an entirely positive experience: loss of status, being told you're nuts or weak or running away from problems are some of the less than welcome consequences. Some find it a test of friendships, and not all of them survive. Downshifters worry about money, sometimes how they're going to pay a bill, sometimes how they're going to support retirement. Some miss the luxuries, but often it's a question of adapting to a new financial status. For some, the slower pace is in fact more stressful.

When downshifting involves a rural move it is not always as idyllic as people hope. Often the country house comes with a commute, maybe even as much as two hours at each end of the day. A property can take a lot of time to manage. Then there are those who find while country living was good while the children were young, as they've got older, the trips into town increase, and it might even seem easier to head back to town full-time.

VOLUNTARY SIMPLICITY

Taking the idea of downshifting a step further are people who may identify themselves with voluntary simplicity. Schor says simple-livers in America are more likely to be women, middle-class, white and without young children.

They tend to be middle-class and well educated and able to manage the world around them. They are socially and personally confident, self-reliant and independent and in stark contrast with traditional poor, they have options—including re-entering mainstream culture if they want to at any point. Some are reformed shoppers, most have sought a simpler life because of work pressure, some are financially independent and a large portion are involved in voluntary work of one kind or another. Common strategies of people who voluntarily want to simplify their lives are:

- downscaling to a smaller house
- driving a used rather than new car
- shopping at thrift and second-hand stores
- avoiding restaurants, first-run movies and expensive entertainment;
- experimenting with bartering services.

Sometimes in these circles, says Schor, the issue of saving money becomes a competition that ends up being 'every bit as self-defeating as spending money'.

The tree change

The latest flux of city dwellers who move to the country have been labelled in Australia as part of a 'tree change', a term coined by the media in the wake of another social phenomenon, the sea change. Social researcher Neil Barr says tree changing is a number of phenomena rolled into one:

- Well-heeled 'shifters' buy amenity farms—perhaps with olive trees or vines—that are expensive, maybe with views or near to a major centre.
- Budget bohemia: where cheap land, abandoned by traditional farming, is purchased, sometimes with a view to protect biodiversity, or, says Barr, with a degree of 'counter-culture aspiration'.
- People seeking out a particular culture that's become established in a small town. It might be a gay community, folk music, rock climbing or art. Some areas first attracted low-income arts earners, but are now attracting people with money.
- People seeking better housing value often move to small rural towns, driven out of the cities by high prices. These can include retirees, people from business failures and people receiving benefits. The impact of these 'migrants' on a town depends, according to Barr, 'on the mix and the clash of cultures'.

What's in a word? Alterpreneur

This play on 'alternative' and 'entrepreneur', refers to people who leave their jobs to start their own business, not so much to make money but to improve their standard of living, gain more control over their lives and generally be happier.

Although Duane Elgin published a bestseller in the US in 1981 called *Voluntary Simplicity*, the term had been used for many decades. The idea of living simply goes back as far as people have consciously thought about their manner of living, as this excerpt from Richard B Gregg's classic, *The Value of Voluntary Simplicity*, shows: 'Voluntary simplicity of living has been advocated and practised by the founders of most of the great religions: Buddha, Lao Tse, Moses and Mohammed—also by many saints and wise men such as St Francis, John Woolman, the Hindu rishis, the Hebrew prophets, the Moslem Sufis … Our present "mental climate" is not favourable, either to a clear understanding of the value of simplicity or to its practice. Simplicity seems to be a foible of saints and occasional geniuses, but not something for the rest of us.'

Voluntary simplicity is an inner and outer condition, says Gregg, with a perspective that has remained surprisingly contemporary: singleness of purpose, sincerity and honesty within, avoidance of external clutter, of many possessions irrelevant to the chief purpose of life; an ordering and guiding of our energy and desires and a partial restraint in some directions in order to secure greater abundance of life in other directions.

The gist of voluntary simplicity seems little changed, although the trappings may be different—computers are popular for email, research and writing, even among simple-livers.

Elgin's book embraces what it called the tenets of voluntary simplicity—frugal consumption, ecological awareness, and personal growth. In short, voluntary simplicity is a way of living that is 'outwardly more simple and inwardly more rich'. There's no dogmatic formula for simpler living, says Elgin, but some of the aspects and attitudes he associates with the approach are listed below. (Warning: it does not read like a blueprint for a simple life.)

- Investing the time and energy in family and friendships with activities, such as walking, making music together, sharing a meal or camping.
- Developing a full spectrum of potential: physical, emotional, mental and spiritual.
- Feeling connected with the Earth and concerned for the poor.

- A lower level of personal consumption, which involves going on less commercialized holidays.
- Eating simpler and less processed foods.
- Less clutter and complexity in people's personal lives.
- Greater self-reliance by learning basic carpentry, plumbing, appliance repair, gardening and crafts.
- Fostering community by a preference for smaller scale living and working environments that encourage face-to-face contact.
- Becoming involved in volunteering and civic affairs.
- Getting involved in worthwhile causes, such as protecting rainforests, saving animals from extinction or boycotting goods and services from unethical companies.
- Transformed transport: more public transport, car pooling, smaller and more fuel-efficient cars, living closer to work, riding a bike and walking.

David McClements (1936–)

David McClements, an Ontario-born American who later moved to New Zealand, practises what he calls Extreme Voluntary Simplicity. He has reduced spending to a bare minimum, managing on US$950 ($AU1250) a year, with $US450 (AU$595) going on food. He owns the house where he and his wife live, and much of the rest of the money goes on rates.

'I am now free from the boss's pressure to produce more and keep up with the Joneses. It's not exactly a religious decision, but it's based on some of the same basic impulses,' he says on his website. He's living off the 'capital' of a horde of clothes and hasn't thrown any out for a couple of decades. In 1992, aged 56, he featured on the front page of the *North Shore Times Advertiser*, sporting bare feet and carrying a packed rucksack. At that time, the weekly shop cost him around US$71 (AUS$94), and fed a family of five, including two teenagers and a 20 year old. Living with less money means more careful budgeting: 'We realised we just had to think three times before buying anything.'

SIMPLE LIVING

Our life is frittered away by detail. Simplicity, simplicity, simplicity! I say, let your affairs be two or three and not a hundred or a thousand. Keep your accounts on your thumbnail.

HENRY DAVID THOREAU (1817–1862)

What is simple living? It could encompass any of the following ideas: unadorned country living, back to the land, arts and crafts revivals, organic gardening, environmental conservation, recycling, anti-nuclear, urban cooperatives, wilderness expeditions and frugality. All this and more, says David Shi, author of *The Simple Life: Plain Living and High Thinking in American Culture*. It doesn't have a fixed meaning and throughout its history has always represented a 'shifting cluster of ideas, sentiments and activities'. While in different times and places, the emphasis has changed, the underlying assumption has always been that making money and accumulating things should not smother the soul, the life of the mind or the cohesion of the family. Some of the ideas over time have included: a hostility to luxury; suspicion of riches; reverence for nature; rural rather than urban ways of life and work; self-reliance through frugality and diligence; nostalgia for the past; scepticism for modernity; conscientious, rather than conspicuous consumption; a taste for the plain and functional.

Over the centuries philosophers, thinkers and writers have had much to say about simple living and the clash of the material world with the world of ideas and the spirit. But praising simplicity can be easier than living it. Ralph Waldo Emerson discovered he didn't have the stamina for a simple life of physical work, found the vegetarian diet too bland, and his wife and children declared they couldn't do without servants.

- Socrates (470–399 BC): Ideas should take priority over things. 'Men are to be esteemed for their virtue, not their wealth.' He recommended a golden mean between poverty and wealth.
- Aristotle (384–322 BC): Lead a balanced life with moderation in things material and exertion in intellectual matters. 'The man who indulges in every pleasure and abstains from none becomes self-indulgent.'

- In 1629, Puritan settlers, led by John Winthrop, landed in Massachusetts Bay and started a new colony. 'The simple life may have seemed both necessary and reasonable to the original Puritan leaders faced with carving out a Christian utopia in a "howling wilderness",' comments Shi.

  By 1634 the new colony was already struggling to uphold its original Puritan ways. The Massachusetts General Court was concerned about the appearance of 'new and immodest fashions' and ordered that no man or woman make or buy clothes of 'great, superfluous and unnecessary expenses'. One year later, they specifically prohibited: 'immoderate great breeches, knots of ribbon, broad shoulder-bands and rails, silk rases, double ruffs and cuffs.'

- In the 17th century, George Fox played a central part in the founding of the Religious Society of Friends in England. Its members, known as Quakers, believe that a person should live his or her life simply to focus on what is most important and ignore or downplay what is least important. This is known as the Testimony of Simplicity. It centres on being more concerned with your inner condition than your outward appearance and with other people more than yourself. A person's spiritual life and character are regarded as more important than the quantity of goods a person possesses or their monetary worth.

- The Transcendentalists were a colourful group of poets, writers and philosophers who lived around Concord in the US between 1830 and 1850 and held interest into the late 1870s. Most famous of these are Ralph Waldo Emerson and Henry David Thoreau. They appealed for a more enlightened approach to getting and spending. They believed life was too precious to waste on 'the mere pursuit and enjoyment of things', says Shi. They sought simpler ways of living that reduced material needs so they could more easily pursue spiritual truths, moral ideals and aesthetic impulses. William Henry Channing expressed their credo: 'To live content with small means; to seek elegance rather than luxury, and refinement rather than fashion; to be worthy, not respectable, and wealthy, not rich; to study hard, think quietly, talk gently, act frankly ...'

- On Walden Pond. Thoreau famously lived for two years in the woods at Concord, not as is often suggested, to live cheaply but 'to transact some private business with the fewest obstacles'. Nor was it a hermit's life. The hut was only a mile or two out of town and he had plenty of visitors, so that the cabin rang out with 'boisterous mirth' many times. His mother and sister visited most Saturdays, bringing him something to eat, and he strolled into town every couple of days. He tried—not successfully—to persuade an impoverished and barely surviving woodsman and his family to reorganize their lives, recognizing that coffee, butter, milk

John Woolman (1720–1772)

Born into a large and pious Quaker family in Northampton, West Jersey in the US, John Woolman apprenticed himself to a tailor and in 1746 opened his own clothing and dry goods store. His aim was to 'get a living in a plain way without the load of great business and have opportunity for retirement and inward recollection'. He rigourously applied his religious scruples to his business practices, attempting to dissuade poorer customers from purchasing beyond their means and going into debt, and refusing to sell 'mere luxuries'. His trade prospered, triggering a tension between piety and profit. After several attempts to curtail his business, he warned customers he would close shop.

He decided to make a living as a tailor, supplementing his income with teaching, tending an apple orchard and working as a scrivener. He was also an itinerant minister and in 1772 visited England, where he was keen to witness the social conditions in the North. He walked from London to Yorkshire because of the hardships that stagecoaches caused men and horses alike. 'So great is the hurry in the spirit of this world that in aiming to do business quick and to gain wealth the creation at this day doth loudly groan!' he said. He contracted smallpox at a Quakers Meeting and died soon after. He is remembered especially for his ability to balance a strong work ethic with a spiritual ethic.

and fresh meat were not necessities: 'If he and his family would live simply they might all go a-huckleberrying in the summer for their amusement.'

- The Arts and Craft Movement. Led by William Morris, the British poet, artist and architect, and John Ruskin a writer and reformer, the Arts and Craft Movement of the late 19th century rejected mass-produced reproduction furniture in favour of simplicity, good craftsmanship and good design. Its proponents saw the worker as a cog in the wheel of progress, living in an environment of shoddy machine-made goods, based more on ostentation than function. It took hold in both Britain and the US but in the former, the high quality and the decent wage paid to the craftsmen meant goods could only be afforded by the upper class. A social and artistic movement, its philosophy was the synthesis of nature, love of craft and simple living.

- Progressive simplicity—a simplicity for therapy's sake—was attractive to a number of harried members of the professional class in the US at the turn of the 20th century. Centred on the concept of spending time and money wisely, it consisted of productive occupation, civic involvement and careful control of material desires and mental and physical energies. Shi quotes an editorial from the *Independent* contending that simple living is 'the only possible relief from the nerve destroying complexity of modern civilization' and makes sense, on both economic and psychological grounds to the many 'overpressured' bourgeoisie.

I love a small house, plain clothes, simple living. Many persons know the luxury of a skin bath—a plunge in the pool or the wave unhampered by clothing. That is the simple life—direct and immediate contact with things, life with the false trappings torn away ... to see the fire that warms you ... to be thrilled by the stars at night; to be elated over a bird's nest or over a wild flower in spring—these are some of the rewards of the simple life.

JOHN BURROUGHS, AN ESSAY ENTITLED, 'WHAT LIFE MEANS TO ME'
IN *COSMOPOLITAN*, 1906

- Gandhi's simplicity. Mahatma Gandhi, the spiritual and political leader who was assassinated in 1948 was committed to simplicity and believed that a person involved in social service should lead a simple life. He first simplified his own life by denouncing the Western lifestyle he was leading in South Africa. He called this 'reducing himself to zero'. He made and washed his own clothes, the traditional Indian *dhoti* and shawl, woven with a *charkha*, and lived on a simple vegetarian diet. Gandhi spent one day of each week in silence, believing it brought him inner peace and drawing on the Hindu principles of *mouna* (silence) and *shanty* (peace).

- *The Good Life*. The popular BBC TV show which ran from 1975–1978 featured Tom and Barbara Good, who decided to give the self-sufficient life a go in suburban Surbiton. The main character, Tom, decided on his 40th birthday, that he could no longer take the assignment to design plastic toys for breakfast cereal packets seriously and quit his job. They generated electricity using methane from animal waste, thanks to pigs Pinky and Perky, a goat called Geraldine and several chickens. The gardens were turned over to fruit and vegetables, while bartering surplus produce was the means to obtain the essentials they could not make themselves. Their trials and tribulations made *The Good Life* one of Britain's most successful situation comedies ever.

- Self-sufficiency. The simple life has usually equated with at least partially, a more self-sufficient one. Dreamers and realists alike were boosted by the 'sage of smallholding' John Seymour's *Complete Book of Self-Sufficiency*, published in 1975, which has since sold over a million copies and been published in 20 languages. (It was the kick-starting publication for young publishers Christopher Dorling and Peter Kindersley.) It covered topics such as ploughing the fields, milking the cows, creating an urban organic garden and harnessing energy. A new edition was released in 2003 with a preface by *Small is Beautiful* author E F Schumacher.

COMMUNITIES WITH INTENTION

It can be hard to go it alone and live simply in a materially cluttered and money-driven society. Many people make the choice to start or join communities that share a different set of values—whether inspired by religious belief, concern for the environment or a less financially oriented life. According to environmental sociologist, Bill Metcalf of Griffith University in Australia, there are between 150 and 200 communal groups in England, perhaps 2000 in the US, around 280 in Israel, somewhere between 150 and 200 groups in Australia, 50 in New Zealand and several hundred in Japan. While not all of these are concerned with simple living, many are concerned with aspects of it. Professor Jim McKnight of the University of Western Sydney estimates at least half of Australia's 100,000 or so communards hold to voluntary simplicity in some form. 'It is clear that communards, of whatever

A day in a life at Fruitlands

The moral community, Fruitlands, was founded in 1843 in Harvard, Massachusetts in the US, financed by English journalist and reformer, Charles Lane. Bronson Alcott, father of author Louisa May Alcott, was one of 11 adults who joined forces to strengthen their spirituality, live simply and self-reliantly. Residents turned their backs on the market economy and turned their hands to subsistence farming and bargaining. It was no holiday.

The day began at dawn with a plunge in the cold pool, a music lesson and breakfast of nuts and grains. They worked till noon, stopping for a vegetarian meal and 'interesting and deep-searching conversation'. Afterwards it was back to the fields for the afternoon, then supper, discussion and sleep. That was the initial plan, but it was soon discarded because the men paid more attention to conversation than crops, and the women found themselves taking up the slack. The community disbanded as winter approached and residents found themselves lacking adequate shelter and food. The project is remembered fondly and the site of Fruitlands is today a museum.

shade of radicalness, live more environmentally sustainable, less materialistic lives, and are more content with their lifestyles than are their non-communal neighbours,' says Metcalf in his 2001 paper, 'Diggers and Dreamers'. A handful of the better known communities are outlined below.

Christiania, Copenhagen

The partially self-governing 'village' in the Danish capital of Copenhagen was founded in 1971 when a group of hippy squatters took over an abandoned military barracks. It has managed so far to survive many scandals and attempts to close it by the government. Hard drugs have been banned since 1979 and hash stalls, once openly selling on Pusher Street, disappeared from view in 2004.

The 1000-strong community that occupies the carless area of 34 hectares, attracts more than one million visitors each year. Houses are built by the inhabitants, but not owned. When there's a vacancy, it's advertised in the Christiania newspaper and applicants are invited. 'No money passes under the table at Christiania,' its guidebook explains, 'so you don't need a fortune to move in.' The grounds house numerous art galleries and four day care centres for children. It was one of the first places in Denmark to provide low-cost high-speed internet connections. Christiania bikes—solid load-bearing tricycles with various carrying boxes—were designed about 20 years ago and are now exported all over the world.

Findhorn, Scotland

Founded in the 1960s by Peter Caddy, his wife, Eileen, and their friend Dorothy Maclean, the Findhorn community hosts several hundred people working 'on the values of planetary service, co-creation with nature and attunement to the divinity within all beings'. It runs nearly 200 week-long courses a year, organizes conferences, training, worldwide pilgrimages and outreach programmes of educational workshops. In 1972 it was registered as a Scottish charity under the name, the Findhorn Foundation. Today it describes itself as 'the central educational and organizational heart of a widely diversified community ... spanning dozens of holistic businesses and initiatives ...'.

The Ecovillage Project began in the late 1980s with the building of a wind-energy generator and several eco-friendly community buildings. Sustainable housing (there are now 40 houses) is gradually replacing the original community caravans. In the 1990s the community built a biological sewage treatment plant they call 'The Living Machine'. Residents of the Findhorn community abide by the Common Ground, its 14 core values: spiritual practice, service, personal growth, personal integrity, respecting others, direct communication, reflection, responsibility, non-violence, perspective, cooperation, resolution, agreements, and commitment to the spirit of the Common Ground.

Riverside, New Zealand

In 1941 a group of Christian Pacifists moved to a 12-hectare farming property near Nelson, to adopt a cooperative way of life as a practical alternative to 'normal society's' competitive ways, which they saw as a major contributor to war.

Today, the community occupies 208 hectares. Its main income is dairy farming and a commercial orchard. It is also home to a public garage, a café, a small hostel, an organic vegetable garden, an organic home orchard, a pine forest, a native plantation, sheep, one pig, chickens and ducks. The members, who currently number 19 adults and

---

Royalty to Rags: Siddhartha, The story of Buddha (563–483 BC)

The princeling Siddhartha was born in the Gautama clan among the Sakkas, a people who lived on what is now the border of India and Nepal. He renounced royal family life to study under various spiritual teachers. Seeking his own way, he 'practised self-mortification', which he then rejected in favour of moderation, finally achieving a spiritual 'realisation' after a night of soul-searching beneath a tree in a place now known as Bodhgaya. He spent the rest of his life giving spiritual instruction to an ever-growing number of disciples. When he died, aged 81, he had a large and well-organized following.

17 children, aim to eat a shared lunch and one evening meal together each week. Assets are owned by a registered charitable trust. Members share the use of two minibuses and four cars; most work on site. Decisions are arrived at by consensus at weekly business meetings. Adults receive the same cash income plus an allowance for each child or dependant, while earnings from outside the community go into the general account. All power, telephone charges (apart from tolls) and medical expenses are paid from the community's general fund.

Let your life speak

All you need for living are a few possessions, simplicity of spirit, and readiness to answer to the divine spark in every person.
ROBERT LAWRENCE SMITH, *A QUAKER BOOK OF WISDOM*, 1999

Says Robert Lawrence Smith, author of *A Quaker Book of Wisdom*, the key question for Quakers following the tenet of simplicity, one of the cornerstones of the Quaker faith, is 'What do I need?' The idea of simplicity touches the spirit, he says, but while simplicity of lifestyle is not about forsaking worldly goods, someone with materialistic preoccupations is 'ill-prepared' to sit in silence and listen for the 'still small voice of God'.

Many young parents become fixed on the problem of how to deal with their children's 'marketing-induced materialism'. The Quaker response is, 'let your life speak': parents must first order their own priorities, and not let 'superfluity' get in the way of attempting to live a simple life. 'What counts,' believes Smith, 'is our ability to recognize the small miracles sprouting in our midst and to share them with others.' Pay attention, he says, to that feeling deep inside, that your life should be less cluttered and less stressful. Simplicity is like getting your mind in shape—you feel more in control, more centred and more effective. It's about living to the point.

Eileen Caddy (1917–)

Best known as a founder of the Findhorn community near the village of Findhorn, Scotland, Eileen Caddy was born in Alexandria in Egypt. Her father was a director of Barclays Bank Dominion, Colonial and Overseas. She married Squadron Leader Andrew Coombe in 1939 and after a divorce, married Squadron Leader Peter Caddy in 1953. She was part of a circle in the 1950s that surrounded Peter's first wife, Sheena Govan, and also included Dorothy Maclean.

Eileen, Dorothy and Peter managed the Cluny Hill Hotel near Forres, Moray, Scotland, for several years. When the work came to an end, with nowhere to go and little money, Eileen and Peter moved with their three sons and Dorothy, to a caravan. They started to grow food organically, and despite being on sandy soil, the garden flourished. They claimed to be guided by nature spirits. Whatever the reasons, the garden and its 40-pound cabbages attracted national interest, and by the 1960s a community had formed around the three friends. Eileen claimed to receive guidance during meditations from an inner divine source she called the 'still small voice within'. In 2004 she was awarded an MBE from the Queen for her services to spiritual inquiry.

CHOOSING BETTER

The traps and snares of modern life have made the pleasures that are right there in front of us harder to recognize.
ROBERT LAWRENCE SMITH, *A QUAKER BOOK OF WISDOM*, 1999

It's very easy to get caught up in the material world and the pursuit of wealth. And easy too, to forget the riches of the natural world and a life of ideas and friendship. Choosing to risk a transformation can lead to something 'rich and strange' and maybe even a different way of life. Money can transform, but it's not the only way to change rags to riches. Downshifting desires or choosing simplicity can reduce the budget and perhaps even provide a richer life.

TAKING STOCK

DOWNSHIFTING

1. Are you tempted to downshift but not sure how to go about it? Planning is key and preparing for reduced spending will add to the success of your venture.
   Think about:

(a) reducing debt. Paying off credit cards, and other debts, such as car loans and personal loans.

(b) changing expectations. Eating out once a month not once a week; or twice a year, not twice a month, and consider buying second-hand sometimes.

(c) reducing spending. Cutting back on luxuries, trying delay tactics to reduce weekly spending and looking closely at your budget to identify possible savings.

(d) analyzing values. Investing in the things you deeply value, whether it's music, your family or your nearby native bush.

2. Do you yearn for a simpler life? What are the complications in your life you'd like to see the end of?

3. When you read about others' attempts to live more simply, which aspects appeal most to you (for example, environmental, spiritual, less commercial)?

4. How practical are these changes for you? What are some easy first steps you could take to move towards a simpler life?

... our bodies are fighting against a deeper rhythm ... described as an 'echo of the sun'.

RUSSELL G FOSTER AND LEON KREITZMAN,
RHYTHMS OF LIFE, 2004

7. NATURAL RHYTHMS

TIME IS EMBEDDED IN OUR GENES,
JUST AS IT IS IN EVERY LIVING THING
ON EARTH. HUMANS HAVE FOUND
WAYS—CLOCKS AND ARTIFICIAL
LIGHT—TO RESIST OUR BIOLOGICAL
RHYTHMS. BUT WHAT DOES THIS DO
TO BODY AND SOUL?

BEATING TO A COLLECTIVE TIME

All living beings on this Earth, whether diatoms, corals, spiders, scorpions, squirrels, beavers, kangaroos, bacteria, algae, jellyfish, worms, centipedes, muskrats, shrews or humans, share the fact of a biological clock. This deep-seated mechanism has a role likened to the conductor of an orchestra, and is what keeps an organism beating to a collective time. The clock triggers and coordinates the thousands of processes—almost all the activity—occurring in the body. For all the sophistication of our digital clocks, hand-held organizers and jet travel, we are controlled by these complex masters that reach back to the time when life began.

Survival on Earth means adapting to a home that rotates and spins, bringing night and day and changing seasons, and that survival depends on having a biological clock. It's how salmon know when to spawn, bison to migrate and field mice to hibernate. In short, a biological clock allows them to anticipate the future and attune to their environment in the broadest and deepest sense. Sheep breed so that the lambs are born at a time when there's plenty of new grass to sustain the mother during lactation and the young after weaning; rooks breed at certain time of year in order to feed earthworms to their young before the worms move deeper as spring weather warms and dries out the soil. Evening primroses prepare and later release their scent as the sun descends in the sky, attracting pollinating moths and other night-flying insects.

Even bacteria have clocks that help regulate chemical reactions, and it was probably in bacteria that biological clocks first developed. The first cyanobacteria appeared more than 3.5 billion years ago. These water living photosynthesizing bacteria (sometimes referred to as blue-green algae, although they are now known not to be algae) remain one of the largest and most important bacteria today. They have changed little in billions of years, but their environment has changed dramatically.

Early Earth revolved more rapidly and its days were shorter. Tides were greater and storms more severe. The sky was steely blue, dark and hazy with dust storms and volcanic clouds; there was almost no oxygen. We can thank the bacteria, the first life, for producing our oxygen-rich atmosphere, but it took billions of years. Ultraviolet-absorbing ozone was in short supply so the Earth's surface was blitzed with lethal ultraviolet light. A biological clock could regulate reactions so that the bacteria fixed nitrogen in the night and photosynthesized during the day—reactions that can't take place at the same time as the former can't happen in the presence of oxygen. It also may have timed cell division, by shutting it off when the light was at its most damaging, thus protecting valuable DNA.

Biological clocks explain why the dawn chorus can start before the first light appears. It is not a response to the rising sun, it is the birds' internal alarm clocks at work, which wake them to welcome in the sun. Biological clocks allow organisms to mould their lives around natural rhythms making it possible to exploit the conditions they find. They work both within the organism itself, for example, in waking every morning, and within groups, by coordinating breeding activities. Biological clocks are so ubiquitous they are almost a hallmark of life itself.

THE SEARCH FOR A BIOLOGICAL CLOCK

The painstaking search for the mechanism of the biological clock is meticulously recounted in Russell G Foster's and Leon Kreitzman's book, *Rhythms of Life*. It's a search that's involved putting mimosa stems in dark cupboards (in 1729 French astronomer, Jean Jacques d'Ortous de Mairan observed how it opened and closed its leaves periodically despite the darkness); watching cockroaches on a miniature running wheel in differing periods of light and dark; shining light on the back of the knees (one theory held that humans had photoreceptors (or light receptors) there, but it could not be confirmed) and many human attempts to live (temporarily) deep underground away from the influence of light.

By the 1960s the majority view was that life responded to an internal mechanism—although they didn't yet know what it was. A minority view still held out for circadian rhythms being explained by external forces, perhaps from a geophysical source, such as magnetism, electro-magnetism or cosmic radiation.

HOW DOES A BIOLOGICAL CLOCK WORK?

Time works across all scales: from the planetary, through to the molecular. And at the basis, a biological clock comes down to an oscillating molecular system made up of different proteins.

Very simply, a biological clock involves a number of mechanisms.

- Entrainment. Clocks get reset every day at sunset and sunrise, and this way, an animal's internal time stays attuned to 'astronomical time'. Entrainment explains how we eventually readjust after a period of jetlag, our clocks are not just set once and that's it, they are subtly corrected every day according to local conditions.

- Zeitgeber. While organisms have their own internal clock mechanisms, they rely on an external 'zeitgeber' or entrainment signal to bring them in line with 'local time' each day. This explains how animals can change their rhythms as the days shorten and lengthen each season. Light is the entrainment mechanism for humans.

- Light. The cogs and wheels of the biological clock are the rotation of the planet and light. The eye contains light receptors, but the eyes don't have it all as far as receptors for circadian rhythms. There are other receptors, called photoreceptors, and in some animals, the clock mechanisms are distributed about the body. In humans, the photoreceptors in the eye associated with the circadian clock are not the same ones we use for sight. So, although some blind people experience free-running circadian rhythms, some others have functioning circadian receptors so they respond to the entrainment signal of light, even though they cannot use light to see.

- Melatonin. Known as the Dracula hormone, because it only comes out at night, melatonin is released by the pineal gland, surging into the bloodstream at about 9 pm each night and preparing the body for sleep. Light prevents its release at any other time by putting a break on the release mechanism.

- The third eye. Birds have clocks in their eyes and the Linnulus crab has a photoreceptor in its tail. The human 'master' clock is found in a part of the brain that coincides with what has been referred to as the 'third eye'. It's called the suprachiasmatic nucleus (SCN) and consists of a group of about 20,000 cells in the anterior part of the hypothalamus in the brain. This master clock, the SCN, is the circadian pacemaker of all mammals, and through its influence on other parts of the brain and other organs, it generates the circadian rhythm of neuronal and hormonal activity, regulating the fluctuations in many different body functions over a 24-hour period. Its position coincides with what Buddhists call the third eye. (To find it, imagine a line running inside your head from the bridge of your nose to the base of your skull. Imagine a second line running about 2 centimetres behind the eyes. Where these intersect is the SCN, a cluster about a third of a cubic millimetre in volume.) In some schools of Buddhism focusing on the third eye, while emptying your mind of thoughts, is believed to bring calmness.

- Free running. What would happen if there was no signal to readjust the biological clock every morning? This is what scientists have observed by keeping organisms in the dark constantly. Instead of being programmed by a light signal each dawn and dusk, the organisms find their own rhythm. This is sometimes a fluctuating one and is called 'free running'. When circadian clocks are kept in constant conditions they run close, but not exactly, to 24 hours. Scientists interpreted this as demonstrating that organisms have their own internal clock, and are not responding to their surroundings alone. In 'real' life, circadian clocks are reset each dawn and dusk to 'local time'.

Waking up to new sleep medicine

In the future, lifestyle drugs and devices might allow us to structure the way we sleep. A 2006 *New Scientist* article, 'Get up and go', explores many of the options, such as drugs for a deeper sleep that restores in half the normal time, wakefulness promoters to go without sleep for several days, electrical devices to switch on the brain and neurofeedback training. Will 'advances' such as these drive us further down the 'sedative/stimulant' loop? Such technology might help us cope with a 24/7 life, but is coping really living?

Circadian rhythms

Over the course of a day we experience circadian rhythms ('circa' meaning about; and 'dia' a day)—the shifting patterns of metabolic and hormonal activity that take place during a 24-hour cycle managed by our biological clock.

Circadian rhythms assign a time for all that needs to occur over a 24-hour period. The programmed regularity is also a way of preventing everything happening at once. Such a basic yet fundamental definition is also one used to describe what mechanical clocks do to our lives—once life gets complex, we need clocks to prevent everything happening at once. From a bilogical viewpoint, it's useful not to need to urinate at night, for instance, and kidney function is reduced accordingly.

Our experience of time and the associated sleep, naps, alertness, mood, body temperature and circadian rhythms are all intricately linked. Body temperature, for example, varies across the 24 hours of each day—when our body temperature is at its peak we experience peak alertness, when it's at its lowest we are in deep sleep, usually at 4 am.

Heartbeat and blood pressure also follow a day and night pattern. We're at our most vulnerable in the early morning hours when the low point in the circadian rhythm means our bodies are least able to resist cardiac or respiratory difficulties. In addition, accumulated research shows:

- tooth pain is lowest after lunch
- proofreading and sprint swimming are best in the evening
- labour pains more often begin at night
- most natural births occur in the early hours
- sudden cardiac death is more likely in the morning
- complex problem solving and logical reasoning is most efficient around noon
- athletic tasks, and those involving physical coordination, are best performed in the early evening around the time of the daily peak in body temperature.

TIME AND CULTURE

Que no son todos los tiempos unos.
(For all times are not the same.)

MIGUEL DE CERVANTES, *DON QUIXOTE DE LA MANCHA*, 1605

In simpler eras our concept of time was linked to our observations of the natural rhythms of the environment. In old German the period of a year was described, not with a single word, but with the expression, 'in bareness and in leaf'. In England, the cuckoo marks the start of spring, while the robin's song marks the beginning of winter.

The Bontoc Igorot, a rice-cultivating people from the Philippines, used to identify eight seasons based around farming: *i-na-na*, 'no more work in rice sementaras' (three months); *la-tub*, 'first harvest' (four weeks); *cho-ok*, 'most of rice is harvested' (four weeks); *li-pas*, 'no more palay-harvest' (10 to 15 days); *ba-li-ling* 'general planting of camotes' (six weeks); *sa-gan-ma*, 'the seed beds for rice put into condition' (two months); *pa-chong*, 'seed-sowing' (five to six weeks); and *sa-ma*, 'seedlings planted out' (seven weeks).

The Nuer tribesmen of southern Sudan divided their year into wet and dry, while Ancient Egyptians had three seasons: inundation, seed time and harvest. Their priests were honoured for predicting the yearly floods. It was important to be able to predict this key natural event in order to coordinate the gathering of a widely dispersed workforce that was called up each year to make the most of the flood for farming purposes. The annual flooding of the Nile was surrounded in ritual and magic, and occurred—so the priests knew—when the sun and the moon were in a particular configuration.

CIRCULAR TIME

The Australian Aboriginal concept of time is usually described as 'circular' and rhythmical rather than the typically Western 'linear' perception, with its clear past, present and future. In a 'circular' pattern of time an individual is in the centre of 'time-circles', and events are placed in time according to their importance. So the more important an event is to an individual or the community, the 'closer in time' it is perceived.

Time was traditionally measured in seasons, drawn from observations of plant and animal behaviour. The Australian Aboriginal Dharawal people of the Illawarra used seasonal plant signs to tell them when animals could be hunted. The flowering of the inland wattle tree told them sea mammals were about; when the apple berry fruit was ripe, pythons could be found in the early morning hunting birds; when the succulent Pig Face flower was in bloom, there were schools of tailor fish to be had in the shallow beach water. These patterns were passed between generations by knowledge-holders.

A WORLD OF TIME

Different concepts of time are a source of frustration and fascination for the traveller, and an important point of study for the diplomat who wishes to understand and avoid offence. 'So time provides a tangible, observable way for groups to define who is and who is not a member,' explains Allen Bluedorn in *The Human Organization of Time*. Differing time values also occur within a country. Mexican-Americans differentiate between 'hora inglesa', the actual time on the clock, and 'hora mexicana', a much more casual treatment of time.

In 1960, Jules Henry, an anthropologist and sociologist at Washington University in the US, spent a year interviewing mostly poor African-American families in a St Louis housing development. For them, one of the biggest differences between their lives and the lives of the surrounding white community centred on their attitudes to time. They talked of CPT (coloured people's time) in which an event, even though scheduled, could occur at any moment during a wide span of hours, or not even at all. This they saw was in great contrast to the highly organized, precisely scheduled world of white people.

Another way different cultures experience time is with ritual. Life cycle rituals are fundamental to the life of a Hindu. Indian psychoanalyst, Sadhir Kakar explains: 'One of the major thrusts of these rituals is the gradual integration of the child into society, with the *samskaras*, as it were, beating time to a measured movement that takes the child away from the original mother–infant symbiosis into the full-fledged membership of his community.'

There are sixteen main *samskaras*, or sacraments, from conception and naming the child, through to when studies are completed, marriage, renouncing the householder's life and funeral rites.

OWL OR LARK?

When the moon is on the wave,
And the glow-worm in the grass,
And the meteor on the grave,
And the wisp on the morass;
When the falling stars are shooting,
And the answer'd owls are hooting,

LORD GEORGE GORDON BYRON (1788–1824), 'MANFRED'

One in ten people are raring to go at dawn says Dr Michael Smolensky, chronobiologist and co-author of *The Body Clock Guide to Better Health*. He calls these people larks. About two in 10 are owls and like to stay up past midnight. Most people are hummingbirds and fall somewhere in between, with less distinct preferences to either the morning or the night. They might not even mind the occasional very early rise for fishing or a late night party every now and then.

Cartoonist Scott Adams, creator of the syndicated strip, Dilbert, told Smolensky that he created his second career by 'discovering' the morning. He started the cartoons during 5 am stints in the mornings before his regular job and even when he left the job to cartoon full-time, he never tried to be creative past noon. Then again, he says his hand isn't steady enough for the inking part of the process until the afternoon or evening. However, when later in his cartooning career he had to coincide with Hollywood workers (mostly owls) he found he needed to change his routine, working to midnight and rising at 7 am.

As a freelance writer, AN has experienced a similar variation in timing:

A few years ago I got up at 5 am for three months and worked for a couple of hours before the rest of the household was up and about. It helped push along a big project and meet a looming deadline. Another time, several times I got up at 3 am to meet a series of deadlines. Once I was up and had had a cup of tea I enjoyed having such a stretch of uninterrupted and productive time. I liked being up in the dark and witnessing the gradual lighting up of the sky and the garden. But eventually I overdid it and combined with moving house, I got sick with a temperature and a cough I couldn't shake for weeks. Now I've got a deep-seated aversion to forcing myself out of bed. Even if work demands the time, I just haven't got the energy: my family's at a different, very busy stage and the demands are high.

Nathaniel Kleitman (1895–1999)

Nathaniel Kleitman was born in Kishinev, Russia, in 1895 and migrated to the US in 1915. He was the first scientist to seriously study sleep and was interested in things like the changes in human efficiency and alertness across the course of a day. A scholar, Kleitman often observed family and friends as well as himself. He kept precise records of his two daughters' sleep habits from infancy to college and once kept himself awake for 180 consecutive hours to study the effects of sleep deprivation. In the 1930s, he measured the performance of a range of tasks such as multiplication, hand steadiness, card dealing and sorting. He found performance rising in the morning to peak at midday, then falling again.

He set up the first sleep laboratory at Stanford University in 1925. In 1938, Kleitman and assistant, Bruce Richardson, lived for one month deep underground in Mammoth Cave, Kentucky in the US. Kleitman said he never slept properly there—perhaps he was distracted by the need to devise and set traps to prevent rats from sleeping with the 'campers'. In 1953 he and associate, Eugene Aserinsky, discovered REM (rapid eye movement) sleep. Known as the 'father of sleep research', Kleitman died in 1999 aged 104.

The characteristics of owls and larks

Owls are notoriously college students and twenty-somethings, who do not really get going until the afternoon, are at their most pleasant later in the day, and at their most alert about 6 pm. An owl usually has the following behavioural patterns:

- They are usually in a rush to get to work or college in the morning because they've woken up late.
- They wouldn't mind an evening job, such as a bartender.
- They might catch up on the laundry or other chores at midnight.
- They can often be found surfing the internet late at night.
- They are more likely than larks to be polo players.
- They wake up one or two hours later on days off.
- They need multiple alarm clocks.
- They cope better than larks with night shifts.

Generally, larks are most active in the morning, tend to be older (most are over 60) and they feel most aware around noon. They work best in the late morning and are chatty and friendly between 9 am and 4 pm. A lark usually has the following behavioural patterns:

- They get up early to read the morning paper with coffee.
- They could handle a morning newsreading job.
- They are more likely than owls to be golfers.
- They fall asleep faster than an owl.
- They don't need an alarm clock to wake up.

Bill Gates, on the other hand, is known to be an owl and in the early days it wasn't uncommon for him and his team to fall asleep at their terminals. JS is similar. A self-employed graphic artist, if she hasn't managed to put in the hours on a task during the day, she'll start again in the evening, after dinner, and if necessary work through till 2 am. She's not a morning person at any time, but will be up by 8 am to get her children off to school. It's a pace she can keep up for months at a time, but not without feeling shattered at the end of each period.

Despite his best intentions, PN is not as good an early riser as he'd like to be. He is easily distracted in the morning, likes to lie in bed listening to the radio over a couple of cups of tea and get up about 8 am. His natural urges are to potter—perhaps preparing a soup for the evening, attending to the garden, carrying out household tasks or shopping. Left to his own preferences, rather than his sense of 'should', he would front up at his desk at 11 am or 12 pm. Observing this, his wife suggested he work with, rather than against, his natural rhythm, 'allowing' himself to potter in the morning and do a 'decent day's work' of around seven hours, finishing at 7 pm.

Whether we're morning people may depend largely on our genes, in particular, one called the 'clock' gene that is known to control our biological rhythms. The first human gene controlling circadian rhythms was discovered by researchers exploring the genetic basis of a rare syndrome that causes people to fall asleep early and wake very early in the morning. The findings were published in *Science* magazine in 2001. They found that a mutation in a gene called hPer2 caused something called Familial Advanced Sleep-phase Syndrome in a family in Utah. The affected family members fell asleep around 7 pm each evening and woke spontaneously at about 2 am. The discovery could one day help people who find themselves suffering sleep problems.

Time signatures

Our morning or evening tendencies are also known as a 'chronotype' or time signature. So, why do time signatures, or chronotypes, vary? Even normal variations have complex reasons, involve several genes and are also influenced by environmental factors. There are several factors affecting people's performance.

- The strength of the zeitgeber or entrainment signal which affects the way we adjust to 'local time' each day. A farmer who is up and outside in the early morning will get a much stronger signal, for example, than an office worker who spends much time indoors.
- Individuals have different 'free-running' periods. For example, each person experiences different periodic cycles that would dominate without the regular adjusting mechanism of dawn and dusk.

- Genetics can affect our master clock, the SCN, in many ways, including the sensitivity of the receptor (interpreting an entrainment signal as either strong or weak).

Factors such as these affect why we perform better at different times during the day and night. Comment Foster and Kreitzman: 'It is impossible to say how much more productive we would be if we timed our activities so that they were in harmony with our time signatures.'

'Early to bed and early to rise makes a man healthy, wealthy and wise.'

So said Benjamin Franklin, echoing the moralistic tones that equate virtue with early rising. Dr Christopher Martyn—a self-reported owl—had always been irritated with the self-righteous tones of Franklin's statement. A researcher from the Medical Research Council's Epidemiology Unit at Southampton Hospital in the UK, he was one of several to put the theory to test. They analyzed data from a long-term study of older people and divided people into two groups, 'larks', who were early sleepers and early risers; and 'owls', those people who slept and got up late. The researchers found nothing to substantiate the saying.

People who were 'larkish' and in bed before 11 pm at night and up before 8 am, did not live any longer, report being any healthier or perform any better in intelligence tests. If anything, 'owls' were slightly wealthier. Martyn guesses the origin of the sentiment has to do with the idea of wasting daylight hours in times when the electric light wasn't quite so universally available. 'And that had to do with how much work you might be able to get into a day,' he says. In addition, people who lay in bed till midday didn't fit well with the industrial work ethic and tended to be viewed rather unsympathetically as undisciplined and lazy. With the rise of shiftwork around the clock, perhaps the judgmental denouncement of late rising will fade.

VOX POP: Are you an owl or a lark?

I used to pay more heed to my own daily rhythms pre-kids, as in thinking of myself as a 'night' person who could get up and do things in the morning if necessary (as in an exercise class at 6.30 am before work) but by preference would sleep very late and stay up very late. But that's no longer relevant. Waking at 7 am is a huge sleep-in in our house, even on a day we're not working. We're all early risers now. FH

There are no doubts that my energy ebbs and flows across the day, but I'm not acutely aware of it. When I have the energy, I like being up early and getting on with things. In the evening I prefer to relax with a glass of wine and not take anything too challenging on. AH

I know that I'm a morning person. I can achieve all manner of things. By the evening I am limp with exhaustion. I still achieve all manner of things—just with less enthusiasm! SE

I'm not super good in the morning. My most productive times are probably mid- to late-morning and the afternoon. Once the sun is getting ready to set I would much rather be at home and even if I stay at work my productivity declines. PN

In the evenings I'm bad. I don't like to go out and socialize in the evening and that can be a problem. I much prefer socializing in the day when my energy levels are higher. ML

I am better in the evening than in the morning. I have never really been a morning person. I used to stay in bed all day sometimes, but I don't like to anymore, as it seems a waste of the day. AE

I am energetic in the morning but by the afternoon I can hardly concentrate. There are periods when I have high energy and feel as though I can tackle the world. Other times it's a struggle to get out of bed. SG

THE PASSING OF TIME

The time would not pass. Somebody was playing with the clocks, and not only with the electric clocks, but the wind-up kind, too. The second hand on my watch would twitch once, and a year would pass, and then it would twitch again.

KURT VONNEGUT, *SLAUGHTERHOUSE-FIVE*, 1969

In 1972 Michael Siffre, a French geologist, spent six months in Midnight Cave in Texas in the US living 'beyond time'. He conducted his experiment with 780 jugs of water, a bicycle machine and a battery of sophisticated monitors that measured his body temperature, cardiac rhythm and the length and nature of his sleep. He was 'divorced from calendars and clocks, and from sun and moon, to help determine, among other things the natural rhythms of human life'. NASA supervised his diet, providing frozen meals identical to those consumed by Apollo 16 astronauts; a professor at the University of Minnesota weighed his daily whiskers (to asses hormonal activity); even the military took an interest in the fact that the last time Siffre went underground, his body rhythms altered to a 48-hour day.

It was a lonely and—temporarily at least—maddening experiment. Siffre even considered suicide at one point, though perhaps not seriously, abandoning the idea when he realized that although his wife would receive his life insurance, his parents would be responsible for the considerable debt he'd accumulated over the years financing his schemes. A highlight of his time in the cave was the realization that another living thing, a mouse he named 'Mus', was sharing his habitat. Wanting a companion, he spent hours devising a way to capture Mus and keep him near. 'Time passes rapidly', he wrote in his diary. Unfortunately, in slamming a dish over the mouse, he caught him on the head and killed him! Time passed slowly again.

HOW WE EXPERIENCE TIME

Why does a watched pot never boil, time pass quicker as we get older, slow when we're waiting and quick when we feel it's running out? There are times when time seems almost to freeze: pivotal moments like near accidents; that moment when the semitrailer that seems to be filling your windscreen and heading straight for you, instead misses you by a hair-breadth. Or, when we are fully attuned to our senses, as this winter swimmer describes: 'There is that moment just after I decide to plunge into the cold water, once I decide and make the tiny adjustments that will send my body forward, there's no going back, yet I feel time stretch as I anticipate the enveloping coldness.'

On the other hand, soldiers have reported losing all sense of time during intense moments of war. Mary Sturt recounts a Sussex Regiment soldier's experience at the front line at the Somme in 1916 in her 1925 book, *The Psychology of Time*. The fresh and 'untried' soldiers experienced for the first time going 'over the top' (attacking from the trenches required the infantry to climb over the top of the parapet before they could cross no-man's-land). The prevailing feeling

Time for a cigarette

Stimulating drugs, such as caffeine and amphetamines, make people underestimate the amount of time that has passed. Hallucinogens, on the other hand, such as marijuana and LSD, slow time, causing people to overestimate the passing of time. People who have recently given up cigarette smoking also have a changed perception of time. A 2003 study from Pennsylvania State University in the US found that time really does pass more slowly when you're feeling desperate for a smoke. Researchers recorded the differences between perceived time and actual time and found that when regular smokers gave up their habit, their perception of passing time was stretched by 50 per cent. The two groups initially had similar abilities in accurately estimating the amount of time that had passed. But when tested after abstaining for a day, most of the smokers estimated a much longer time interval. Does time seem longer because the stopped smokers are more impatient and irritable, or is it just something else to add to feelings of stress and inability to focus? Does it ease with time? Only time, and further research, will tell.

was 'the excitement, if you like, of the chase'. After the first exchange of bombardment the soldier wrote. 'All this turmoil—for the earth rocked like a sea in a storm—had the effect on our untried men of stringing them up to a still further pitch of excitement.'

From the first fire in the early morning to the last moments of light when the company started 'digging in' for the night, appeared to the soldier to last less than half an hour, although it was in fact an entire day. 'This curious delusion ... has remained one of my most striking memories of the Great War.'

The paradox of time is that we experience it in several ways at once. The human experience is one of a multitude of simultaneous and overlapping events. We can watch a kettle boil during breakfast on a long ship journey. Breakfast can go fast, the kettle slow and the journey seem endless. The experience of time in the 'now' is different to our retrospective perception, explains Sturt. Our feelings about time depend on the number of separate events within a period; how pleasant or unpleasant a period of time is; and how much attention we give to time during any given period.

Time stretches

- ... when you're bored. If you are bored, or keep getting distracted, the timekeeper is on and you're more aware of time passing. Psychologist Jean Piaget called this perception 'lived time'.
- ... when you interrupt a task. The more an activity is broken up and interrupted, the longer it seems to take.
- ... when you're passive. Doing 'nothing' can seem to take an aeon: passive activities like listening can seem to last longer than active ones, like taking notes while you listen.
- ... when your mind's working overtime. When mental stimuli makes more mental impressions than usual we feel that time is stretching. In other words, the more you notice change during an interval, the longer you judge that interval to be; for example, if you're waiting for a friend at an airport and lots of people keep coming by, it might seem like it is taking a long time for your friend to appear.

Time flies

- ... when you're having fun. Or, more specifically, when you are fully engaged in an activity. This is because, with your entire focus on the task at hand, you switch off your timekeeper. It can be something fun, but also something like an exam, that you are fully absorbed in, and maybe—pleasantly or not—surprised when it's over.

- ... when you're asleep. In fact, time doesn't even seem to have passed sometimes, when you wake up again. Typically, when we wake up, we can be quite disorientated as to the time—hence stories of people waking, getting dressed and setting up in their studies, only to realize it's 3 am, not 7 am in the morning.

- ... when you are older. A day seems to last longer for a child than an adult. One possible reason for this is that with increasing age, each segment of time is a decreasing percentage of the person's total experience. An hour for a newborn who's waiting for food, seems a very long time, and is more like asking an elderly person to wait for a week! Also, children are less consistent than adults in their estimation of duration, perhaps because they are less able to compensate for differences in the nature of the task or their personal motivation. Elderly people, on the other hand, often find time shorter, probably because they are less likely to notice changes that they've become accustomed to. Learning about time takes time. Typically, young children confuse age with height, assuming anyone taller than them is necessarily older too.

- ... when you are motivated. The more motivated you are for a task, the shorter time it seems to take. In addition, the less motivation you have, the more likely you are to lose attention and keep breaking off, and the longer again it seems to take.

- ... when you're undergoing sensory deprivation. Relatively complete sensory deprivation such as prolonged stays in isolation chambers compresses the experience of time. Time seems to pass about twice as fast according to the *Encyclopaedia Britannica*, even though unpleasant.

RESIST ROUTINE

Dinah Avni-Babad, a psychologist at the Hebrew University in Jerusalem, offers another possible explanation to why the years flash by as we age. 'Want time to pass more slowly?' she asks in an article called 'Shake Up Your Life' published in *Psychology Today*. Her research showed that everyday routines shift our brains to autopilot, whereas new experiences pack the brain with new perceptions. Routine is in some ways like inaction, and the fact that generally we encounter less new experiences as we age, explains why the years seem to go by faster.

BEATING TO AN ARTIFICIAL RHYTHM

Little children can keep time to a march or dance tune, and such dancing to music involves an appreciation of the rhythmic time because we need to anticipate the beats. When we fail to anticipate, we cannot 'keep time'.

MARY STURT, *THE PSYCHOLOGY OF TIME*, 1925

It is only a thin veneer of civilization—helped by the alarm clock—that prevents the tyranny of the biological clock from total domination of our behaviour, whether it's eating, sleeping or our mood swings, say Foster and Kreitzman. But despite the core importance of our internal clocks, it's the external ones that we pay more attention to.

Knowing what the time is seems to anchor us, when we wake and it's four in the morning, we feel we should go back to sleep, whether or not we feel alert; if it's 11 am and we had planned a full day, we may even feel panic that we have made such a late start on the day. As Foster and Kreitzman comment: 'In our modern world we need to know the time to tell us what to do.'

Our '24/7' lifestyle, with 'round-the-clock activity' brings about a conflict, witnessed in the struggle to balance our lives and the stress this puts on our physical health and mental wellbeing. When our internal timers are disrupted we suffer from a range of symptoms, from relatively mild jet lag through to far more serious situations that increase the risk of heart disease, as well as depression and sleep disorders, including sleep fatigue that can be the simple reason behind devastating human accident.

THE ELECTRIC BULB

Light, light, light, light,
Strike a bright light
To shine through the night.

KATHLEEN RICH, *RHYMES & JINGLES FOR PRACTICE IN SPEECH TRAINING*, 1952

Artificial light—whether flickering camp fires, smoking candles or glowing light bulbs—allows us to stay awake and active longer and potentially shortens our sleep schedule. The advent of the light bulb created an environment strong enough to disrupt circadian cycles. Bright lights during a night shift are helpful, but turning on the lights at home when you get up at night can disturb your sleep cycles. Light tells us it's daytime, so it's confusing for our bodies if that's not the case. While we live under more artificial light, many of us are also exposed to less natural light than in previous eras. '… we all have set up house in an electric cave, each of us master of his own schedule,' comments William C Dement in *The Promise of Sleep*.

Hot stove and hot chicks

As explanation of his theory of relativity, Albert Einstein is often quoted as saying that although sitting next to a pretty girl for an hour feels like a minute, placing one's hand on a hot stove for a minute feels like an hour. Or, scientifically speaking, the interval between two events are perceived differently in different circumstances.

THE ALARM CLOCK

Hand in hand with light that delays the onset of sleep, is the alarm clock that brings sleep to a halt. Historians usually point to the Industrial Revolution as the major 'event' that changed our relationship with time, but in fact, the thin end of the wedge came much earlier, as we discovered ways to tell the time. And even after sundials were invented, not everyone would have had access to them, and they clearly didn't work around the clock, so to speak. We used different cues to know the time. In the Bible, for example, we can read how Jesus Christ prayed at daybreak when the cock crowed, again after noon when the sun was highest in the sky and in the evening when three stars were visible. Buddhist monks in some places rise when it is light enough to see the veins in their hands when they hold them up to the sun.

We have become accustomed to a different state of wakening. Our ancestors needed to wake in an alert state if they and their families were to survive the perils of the wild—no shuffling around in a dressing gown with a mug of tea while they woke up. We needed to 'entrain' or realign ourselves with the changing dawn and dusk, to adapt to being ready for the day on waking.

THE ARTIFICIAL SHIFT

Perhaps the most striking demonstration of what happens when we disrupt our circadian rhythms is the resultant effect on the health of shiftworkers. A myriad of biological processes are knocked off balance, with serious and measurable consequences: more cardiovascular disease and greater risk of developing peptic ulcers, are some examples. Shiftworkers experience more sleep problems, as you might expect, with resultant chronic fatigue, excessive sleeping as well as difficulty sleeping. Shiftworkers also experience higher rates of depression, substance abuse and divorce.

Nor do we adapt to shiftwork. We might be able to adapt our social routines, but our bodies aren't tricked. 'Even if you've been on night shifts for 20 years or more your body clock does not shift to the demands of working at night,' says Russell Foster. 'The health consequences have been linked to smoking a packet of cigarettes a day, so it's very severe.'

Digestion is a daytime function according to the body clock and it can only partly shift to night-time with different working hours. The irregular mealtimes that can accompany shiftwork can disrupt hormone, acid and enzyme secretion. For example, if acid is secreted in the stomach in response to eating, when protective agents are not, over time it can lead to stomach ulcers.

Blood pressure is usually lower at night, but because night workers are up and about, their blood pressure remains at levels usually associated with being awake. A study by Joseph Schwartz at the Cornell Medical Center monitored the blood pressure in 100 female nurses and found those working evenings and nights were six times more likely to be 'non dippers' than day workers—they were much less likely to experience that reduction in blood pressure that is normal for the human body. They also had higher average blood pressure overall.

A better shift

If shiftwork is unavoidable, you can try reducing the impact on your health by taking positive action.

- Set up the conditions for good sleep. Keep the bedroom dark and cool, reduce noise with heavy curtains, lower the ring volume on the phone and switch on the answer phone.
- Exercise can be tricky to fit into your schedule, but try at least to keep active in general, even if it's just backyard soccer with the children. Avoid vigorous exercise in the last two to three hours before bed.
- Having regular meals is kinder on your digestive system. Limit caffeine intake and eat lots of fresh fruit and vegetables.
- When you are at work, do dull or boring tasks early on in the shift, and the most interesting ones last, recommends Dr Smolensky.
- Have breaks, stand up and stretch frequently. Consider napping where appropriate.

SLEEP DEPRIVATION AND SLEEP DISORDERS

Shiftworkers find it harder to sleep in the day. Humans are designed to sleep at night, so even if you can sleep in daylight hours, it's not usually for as long. And if you're leaving work at 7 am, you get a blast of light that sends a 'wake-up' signal to your biological clock, at odds with your intention to relieve your tiredness and sleep. Daytime is noisier too. According to studies, night workers sleep for two to four hours less on average than when working in the day. Shiftworkers as a whole also rely on alcohol more as a sleeping aid and sleeping problems sometimes persist even when a shiftworker goes back to working normal hours.

But it's not just shiftworkers who are sleep deprived. Professor Stanley Coren from the University of British Columbia in Canada, is among those who believe that Western society is chronically sleep deprived. Author of a book called *The Sleep Thieves*, he told Radio National in Australia on the *Health Report* in 2000: 'Basically it appears that evolution wanted us to have between nine and 10 hours worth of sleep out of every 24, and given the fact that in the Western world the average amount of sleep is seven to seven and a half hours, that means that on average we're about one and a half to two hours sleep deprived.'

The magic figure is not certain, however, and it changes throughout life. The US National Sleep Foundation says most adults need between seven and nine hours sleep a night to feel their best. Children aged between five and 12, need between 10 and 11 hours sleep, while teenagers need between eight-and-a-half and nine-and-a-half hours a night. Teenagers also typically have a delayed sleep agenda—tending to feel sleepy later in the evening, and wanting to sleep in the morning, a schedule at odds with school hours.

It is certain, however, that we sleep less than we did a century or so ago. Dr David Joffe, Secretary of the Australasian Sleep Association, told Radio National in Australia: 'A hundred-and-fifty years ago you went to sleep when the candle burnt out, and got up when the sun came up. And those kind of cues are no longer there in our society. You go to sleep when you turn off the television and you get up when the clock radio goes off. And there are increasing societal pressures that we think are impacting upon people's sleep performance, and their ability to get good quality sleep.'

Taking sleeping tablets is also a sign that all's not well in the land of nod. About 10 per cent of Americans report that they regularly struggle to fall asleep or to stay asleep throughout the night. In the US in 2005, doctors prescribed sleeping pills around 42 million times according to research company IMS Health, a figure 60 per cent up on 2000.

What no-one doubts, is that chronic lack of sleep causes serious health problems: infections, lowered lymphocyte count, bowel problems and in some cases, depressive illnesses.

How long is a shift?

Working long shifts is worse than working short shifts. Eight-hour night shifts are optimal and 12-hour night shifts are acceptable only if workloads are light according to studies reported in the *Journal of Sleep Research*. Night shifts longer than 12 hours, and daytime shifts longer than 16 hours have consistently been found to be associated with reduced productivity and more accidents, write Leslie Olsen and Antonio Ambrogetti in the *Medical Journal of Australia*. In addition:

- The later the night shift ends, the less sleep is obtained that day.
- Short periods of night work (one or two shifts) are better for intellectually demanding tasks because the accumulated sleep deficit is less.
- For most people, rotating forward through day, afternoon and night shift is better than backwards (night, afternoon then day).
- The best speed of rotation (a cycle over several weeks or several days) is still in debate. While a longer period in a shift should in theory allow better (if partial) adaptation, in reality, exposure to the sun after a night shift is enough to prevent adaptation, and days off are usually just that: days, not nights.

ACCIDENTS

Says Stanley Coren: 'I'll give you an example of just how sleep deprived we are as a society. Every year in the spring, we shift to daylight-saving time, and on that day the nation loses an hour's worth of sleep, and because God's a good researcher, in autumn we have a control group.'

Traffic statistics in Canada show an increase in traffic accidents of 7 per cent coinciding with the hour's loss of sleep. In autumn, when you get the extra hour of sleep, accidents decrease by 7 per cent.

'We are so chronically sleep deprived as a society that a single hour's worth of sleep gained or lost will shift the likelihood of accidents by 7 per cent in either direction. That's scary,' says Coren.

It's a story repeated elsewhere. The National Transportation Safety Board in the US found that in crashes involving a heavy truck, almost a third of those that killed the truck driver were probably caused by fatigue. Another third or so are caused by alcohol, and notably, alcohol increases feelings of sleepiness.

'At the low point of the day, and after missing some sleep, people fail to see things they seldom overlook when fully alert,' writes Dr Smolensky. Many of the major accidents of the 20th century occurred, experts believe, because of lack of sleep. Here are some examples.

- The Exxon Valdez ran aground at 12.04 am on 24 March 1989 depositing 11 million gallons of crude oil off the coast of Alaska. The third mate who was in charge had worked a physically demanding day previously and slept only five hours in the previous 24, a sum that included a nap in the afternoon.

- The Presidential Commission that investigated the *Challenger* space shuttle explosion that killed seven astronauts concluded that contributing factors included: excessive overtime of the launch crew, irregular working hours, insufficient sleep and fatigue.

- The Chernobyl nuclear plant accident in Kiev occurred at 1.23 am on 26 April 1986, and was one of the worst nuclear disasters of all time. While faulty equipment design was partly blamed, Soviet officials also blamed human error: the engineers on duty had been at work for 13 hours or more.

A GOOD NIGHT'S SLEEP

As the sun sets, a delicate timing device at the base of our brain sends a chemical signal throughout our body and the gradual slide toward sleep begins. Our body becomes inert, and our lidded eyes roll slowly from side to side. Later, our eyes begin the rapid eye movements that accompany dreams, and our mind enters a highly active state where vivid dreams trace our deepest emotions. Throughout the night we traverse a broad landscape of dreaming and nondreaming realms, wholly unaware of the world outside. Hours later, as the sun rises, we are transported back to our bodies and to waking consciousness.

WILLIAM C DEMENT, *THE PROMISE OF SLEEP*, 1999

A good night's sleep is a gift to mental and physical health. There's no magic formula that will suit everyone, but experts tell us to try the following if we're having sleep troubles.

- Get up at the same time each day. This helps to regulate your rhythms more than anything else.
- Try going to bed 15 minutes earlier than normal. If you suspect you may not be getting enough sleep, try going to bed earlier for one week and see if you feel more alert during the day.
- Create bedtime rituals. Take time before going to bed to wind down from the day's activities to prepare yourself mentally for sleep.
- Dark and light. Keep your bedroom dark for best sleep and open the curtains straight away in the morning.
- A cool bedroom is most conducive to sleep. This is because it helps your body naturally fall in temperature, which helps you get a more restful sleep.
- Go to bed when you're sleepy. If you've been having trouble getting to sleep, don't go to bed too early, turn the lights low, relax and go when you're feeling tired.
- Don't rely on alcohol to make you sleep. A drink or two in the evening may seem to help you fall asleep, but its rebound effect means you can be awake in the early hours.

THE FUTURE OF TIME

Technological advances take us further and further from the basic biological rhythms we evolved with. At the same time, medicine, in particular a branch called chronomedicine, is discovering just how significant timing is for optimal health care. The fact that different body processes perform differently throughout the day can mean there are optimal times to give certain medicines.

We might kid ourselves that we can do with less sleep, but the evidence disagrees. Our round-the-clock society, however, looks here to stay, so it's likely we'll try to learn to better cope with living against our clocks and try to understand the role of good lighting, optimal shift times and rotations, and better exercise and nutrition to counterbalance the toll of night shiftwork.

Resolving the work–life balance, say authors Foster and Kreitzman, is not possible without understanding the underlying biology—a struggle to balance the tension between the way we want to live and the way we're built to live: 'We have to make choices. We are diurnal creatures but we live in a 24-hour world.'

TAKING STOCK:
CIRCADIAN RHYTHMS

1. Are you an owl or a lark?

What time in the day do you function best? If you haven't worked it out yet, think over your answers to the following questions.

(a) What time would you get up if it were entirely up to you? How different is that to the time you do in fact rise?
(b) If you went to bed when you really felt like it, what time would that be? Is that earlier or later than your usual bedtime?
(c) Do you need an alarm clock to wake you up in time?
(d) Is it hard to get out of bed in the morning?
(e) How alert are you in the first half-hour after waking? How tired? Do you have a good appetite?
(f) Which time slot would you choose for an important two-hour test? 8 am, 11 am, 3 pm or 7 pm.
(g) If you had to do two hours of hard physical work, when would you choose to do it?
   8 am, 11 am, 3 pm or 7 pm

2. Highs and lows

Body temperature varies across the daily cycle. If you're interested to see how yours varies, and when you experience your highs and lows, take your temperature first thing in the morning before you get out of bed, and every two hours until you go to bed again. Peak alertness coincides with peak temperature.

We think that our machinery and technology will save us time and give us more leisure, but really they make life more crowded and hurried.

RICHARD GREGG,
THE VALUE OF VOLUNTARY SIMPLICITY, 1936

8. THE COST OF COMFORT

HOW DOES MONEY AFFECT THE WAY WE USE AND EXPERIENCE TIME? DOES THE PURSUIT OF MATERIAL POSSESSIONS AFFECT OUR WELLBEING AND HAPPINESS?

MONEY — IN THE FORM OF AN EFFICIENT ECONOMY OR A PAID JOB WITH START AND END TIMES — CHANGES ATTITUDES TO TIME, AS WELL AS THE PACE OF LIFE. THE MORE OUR LIVES DEPEND ON MONEY AND WHAT IT CAN BUY, THE MORE WE ARE SUBJECT TO A NARROW, MATERIALISTIC VIEW OF LIFE. PERHAPS THERE IS A PRICE TO PAY FOR COMFORT AFTER ALL.

RELAXED RHYTHMS

In 1998, social and psychological anthropologist Kevin Birth stayed six months in the small village of Anamat in rural Trinidad. His quest was to study their attitudes to time. Some of the hot observation spots for his research were the rum shops, taxi stands, the recreation ground during cricket games and places in the nearest market town where people from the village would loiter.

One of his first encounters with Trinidad time was a placard displayed in many of the rum shops: 'Opening and closing hours: any day and any time'. When pressed as to what it meant, one shopkeeper explained: 'Sometime I open early. Sometime I don' open at all. I open when there are customers. When there are none, I close the shop and take a little five.' In Trinidad, 'any time' is a recognition of the different needs and rhythms of a diverse customer group: taxi drivers, factory workers, agricultural labourers, school children, the underemployed and homemakers.

While careful questioning filled his working days, off-duty Birth found himself slipping into the role of soccer fan and taking an interest in *parang* (a popular Trinidad music style), by becoming a *parrendero* (a band member)—roles which deepened his understanding of Trinidad time.

'I discovered that people utilize many different conceptions of time and these are distributed in complex ways over social contexts and statuses. Finally, I became concerned not only with these times that individuals possessed but the fashion in which they deployed these times,' he says in his book, *Any Time is Trinidad Time*, a fascinating exploration of the different ways people live in time, even in the same place and society.

People living in Anamat felt the influences of both agrarian and industrial time. Ethnic groups of French, Venezuelan, Amerindian, Indian and African Creole have, over time, been moulded into two main groups, Indian and Creole, around which centre clichés about present orientation and future orientation. Villagers did use alarm clocks, Birth noticed. But rather than use it as a signal to get up, it was usually turned off as soon as it sounded, and people simply went back to bed. Other wake-up signals, particularly for gardeners, were getting friends to wake them, waking to the sounds of dogs and roosters stirring, and waking to the sound of increased traffic on the road.

Where many different cultural traditions meet, the diversity of times is great, says Birth. And so too potential conflicts. Ideas of time are contested and used in ideological struggles about cooperation, hierarchy, group definitions and power.

Multiple times in Trinidad

Central to understanding time in Trinidad are three idioms, says Birth.

- 'Any time is Trinidad time', a phrase that comes from a calypso by Trinidad singer, Lord Kitchener.
- 'Jus now' is a phrase open to interpretation, but something like 'don't get impatient! S/he's coming …'
- 'Long time' can mean something akin to 'the olden days'. Quite what it means depends on the person, it could be 10 to 20 years ago, or reaching back to a different era.

The phrases, investing time, time budgeting and time management were foreign to the villagers, but some were familiar with the idea of 'time is money'. These tended to be doctors and business people (who tended to have more contact with American English and also to have an American English education) and the tailors and taxi drivers they came into contact with.

In Trinidad, Birth noticed, people use their knowledge of other people's social activity as much as they do clocks, to organize appointments. For example, young men tend to go to the soccer fields in the early evening at the time they expect enough people to have finished work; shopkeepers might open shop when they see the first school children on the road after school finishes—a variable time since sometimes a water shortage means school ends early. This means they can get on with jobs around the house at the same time.

Schools (with missionary origins) and industry (with global economic influences) keep more or less clock time, while small-scale farming, artisans and tradespeople mostly create their own routines. And one of the attractions of staying in farming is seen as the freedom not to have to submit to being told what to do and when to do it.

Many people's lives in Anamat intersect several time views. Ranjit, a farmer with a small shop manages the commercial cycle of candy making and delivery, the farming cycle of harvesting and processing cocoa, and the daily business cycle of his shop. Many jobs that do revolve around clock time also have the added flexibility of early starts or early finishes so that people have the time to 'make garden'— cultivating small strips of land for extra food.

Clock time versus event time

During Birth's stay in Trinidad he witnessed many examples of the difference between what's called 'clock time', adhering to the clock, respecting timetables and so on, and 'event time', when the duration or timing of an activity is related to that activity. You harvest the tomatoes until you've finished them all (event time); respectability in Anamat is partly earned by getting your children to school on time (clock time).

Life tends to be faster for those living on clock time, but it's not just about speed. When event time reigns, schedules follow activities rather than activities following schedules determined by the clock. As Birth witnessed, although some cultures seem to be predominantly run on clock or event time, activities themselves create their own times. All around the world people get fed up waiting for doctors. That's because we make an appointment based on clock time, yet the doctors' time use is an event-centred activity—they have to examine, discuss and possibly treat a patient. The time slots might be uniform, but the patients, and the times it takes to treat them, are not.

Plantation time

While the Caribbean sugar plantation system emphasized clock time and time discipline, workers themselves did not have time pieces. Instead, it was the overseer's job to keep time. Bells rang, shells blew to regulate work starts, pauses and ends. In one Jamaican plantation, an overseer destroyed an apprentice's hourglass; this way it was the overseer who maintained utmost control and power over time.

Slow life on the Malay Peninsula

For the Kelantese people of the Malay Peninsula, slowness is a deeply embedded social norm. Hurrying is considered a breach of ethics. At the core of their social rules, known as '*budi bahasa*' (the language of character), is a willingness to take time for visiting and paying respect to friends, relatives and neighbours. Rushing is associated with greed and shows too much concern for material possessions. It also shows disregard for the *budi bahasa*. These people are not industrialized and the demands on their time are relatively few and simple.

COMPLEXITY AND TIME

Living by the clock allows for greater complexity of events. 'The primary function of clock time, it may be argued, is to prevent simultaneously occurring events from running into one another,' comments Robert Levine in *A Geography of Time*. Once you're knee-deep in such a way of life, Levine argues, you rely on the clock to help you maintain your flow and keep the cog of events moving. The clock controls the traffic of appointments, pick-ups, shopping times and task deadlines. Simpler ways of life and simpler societies can avoid clock time because the demands on their time are distinct and uncomplicated.

In Burundi, in Central Africa, harvesting begins when the dry season starts, and the growing season when rain returns, appointments are more likely to be set according to the activity of cows than hands on the clock. They might be set for the time 'when the cows are grazing in the morning'; or for a time near midday 'when the cows are going to drink in the stream'; and a later time in the day, 'when the young cows go out' (they're kept in the shade for a few hours to prevent them drinking too much). An hour or two either way is not important, and nobody minds if, for example, you've led the cows out an hour later because of a hot day. Precision is impossible, and not sought.

Meeting during evening hours calls for phrases such as 'who are you time'—when it's so dark that you need to greet people with 'who are you?' Similarly they have times for 'when nobody awake', or 'when the rooster sings'.

Aldwyn Roberts, Lord Kitchener (1922–2000)

Born in the the Caribbean state of Trinidad and Tobago into a family
of six, Lord Kitchener, or Kitch as he was also known, had to leave
school at the age of 14 following the death of his parents. He began
composing calypsos from the age of 10 and got his first job as a singer
in 1936, serenading employees of the local Water Works. He became
internationally known after his move to England in the 1950s, where he
married an English woman, Marjorie. He remained popular in Trinidad
and his compositions were often played in the annual Trinidad Carnival.
The subject of time came up a few times in his lyrics in his first hit song
of 1939, 'shops close too early', and the phrase, 'any time is Trinidad
time' comes from his song, 'Trinidad Time'.

VOX POP: In much contemporary social criticism,
long work hours are seen as part and parcel of
the work-to-spend cycle. Is work about money or
other rewards?

What makes work different is that you do it for money and that
makes it feel different to the same tasks outside the financial arena.
But work is not about how much it earns you—although as a part-
time writer working from home, when my income dips, I sometimes
feel that my work is regarded as less important than my husband's.
When I challenge that thought, I realize it is irrational, and I remind
myself that there is lots more than money that I bring into the
workings of our family and household. AH

For me, work is about learning and contributing something
worthwhile, and money has always been a secondary factor. ML

Money's nice, but there are lots of things I wouldn't do for it. One of
them is work. To be in control of my own time is much more
important. EBW

I don't earn a lot of money and think that it is more important to be happy in your work than to be rich, but the more money we have the more choice we have in doing more with the time we have and our enjoyment of it. CL

Work is not about the size of my income. I find that totally irrelevant. It is about other rewards—being respected as an author, as someone committed to heritage and the arts through my hotel business. SG

I like the independence that comes from working and I like knowing that I've earned my pay check myself. AE

Time and the labour-saving device

What kind of rule is this? The more timesaving machinery there is, the more pressed a person is for time.
SEBASTIAN DE GRAZIA, *OF TIME, WORK AND LEISURE*, 1962

So-called labour-saving devices do not always deliver the promise. Instead of saving time, they do the opposite. Nowhere is this more apparent than in the case of housework. Ruth Schwartz Cowan won the Dexter Prize in 1984 from the Society for the History of Technology, for her work which she published in a book, *More work for Mother*. One of the consequences of a greater distribution of household appliances, Schwartz Cowan points out, is that more women are doing it all themselves, where in previous decades, they might have paid for home help, or sent laundry out, for example.

Home life is cleaner in modern society, she says, perhaps even more pleasant, but women put in more hours to keep it that way. Washing machines make it feasible that sheets are changed every week, while vacuum cleaners introduce a 'senseless tyranny ... of immaculate floors', says Schwartz Cowan. Labour-saving devices might save labour—but because of ripple effects, like the ones described, they don't appear to free up our time.

WORKING WITH THE CLOCK

Moments are the elements of profit.

LEONARD HORNER, ENGLISH FACTORY INSPECTOR,
QUOTED IN MARX'S ECONOMIC MANUSCRIPTS, 1861–63

When the first mechanical clocks appeared sometime in the
14th century, *werkeglocken* (work clocks) chimed to signal when textile
workers should come to work, when they could eat and when they
were free to leave. Uprisings to silence the time of the cloth makers
were common and punishment harsh. In Commines, France, in the
1300s, the fine for damaging a clock was £60; if used to signal revolt,
the punishment was death.

Even before industrialization, clock keeping and time slotting was
creeping into the experience of life. This description of Mediaeval
England in David S Landes book *Revolution in Time: Clocks and the
making of the modern world* describes it succinctly: 'As commerce
developed and industry expanded, the complexity of life and work
required an ever larger array of time signals. These were given, as in
the monasteries, by bells: the urban commune in this sense was the
heir and imitator of the religious community. Bells sounded for the
start of work, meal breaks, end of work, closing of gates, start of
market, close of market, assembly, emergencies, council meetings,
end of drink service, time for street cleaning, curfew and so on ...'

Editor, Charles Dudley Warner, summed up the feelings workers
have had over the centuries when he wrote in 1884: 'The chopping up
of time into rigid periods is an invasion of individual freedom and
makes no allowances for differences in temperament and feeling.' The
real problem has always been that of power, however. A timekeeper
has power over you, and that is what people resent.

MONEY MAKES THE WORLD GO FASTER

Whether or not money makes the world go around, it does make the
world go around faster. Or, to quantify more accurately—according to
Robert Levine, professor of psychology at California State University in
the US—the greater the economic wellbeing of a place, the faster the

pace. He's in no doubt and says, 'the number one determinant of a place's tempo is economics'.

To back his statement, he and researchers travelled to 31 countries around the globe, visiting several major cities in each, and measured three indicators of the pace of life. He measured the average walking speed of randomly selected pedestrians (35 of each sex) over a 60-feet stretch, during the morning rush. He also measured the time it took a postal clerk to serve stamps; and the accuracy of 15 randomly selected bank clocks in main parts of the city. These measurements were then statistically combined into an overall 'pace-of-life' score.

The greatest scores were in the wealthier North American, Northern European and Asian countries, while the slowest paces were recorded in third-world countries, particularly in South and Central America and the Middle East. Levine found a direct relationship between the speed of a place and its gross domestic product per capita, to its citizens purchasing power, and to how well people on average were able to meet their minimum needs. 'People from richer and poorer countries do, in fact, march to different drummers,' he concluded.

So, does a fast pace produce a better economy? Or do the pressures of the economy cause an increase in pace? A bit of both, believes Levine. Places with healthy economies tend to put more economic value in time, and places that put more value on time are more likely to have active economies.

Levine found a number of other predictors of speed: the bigger the city the faster the tempo, and the hotter the climate the slower the pace. Where social relationships are deemed more important, there is a more relaxed attitude towards time. Levine tested the theory and found it true; greater individualism was highly related to faster tempo. Individualistic cultures tend to be faster than collective ones.

ARE FAST PLACES MORE MISERABLE?

The dreamy, slow pace of the tropical beach, waves lapping, boats bobbing ... nothing more to do than turn the page of the book in our hand, or even put it down and snooze for an hour or two. The slow life is often extolled as the happy one. But are people who experience a slower pace in fact happier? Levine compared the pace-of-life data he collected with life-satisfaction data from a number of government sources, as well as from international happiness researcher, Dr Ruut Veenhoven.

The result? Faster places are happier places, even though living at a faster pace meant people experienced more smoking and cardiac problems. Levine looked to economics to solve the apparent paradox. Although money making and productivity create time urgency and individualism—and an associated economic vitality—these forces are by no means entirely negative. Yes, they create stresses, but they also provide material comforts and a higher standard of living, both of which, argues Levine, enhance the quality of life. 'Ultimately, how we structure our time is a choice between alternatives. A rapid pace of life is neither inherently better nor worse than a slow one,' he concludes.

PACE OF LIFE AND SOCIAL RESPONSIBILITY

If you want something done, ask a busy person to do it.
LUCILLE BALL (1911–1989)

US social psychologist, Stanley Milgram, held that the fast tempo in modern cities overwhelms people with more sensory stimulus than they can process, with the result of psychological overload and a screening out of anything not related to reaching your own goals— whether it's a bus to catch on a crowded street, or the ingredients of a meal to be bought in the supermarket. But Levine's experiments with a variety of tests—from dropping a pen to 'losing' a letter and observing how many people helped—showed their was no correlation between pace of life and willingness to help. Even people with a fast pace of life can find the time to help others, he concludes.

MONEY GIVES US LESS FREE TIME
Not only are developed countries faster, their citizens have less free time. Industrialization and its multitude of ramifications means it's

not a case of earning enough in a shorter time and having more time at your disposal. This relationship between economic wealth and time poverty also shows up in time-use analysis within countries.

In fact, US anthropologist, Allen Johnson, argues that industrialization triggers an evolution in time, from time surplus to time affluence to a society that suffers time famine. In China, as you approach the tourist site of the Terracotta Warriors, near Xian, you'll see dozens of umbrella-sheltered stalls selling fruit. In November it's pomegranates. As no-one seems to be buying, and they are all selling the same produce, it's hard to imagine how it is worth their while sitting there hour after hour. But time is of little value. It's not an issue of wasting time, they have all the time in the world but very little cash, so even if they make only a little money, it's useful currency.

Johnson argues that increasing efficiency of production puts productivity pressure on the individual to keep the system going by consuming more goods. Time becomes divided into productivity time or consumption time. The argument has many elements in common with suggestions explored in earlier chapters, that we're caught in a work-to-spend cycle.

POLYCHRONS AND MONOCHRONS

Another way of looking at time is to note the differences between 'monochronic' and 'polychronic' attitudes to time. First noted in 1959 in Edward Hall's *The Silent Language*, the terms can be applied to individual people and to cultures.

Monochronic people or cultures tend to pay more attention to clocks. Much of Western culture is monochronic—with a focus on achievement and on the other hand a more linear understanding of time.

Polychronic people and cultures are more event-oriented. For example, in a polychronic society if two people are deep in conversation, yet have an appointment, they would rather finish the conversation and be late for the appointment, than artificially break it up. Polychronic time use tends to put several activities into the same 'clock block' or block of time—for example, combining several household chores, combining a household activity with childcare or a work activity with social interaction. Cultures from Asia, Africa, the Middle East and South America are often described as polychronic.

Are you polychronic or monochronic?

It is possible to have a mixture of attitudes, but usually people tend towards one type more than another. Do you recognize any of these traits in yourself?

Polychrons are more likely to:

- reschedule activities in response to demands.
- think of other things while doing something.
- combine routine tasks to free up time for important tasks.
- have a flexible schedule and not plan exactly when to do things.
- consider that it's not fun just to do one thing at a time.
- break projects into parts.
- change activity from one to another during the day.
- thrive on change, variety and spontaneity.
- feel constrained by strict limits placed on their behaviour.

Monochrons tend to:

- report they have less time than last year.
- when waiting, prefer to spend the time passively, without additional activity.
- be thrown off by indefinite blocks of time and loosely planned agendas.
- prefer to focus on one task at a time.
- view having to take on a second task as an interruption or intrusion.
- are happy with schedules.
- prefer to leave plans unchanged once they're made.
- regard punctuality and promptness highly.

A study of 112 residents of Philadelphia, Pennsylvania in the US questioned adults between the ages of 18 and 65 (68 per cent with some college education) about their attitiude to time and organization. After questioning, people were assigned with a mono or poly characteristic. The results of the study found:

- Polychrons perceived they reached their daily goals more than monochrons. (This was unexpected and unexplained in the study.)
- Monochrons are more upset at changing schedules, possibly when imposed by someone else.
- Polychrons are less upset by change and more likely to instigate change.
- Polychrons reported performing better under pressure and may be better suited to high-pressure jobs and situations.
- Monochrons are more likely to procrastinate, possibly to carry out their preference for doing one thing at a time.

While it may be true that we tend towards one attitude more than another in terms of polychronicity and monochronicity, both people and cultures usually show characteristics of both. It is easy to find examples of this. PJ gets unnerved when he needs to do more than one thing at a time. He'll happily cook dinner for the family, but is irritated if the phone rings, or a child asks for help … let alone try and combine with anything else such as getting a fire going. In that respect he is typically monochronic. But while he wants to be 'left alone' to get on with one task, followed by another, he doesn't have the monochronic respect for timetables and in fact hates them. Although, true to the monochronic time type, he's less able to opportunistically use unexpected free time as he explains.

A less scheduled existence would be preferable. I sometimes find that 'open' periods of free time arrive unexpectedly and are therefore hard to plan for and use constructively. Sometimes mad rushes are followed by periods of relatively unusable free time. A good example of this is 'the dictatorship of the train'—this happens when I have to catch a train into town, a journey of over 80 minutes. I rush madly to get things ready (iron clothes, pack laptop computer, camera, tape recorder, mobile phone and other necessities) and catch that train. If I forget any of them, I face problems, for there is no going back to get them when I am on the train. So preparing for the train is stressful.

There are times when I arrive on the station platform, panting and stressed out, to catch the train by just two minutes or less. Once on the train, I find myself suddenly faced with over an hour of time to spare. What a pity I can't 'even out' that time. But no, the dictatorship of the train means that the time before the train departure is frenzied, whereas once on the train, there's little to do but read, write or look out the window.

In *A Geography of Time*, Robert Levine describes how the Japanese typically combine mono and poly traits. His own research found the pace of life to be very fast in Japan. But he later found this didn't necessarily mean that the Japanese revered the clock in quite the same way as the typical Western manner. Business meetings start less punctually and in a more staggered 'sluggish' way; and may not have a set ending; people may come and go, it's understood; and if a part of the meeting does not concern you, it's considered just fine to make a cup of tea, or even fall asleep.

TEMPORAL FLEXIBILITY
While it's easy to make generalizations about a particular culture or country's attitudes to time, people within that culture may in fact be much more flexible than we imagine, and even in a culture that values punctuality, an individual may be more concerned with their own promptness than others'.

Whether you like to combine tasks also depends on the tasks at hand. Working on a PhD while supervising toddlers would be a test for the most robust polychron, while even a self-confessed monochron may not have trouble eating a pizza in front of the TV on a Friday night. The setting too, can change our attitude to time. We may approach work with monochronic efficiency, but prefer a more polychronic and flexible take on time when we clock off.

In fact, being able to switch between attitudes to time is a useful skill. Staying flexible about schedules can sometimes be more productive, for instance. Sometimes we need to respect and understand another person's sense of time to avoid offending them. Being able to adhere to a timetable—in order to catch a train, for example, is a necessary aspect of participation in today's job market. When we have an overwhelming job ahead, it can help to prioritize and tackle one job at a time.

THE ART OF DOING NOTHING

In our monochronic, clock-watching society, keeping busy is generally considered a good thing. Doing nothing, in contrast, is seen as a waste (although if you 'disguise' it as something socially acceptable, like meditation, you might be all right). Even time off is planned. 'It sometimes seems as if life is constructed with the primary goal of avoiding the awkwardness and the terror of having nothing to do,' comments Levine.

But in many other cultures, there is less of a distinction between activity and doing nothing. Friends may drop by and simply sit in silence—even for hours at a time. In the Trinidad village of Anamat, one of the main activities that occur around the small number of shops was 'liming' or, as Kelvin Birth describes it, 'the art of doing nothing with one's peers, until there is something to do; talking about nothing in particular unless there is something important to discuss.' Liming starts early in the day and continues until dark, sometimes beyond. Men tend to lime around the shops and on the road, while women gather in the front porches of the houses or underneath houses built on platforms.'

In her memoir, *Lost in Translation: A Life in a New Language,* writer Eva Hoffman describes the Balkan time she experienced during her travels through Eastern Europe. She was struck by the number of times she found herself sitting silently, facing others, with a Zen-like acceptance and lack of awkwardness. Eventually she came to an understanding of the acceptance of silence and inactivity. 'Something always happens next: the principle of I've been slowly soaking in ... the world doesn't run out, and neither do human beings ...'

DOING NOTHING: *MA*

The Japanese have a concept called '*ma*' which not only refers to the spaces between objects but also between activities. What isn't said or done is as important as what is. For example, in Japanese societies people are often brought up to believe it is rude to say 'no'. Instead, people are expected to listen carefully to the length of silence before replying 'yes'—the longer the silence, the more likely the 'yes' really means 'no'.

MATERIALISM

Riches are not from abundance of worldly goods, but from a contented mind.

MOHAMMED (570–632)

Everyone needs a certain amount of material goods and most people care to some degree about their possessions. But is there a point when being too materialistic, too focused on the material aspects of your life, makes you less fulfilled and less happy?

When stopped and asked, many people do feel that society is too materialistic.

- In surveys in the 1990s in America, says Juliet Schor in *The Overspent American*, 75 per cent of respondents agreed that America was too materialistic, greedy, addicted to shopping, spent wastefully and had lost the values of thrift and prudence.
- An Australian Institute survey conducted in 2004 asked 1600 people whether or not they agreed with the statement, 'Most Australians buy and consume far more than they need: it's wasteful.' Across all age groups 80 per cent of respondents agreed that more was consumed than necessary.

213

- Similarly people agreed to statements that a high percentage of Australians were focused on working and making money, and as a result did not spend enough time with family and community. This kind of materialistic society, the respondents agreed, made it harder to instil positive values in children.

WHAT DO WE MEAN BY 'MATERIALISM'?

The problem is not that people own things: the problem is that things own people.

CLIVE HAMILTON AND RICHARD DENNISS, *AFFLUENZA*, 2005

In the book, *The Meaning of Things: Domestic symbols and the self*, psychologist Mihaly Csikszentmihalyi explains his understanding of materialism. The problem with materialism, he says, is that we don't leave enough 'psychic energy' to cultivate the self, to interact with the rest of the world or attend to the broader purposes of life. When things take up our time—in acquisition and maintenance—their real value in the context of our lives as a whole declines. Instead of liberating our psychic energy, 'the things bind it to useless tasks. The former tool turns its master into its slave.'

Meaning is the ultimate goal in life, he says, not material possessions. The fruits of technology that fill the contemporary home, will not deliver us more satisfaction or happiness. Advances on the material front, in the battle for value and meaning in life, are mere skirmishes warns Csikszentmihalyi.

Csikszentmihalyi interviewed hundreds of people about the items in their homes. He found a striking anomaly. On further probing he found the people who most loudly protested about being asked about material possessions, saying people were more important, were the ones who were most isolated and lonely. Total obsession with 'things' meant people had to rely on the symbolic meanings of things to get meaning out of life, yet a denial of their importance wasn't a good sign either. The optimal attitude, he found, was where people used things to express, objectify and 'strengthen meanings and relationships without becoming entirely dependent on the objects themselves'. The four-poster rosewood bed is cherished because a grandmother was born in it, not for its cash value; a photograph in a silver frame is loved because it shows a youngest child with their first erupted tooth; a bracelet is treasured because it was a first gift from a then-young husband; a pottery jug reminds you of a carefree day years ago.

Other views on materialism include:

● Market economy. Materialism is a dependence on the market economy, which makes it difficult to express our identity and be acknowledged for who we are. The result is a feeling of impotence and of not being recognized, so people spend on material possessions as comforters.

● 'Having' identity rather than 'doing' identity. Some say materialism is where you create identity from what you consume rather than what you produce or 'do'—which is just what advertisers would like us to think.

● Marketed participation. Where consumption is marketed as a way of participating in society. Get this mobile phone/power drill/ leather sofa and join in, be like the rest!

● Consuming religion. We are prone to being converted to the religion of consumerism and materialism, says Richard Ryan of the University of Rochester in the US. And the result is, he says, an economic landscape, where 'selfishness and materialism are no longer seen as moral problems, but as cardinal goals of life'. We evaluate our lives not by looking inwards, he says, but by looking out and seeing what we have.

DO MATERIAL GOODS MAKE YOU HAPPY?

Research by Tim Kasser, author of *The High Price of Materialism*, emphasizes that a materialistic perspective on life might get you some of the material possessions you covet, but it won't get you more satisfaction with life. In fact, it could make you less satisfied.

The love of money is the root of all evil, the Bible tells us. Kasser too, found that merely aspiring to be wealthy or have more possessions can be associated with greater unhappiness—greater anxiety and depression, less rich relationships, more TV watching and even more anxious dreams. But does a materialist slant make you more likely to be unhappy? Or does being unhappy make you more materialistic?

A bit of both, Kasser believes. Desire for more possessions drives a frantic pace of life, he says, 'rather than providing paths to freedom and autonomy, people feel chained, pressured and controlled …'.

Materialism breeds in people who are uncertain in love, self-esteem, competence or control, he believes. But not everyone agrees with his position. Other research, according to *Monitor on Psychology* (the electric journal of the American Psychological Association), shows that while generally people who are less materialistic are most satisfied with life, materialistic people are quite happy when their material needs are being met: 'If they've got the money and their acquisitive lifestyle doesn't conflict with more soul-satisfying pursuits.' But if you're a materialist in material need (or want, more likely), it's an unhappy situation. If you're a poor materialist—tough.

Kasser also found links between materialism and narcissistic attitudes. He wasn't overly surprised as both relate to external validation and a desire for others' praise. He sees favouring possessions, attractiveness and popularity as materialistic values; and money, image and fame as typically materialistic goals that bring more physical and psychological difficulties. All in all, he concluded the more central a role we give to material things, the lesser our quality of life.

Work by Ed Diener, Alumni Professor of Psychology at the University of Illinois confirms the effect of overvaluing material goods and wealth. He and Shige Oishi (Assistant Professor of Psychology at the University of Virginia) collected data from over 7000 college students in 41 different countries. They found a link between putting value on making money and a diminished life satisfaction. They concluded that while money per se does not make you unhappy, the pursuit of money is linked to unhappiness.

FAMILY AND MATERIALISM

A materialistic outlook on life also has profound effects on family life. When a family environment doesn't meet a need for security, many children, says Kasser, respond by adopting a value system that emphasizes wealth and possessions. Less nurturing parenting styles produce materialistic children. In a study by Geoff Williams and Jacob Cohen, in 2005, the parents of teenagers with materialist values were found to be possessive of their children, used harsh punishments, provided little structure in their children's day-to-day lives and were inconsistent with rules about behaviour.

Another study showed children of divorced parents were also more likely to develop materialistic values—because, its authors speculated, of the 'diminution of interpersonal resources such as love and affection'.

A paper published in the journal, *Child Development*, in 2003, by Suniya Luthar, a professor in psychology and education at Columbia University, makes a link between affluence, drug use, anxiety and depression in children. While pressure to achieve may make children in some affluent sectors of society more 'at risk' than lower socioeconomic groups, isolation from parents was also a factor, and this was seen as directly linked with wealth. 'Inordinate emphasis on material success' has a diminishing effect on other aspects of child development, such as close relationships. In addition, Luthar found material affluence inhibited the formation of support networks as services tend to be purchased and not shared. The 'subculture of affluence' also placed an emphasis on personal autonomy and control—and the danger of blaming yourself when you lose control.

Belk's three traits

Professor of Business at the University of Utah, Russell Belk, takes another slant on materialism. He published papers on materialism and wellbeing in the 1980s and by his measurement, a materialistic outlook had three traits:

- Possessiveness. Materialistic people preferred to own and keep rather than borrow or rent.
- Generosity. Materialistic people tended to be unwilling to share possessions with others.
- Envy. Materialistic people envy others' possessions and feel displeasure when others have things they desire themselves.

POVERTY AND MATERIALISM

Circumstances in which people are more anxious about their basic needs creates insecurity and the response of many people is an orientation to materialism. Kasser believes this is due to social environments that lead children to feel unsafe and insecure, and that these unmet needs drive them to pursue materialistic goals.

MATERIALISM AND RELATIONSHIPS

Numerous studies have found that materialistic individuals feel more alienated in their social relationships. Kasser and his wife (also a psychologist) listened to people's dreams and found that those with materialistic values seemed to avoid intimacy and connecting with people in their dreams.

Students who focused on the pursuit of wealth, fame and image reported lower quality relationships with both friends and lovers. Why would chasing material goods affect relationships? Possible explanations are that having materialistic values runs parallel with devaluing close relationships and community involvement, so people don't put the same energy into them and can neglect relationships and care little about whether they're healthy or not. Also, materialistic values seem to taint relationships by decreasing connectedness, intimacy and closeness.

There's something about holding strong materialist values that seems to affect how we relate to others. Shalom Schwartz, Professor of Psychology at the Hebrew University of Jerusalem (now retired), collected data from students, adults and teachers in 40 different countries, and believes it comes down to a conflict between 'accepting others as equals and concern for their welfare' and 'the pursuit of one's own relative success and dominance over others'.

INTRINSIC AND EXTRINSIC GOALS

Kasser makes a distinction between what he calls extrinsic and intrinsic goals. Extrinsic goals equate with his idea of materialism, and focus on possession, image, status and receiving rewards and praise. Intrinsic goals are about personal growth and community connection and are satisfying in themselves.

Shaking off the chains of materialism

If you fear the narrowness of a materialistic outlook is squeezing your experience of life, Tim Kasser offers the following suggestions.

- Keep materialistic aims in balance with intrinsic ones, and let the healthier ones dominate.
- Confront the issues that scare you and might push you towards materialism.
- Jump off the materialist treadmill. Stop believing that what you need to make things better is more money or a new pair of shoes.
- Question your motives. Look at what your real psychological needs are.
- Get active. Change your activities from passive to active, from materialistic to engaging. For example, watch less TV and read more; shop less and listen to more music.
- 'Monkey see. Monkey do.' When it comes to children, the strongest message you can send them is being a good role model. If you act as if getting the latest BMW is important, they'll believe it.

The extrinsic goal system, comments Clive Hamilton in *Growth Fetish*, is 'the modern myth of the consumer society'—self-focused, celebrating the wealthy, powerful, famous and beautiful. Intrinsic goals, on the other hand, are much more aligned with traditional wisdom and religious teaching, which encourages us to believe that happiness is not about things in themselves.

A MATTER OF DEGREE

Where can we draw the line between materialism that enhances our lives and that which diminishes it? Csikszentmihalyi describes two types of materialism.

Terminal materialism

A product of Western culture, terminal materialism is represented by an entire dependence on a market economy, exposing people to basic human fears, such as starvation. 'Material possessions serve as pacifiers for the self-induced helplessness we have created,' he says. The consumption habit can become an end in itself, so that to possess more things (and more status) becomes the drive. Interestingly, many blueprints for a simple life include being more self-reliant.

Instrumental materialism
The possession of things serves goals that are independent of greed and have a specific and limited scope for a particular group of purposes. The important factor, in this definition, is the purpose of owning things. The shallow quest for money and acquisitions is one thing, but goods can, argues Csikszentmihalyi, serve the 'common good'. Instrumental materialism is part of the full unfolding of human life, in contrast to terminal materialism, which shuts out other aspects of it.

THE POST-MATERIALIST
Political scientist, Ronald Inglehart, uses the terms 'materialist' and 'post-materialist'. His bent is societal rather than personal, and focuses on what people think their governments and society in general should be doing. Materialist concerns reflect the need for safety and sustenance, such as maintaining a strong economy, national security and social stability. Post-materialist values reflect 'higher level' needs for esteem, belonging, knowledge and aesthetics, such as freedom, environmental beauty and civility.

The bottom line? If materialism is a coping strategy, it's a pretty shaky one—the real gold is elsewhere.

CONSUMER SOCIETY
In a time-pressured society, one of the most convincing arguments about the cause of materlialistic-induced unhappiness is that a life organized around 'getting and spending' takes you away from what could really make you happy—family and friends, in particular. When chasing wealth eats into your social life, for instance, you might get richer, but you'll probably end up less satisfied with life.

Are you a maximizer or a satisficer?

Nobel Prize winning economist and psychologist, Herbert Simon first coined the term 'satisficing' in 1950.

When it comes to spending money, do you have to look at every option before you feel it's okay to proceed, then worry if you made the right choice? Or are you willing to take a plunge, settle for good enough and leave it at that?

If you seek and accept only the best, you're a maximizer—someone who wants to feel that every purchase and every decision was the best possible. A satisficer, on the other hand, is happy to settle for something that is good enough and not worry about the possibility there might, after all, be something better.

Maximizers do not necessarily have maximum satisfaction, despite the term. Satisificing, according to Simon's theory, is the winning strategy. That is, when the time, money and anguish are taken into account, all things considered, the satisficing attitude wins out.

Looking out at the world with a materialistic viewpoint dramatically changes the social landscape. 'Consumption and materialism drive out religion, and the more a society emphasizes material pursuits and extrinsic motivations as the path to a happy life, the less validity it attaches to the pursuit of meaning or to life's inner evolution,' says Clive Hamilton, in *Growth Fetish*.

THE TYRANNY OF CHOICE

Barry Schwartz, a professor in social theory and action, and author of *The Paradox of Choice*, believes that the wide range of choices we have as modern consumers places us in a position of more stress. Choosing takes time and energy, and there's always the possibility we got it wrong!

Many choices are, on the surface, trivial. Milk or dark chocolate biscuits, this brand or that? But cumulatively, he says, when it comes to choosing between cars, houses, holidays, schools, coffee beans and irons, they add up to a distressing burden. In this information-rich world, filters are increasingly important.

Schwartz's argument goes something like this: The crux of the capitalist market theory is that individual freedom of choice ensures the most efficient production and distribution of goods. A competitive market will 'exquisitely' respond to people's needs and desires. Freedom to choose enables us to tell the world who we are and what we care about. It's also a testament to our autonomy that is built into legal and moral systems. It 'should' give us the feeling of being in control.

But, despite increased choice, Americans, for one, do not feel an increased sense of control, says Schwartz. He says that as the experience of choice and control gets broader and deeper, people's expectations may rise to match. When opportunities become too numerous we feel unable to cope.

In one survey, people were asked if, should they contract cancer, they would like to choose treatment and they said 'yes'. But in cases where people already had cancer, they preferred not to. Surely it depends what sort of choices there are. We might be able to choose between chocolate biscuits, or even between cancer treatments, but we don't get to 'choose' if trucks on the highway are using fuel that pollutes or if junk mail fills our letter boxes. More choice does not necessarily mean more control over our lives. It depends what the choices are about and if they are real choices at all.

Hard though it would be to quantify, Schwartz believes that a sizable chunk of the time that 'should' go to family and friends, goes on decisions: whether to refinance or not, whether to change internet provider, get different health insurance or change credit cards. These create a background buzz of consumer complexity and clutter: quite how much time goes on them and whether that's a significant time is hard to say. But maybe they do take us one step away from the simple life some of us aspire to.

SIMPLER CHOICES

Simplify your life, Schwartz says, by setting yourself rules, routines and standards. While this may not seem like everyone's cup of tea, to some degree most people follow this, more or less. They don't agonize every night about whether to clean their teeth (or not beyond their teens, anyway), or whether to buckle up the seat belt each time they sit in the car. Do the same in a few other areas of your life, and things will run smoother and in a less time-eating fashion.

Chooser not a picker

Decide what matters, Schwartz says. Focus time and energy on the choices that matter and let the rest pass by. Choose less and choose better, or to put it another way, be a chooser, not a picker. While picking is akin to a lucky dip (follow the herd and hope what you pull out is what you need), making a conscious choice takes time and attention in weighing up which options are best or even in deciding that none of the options that present are right.

Grateful for the good things

Accept that 'good enough' is just that, despite marketing and advertising pressure that only the best will do. By remembering what there is to be grateful about in any situation, we can be more satisfied about it and feel less regret. It's about paying attention to the good things in your life, and being less tempted to check out and compare what's going on in the lives of others.

The anticipation of adaptation

Remember that we get used to new situations very quickly. Pleasures will turn into comforts. The new car will not thrill to the same degree in six months time. By not investing so much time in making the 'crucial' decision, it won't seem so bad when it doesn't have that lustre of perfection anymore. Focus on how good things *are* rather than how good they *were*.

Allow for serendipity

Consider your expectations more carefully and remember that even the events you most look forward to can sometimes be 'underwhelming'. Be philosophical about not having your expectations met all the time.

On the other hand, some of the best times are when circumstances and moods coincide to provide something happy and spontaneous: the fish and chips on the beach on a clear night when you didn't realize there was a full moon that night; the book picked up for a dollar at the school fete that turns out to be one of the best reads ever.

WINS AND LOSSES

While the material wealth of the West may give us a better standard of living, have we lost out in other ways? JC wonders: 'We live with the backdrop of a huge pressure to "do". There's always a timetable hovering in the background and we can't just sit back and enjoy life, take it slower, chat ... sit around.'

Balance is an overused word, but it's a fundamental aspect of the happy successful life. Finding balance is about appreciating what you have but not at the expense of what really matters—family, community and spirituality. A society that supports our aims is the ideal. But if it isn't a reality, we need to do what we can to strengthen our own resolve, make sure we pass on the values that we believe matter to our children, and who knows ... we might even make change on a bigger scale too.

Human beings are incredibly flexible. We learn time habits from our families and the society we live in, but we have the ability to switch between concepts. In a rushed world, maybe we can take some lessons from other slower patterns and make time just a little bit more our own.

TAKING STOCK

1. Taking time

How does the earning and spending of money in your life affect your experience of time? For example, do you:

(a) spend a lot of time researching or making purchases?

(b) spend lots of time maintaining expensive equipment and wonder if it's worth it?

(c) bring work home?

(d) find it hard to switch from efficient and fast mode to slow and relaxed?

2. Materialism

(a) Is our society too materialistic? How does this manifest itself in what you read, see on television, hear around you?

(b) What does materialism mean to you?

(c) Are there materialistic aspects of your own life you'd like to change?

(d) Do you worry about the materialistic values of today's children?

*Those who do not attempt
everything accomplish something.*

MENCIUS (372–289 BC)

9. THE VALUE OF TIME

TIME TAKES ON THE CHARACTERISTICS
OF A COMMODITY WHEN WE EQUATE
IT WITH MONEY AND GIVE IT A
FINANCIAL VALUE, AND ALSO WHEN
WE TALK ABOUT WASTING IT AND
MANAGING IT. BUT IT HAS A
DIFFERENT QUALITY TO MONEY AND
DESERVES BETTER TREATMENT.

THE TIME BANK

At the time bank one hour is equal to one time credit. 'Deposits' in these community-based programmes, where time is the currency, are made by giving practical help and support to others and 'withdrawals' are made when people need help themselves. The Time Keeper software keeps track of credits and debits, while a time broker links up participants, matching available services with needs. Time bank statements are issued regularly and credits can be donated to others in the time pool.

The types of tasks that act as currency in the time bank can be simple: making phone calls, sharing meals, giving lifts, conversation in a foreign language, DIY and shopping. Founder of the international time banking movement Dr Edgar Cahn explains the ideals behind time banking: 'Market economics value what is scarce—not the real work of society, which is caring, loving, being a citizen, a neighbour and a human being.'

In the market economy, explains Time Bank UK, money drives transactions. But the non-market economy is not usually considered an economy at all—it's made up of a support network of family, friends, neighbours and community. The time bank provides a way to strengthen these ties.

Activist and civil rights lawyer, Edgar Cahn devised the time bank system while at the London School of Economics during the 1980s. On returning to the US he started Time Dollar USA. His ideas attracted interest from Japan, where there are now hundreds of schemes, many with government backing. The first UK scheme started in 1998 and at last count there were 77 active time banks with almost 5000 participants, and to date 366,877 hours traded. Most are community time banks based in a specific area, aiming to engage local people of all ages and skills. Organizations are also encouraged to join.

Time banks are also being developed in Australia, New Zealand, Norway and Holland and are already up and going in more than a dozen countries around the world, including Canada, Israel, Italy, Korea, Portugal and Slovakia.

IS TIME MONEY?

Benjamin Franklin, the US statesman, is usually credited with originating the phrase 'time is money'. But in fact, the earliest use of a similar phrase was by Antiphon, an Ancient Greek orator, who wrote speeches for defendants in court cases. Around 430 BC he said, 'The most costly outlay is time.'

'Tyme is precious,' said Sir Thomas Wilson in 'A Discourse Upon Vsurye' in 1572. Perhaps Franklins' apt wording 'remember time is money' in 'Advice to a Young Tradesman' in 1748, explains its wide use thereafter.

It could be argued, suggests psychologist, Mihaly Csikszentmihalyi in *Finding Flow*, that money gets its value from time rather than the other way round. 'Money is simply the most generally used counter for measuring the time invested in doing or making something.' He has a point, although, quite how much money is not a simple calculation. It depends on whose time is being used, how skilled that person is, and how rare his or her talents are and—perhaps most importantly, how much they are valued by people willing to pay.

But 'time is money' is certainly a pervasive concept. 'Workers are paid by the hour, lawyers charge by the minute, and advertising is sold by the second,' points out Robert Levine, author of *A Geography of Time*. 'Through a curious intellectual exercise, the civilized mind has reduced time—that most obscure and abstract of all intangibles—to the most objective of all quantities: money.'

The phrase, 'time is money' reflects our willingness to slice and measure time, even in its slightest moments, as well as the ease with which we attribute a monetary value to it.

But the concept of 'time is money' is not universal. Many of the villagers that social researcher Kevin Birth met in Trinidad, for example, did not understand it. Only those who had contact with Westerners or wage earners—particularly those who'd worked for an hourly wage—had a feel for the idea. To feel that time is money requires money to occupy a certain position. Time is not money in a society that has little money circulating; in cultures where there's lots of time, the idea of wasting it is nonsense. If you're not doing one thing, you're doing another, so how can it be wasted?

Most commentators point the finger at capitalism in explaining where the 'time is money' concept comes from. Clearly it was felt and understood in previous centuries, but the close clock-watching and the drive for efficiency is a more modern phenomenon that perhaps accelerated the advance of the 'time is money' ethic. Historian Edward Thompson once remarked that time had become a currency to spend rather than to pass.

According to Juliet Schor, Associate Professor of Economics at Harvard University in the US, 'work ethic' means 'time ethic'. When Benjamin Franklin declared that time is money, he meant that time should be used productively.

'The origins of modern time consciousness lie in the development of a capitalist economy,' Schor says. 'As capitalism raised the "price" of time, people began to think of time as a scarce resource.' And eventually, time and money began to substitute for each other: time could buy money and money could buy time. Meanwhile, time had become a commodity.

Kellogg's Six-Hour Day: More time, little less money

In 1930 W K Kellogg announced that employees at his Battle Creek plant would work only a six-hour day, with a minimum pay cut. This measure, introduced at the height of the Depression, lasted successfully for nearly two decades. He reaped benefits of reduced overheads and reduced labour costs. Accidents declined, while days lost due to accidents were cut by half. The shorter working day boosted morale and efficiency, accident and insurance rates were lowered and the unit cost of production was reduced too.

But after World War II, management saw things differently, abolished the shorter day and replaced it with a system that rewarded higher productivity with pay rises. In fact, it was the workers and the unions who, once the higher pay was in sight, demanded a return to the eight-hour day.

VOX POP: Is time money?

Time has an utterly different quality. If I'm working for someone or putting in time for an institution, then I'm aware of the hours I'm putting in and although I don't try to convert it to a dollar figure, I sometimes think, 'that's a week's work a year I do there ...' or some such. On the whole I think 'money is money'. For instance, if I'm struggling with the housework, I could think it would be better to pay someone to do it and be freer for my own (theoretically) better paid work, but some martyr streak in me thinks I should do it myself, especially given the precarious nature of the freelance household income. AH

When it comes to working for money, yes, the amount of time spent on it is equated with money. But I don't think spare time should be seen as time that could be spent earning more money—that's not a healthy way to look at it. There are some things I would rather pay someone to do but with many others, if I can do them myself, I will. For instance, I'm renovating a bathroom and am doing the tiling myself and leaving some tasks, like replacing the basin and toilet, to the plumber. It depends what I want to put time into. ML

It's not totally true that time is money. Time can make you money, but it does not have to be your time. For example, I work hard and write a book, I spend the time on the promotions, then I let the book work for me. The aim is to work hard then be organized and let your work continue to work for you when you are onto another project. SG

Marilyn Waring (1952–)

New Zealand feminist and academic, Marilyn Waring, became the youngest member of parliament when she took the seat for the Ragland electorate in 1975, and stayed until 1984. Her 1988 work, *If Women Counted*, points out the shortcomings of ignoring women's unpaid work in economic tallies. She farms goats and sheep on a farm north of Auckland that is organized for simplicity and self-sufficiency.

SPENDING TIME AND MONEY

Time is not money according to a paper 'Spending Time versus Spending Money' by Erica Mina Okada of the University of Washington and Stephen J Hoch of the University of Pennsylvania in the US, published in 2003. They base their findings on a number of experiments in which 360 undergraduate students were questioned about how they'd feel in several scenarios. For example, in one experiment students were presented with the possibility of having a dinner for two or a pair of trainers, and paying for it in money or time. For some the outcome was presented as positive and for others negative.

Both time and money, argue the authors, are mediums of exchange. (Both are academics in the field of marketing, it should be pointed out.) Transactions for goods can be made by paying hard cash (money) or expending effort (time). Typically, there's a trade-off between the two: we're willing to pay a premium for convenience ('saving' time), but also sometimes to pay with time and 'go the distance' for a bargain (saving money).

People 'spend' time and money in a different fashion. We can evaluate money easily, but the value of time is ambiguous and difficult to calculate. As it's harder to pinpoint the value of time, we feel okay about wasting it and rationalizing after the event, whereas a gaping hole in the bank statement is harder to ignore.

Money is highly liquid, it can be saved and is readily exchangeable: a dollar is a dollar no matter the transaction type. But time is perishable, cannot be saved for later, and is not as readily exchangeable.

In addition, Okada and Hoch point out:

- people are more practised at spending money as a currency.
- temporal budget constraints are 'pretty soft', meaning that, with eight hours for working and eight for sleep, there's still a third of a day left over for 'discretionary activities'.
- the value of time is flexible. People adjust the value of time to a particular situation. People don't see their time in terms of how much they earn at work, because during the weekend or in the evening, time has a different quality.

- we have an easier time accepting bad outcomes when we pay with time rather than money. The authors likened this to 'playing with someone else's money' where the outcome doesn't matter as much.

- our flexible attitude to time might be an important part of our 'psychological immune system'. If we viewed time too precisely, life could become very stressful very quickly. But a little latitude in our approach to time means not every moment has to 'stand up and be counted' for us to feel okay about where our time goes.

TOO FAR IN TIME

'Has [our society] perhaps gone too far in the direction of collapsing time into money?' asks Schor. 'The more time substitutes for money, the more difficult it is to establish an independent measure of time's value,' she says.

Time has a different value to money. Time is the big life picture that money is a part of. We can't put a money value on all the aspects of time—they simply aren't part of the narrow market-money view.

But when a 'time is money' mindset dominates, argues Schor, it makes it hard to protect time for ourselves—for relaxation, hobbies and even sleep. The 'time is money' concept threatens to transform a resource that is equally distributed (time) into one that is distinctly unequal (money). Everyone is born with 24 hours in the day, but wealth and income are unequally distributed.

Schor argues that as time outside work becomes more precious, those with money can economize on it. This means that high-paid people can spend money on buying them more free time, by paying for a cleaner, child minder or gardener.

However, this is at odds with research showing that the wealthier a person is the more time-poor they feel. The economic view looks at the relative value of time and money, suggesting that it changes according to scarcity. When we have money but no time, time starts to look more precious.

Polls also support the idea that in many Western countries people feel overworked and would trade money for time if they could. A 1991 survey into time values in the US conducted by the Hilton Hotel

Corporation, found two-thirds of respondents willing to take a salary cut in exchange for time off. 'Time or money?' becomes the question, as if the two were interchangeable forms.

BUYING BACK TIME

Certainly at some point, when money is of little object but time is scarce, people start to 'buy back' their time. According to Robert Levine, we 'buy' back our time by learning ways of doing the unavoidable more quickly or by paying someone else to do those jobs, so that we have time to spend how we want.

It's a concept LB, mother of two, and partner in a business with her husband, is well acquainted with:

Do I want to pay a cleaner? Do I want to paint the house myself? Do I want to pay a babysitter so that I can go to yoga? My attitude to these questions has changed so much in the last 10 years. We now pay for more and more to be done for us so that we can pursue both work and happiness. It's especially important to set aside and pay for time without the children so we can do what we like doing together—like taking two hours to go to a yoga class together. The help we pay for is part of making our working life easier and our family life calmer. The cleaner does a better job than I do. She is quicker and less connected to the mess so less likely to be exasperated.

Nevertheless, there is a great deal to be done to run a home and family, so we still do some cleaning—it doesn't get either of us off the hook. But because we run a business from home I am frequently in the house—separating house and family from business and family is tricky. Part of making that work, is applying the same theory we apply with the business to the home, which is that it is better to pay a specialist to do something that's not your expertise. Financially it's more efficient as it frees us to do the things we are more valuable doing.

THE WAITING GAME

Make 'em laugh; make 'em cry; make 'em wait.
CHARLES READE (1814–1884), RECIPE FOR NOVEL-WRITING IN
SERIAL FORM

If time is money, waiting has a price. In some countries people are prepared to pay—either directly or indirectly—for other people to wait for them. The *gestures* (or middle-men) in Mexico, for example, stand in line for other people. Bureaucratic procedures grind slowly in Mexico, hence the popularity of *gestures*, especially outside government offices. In some cases, the client hands over their papers and calls later to pick them up. In other cases, people literally hire a body to stand in a queue; the night before the visa office opens, for example.

One economist estimated that about 30 billion hours each year were being wasted while shopping in the former Soviet Union because of people having to wait in line. Another researcher estimated that in Moscow alone, people spent more than 20 million hours queuing to pay rent and utility bills.

Levine tells the story of watching people queue for more than two hours to buy shoes in Poland. As soon as they left the shop, many of them offered their purchases on the black market, at prices calculated by how long the purchaser had waited in line.

In the waiting game, status and money give control over time—in certain earthbound ways, at least. If you are powerful, people will wait, and are often made to wait, to see you. The willingness to wait confirms their lower status. Pope Gregory VII (born Hildebrand, around 1020) is said to have made the Holy Roman Emperor Henry IV stand three days and nights barefoot in the snow and ice before agreeing to a meeting.

HOW LATE IS LATE?

If time is a social construct, then being late and what that means is a cultural one. Robert Levine surveyed Brazilians and found they rated people who were always late for appointments as the most successful, while punctual people were considered to be the least successful. Brazilians also thought people who were always late were more relaxed, happy and likeable. But the real reason was because those who were late (who, in other words, kept people waiting) were in fact, those who were more successful, because in Brazil, those who are more important keep their inferiors waiting. 'Lack of promptness is a badge of achievement,' says Levine, and as it is a badge to be envied people don't resent being kept waiting.

Be on time, be fashionably late (if you can work out what that means), but whatever you do, don't be early. In some cultures, half an hour 'late' is expected. If someone says come for dinner at 7 pm, they really mean 7.30 pm. In Sweden and Germany on the other hand, 7 pm means just that and you risk offending if you arrive any later. The one area that is not acceptable across cultures is being early—a definite 'no-no', as you risk arriving before your hosts are ready to receive you and putting them in an uncomfortable position.

Common sense tells us it must depend on the circumstances. To keep someone waiting 30 minutes for a quick lunch appointment that will only last one hour is inconsiderate, to turn up to a stretched out evening party two hours late may be fine. If someone will be waiting for you alone, in possibly awkward circumstances, punctuality is more urgent than if they were at home.

Beware a culture in transition! A consultant in the Philippines, for example, warns that 'although there is a tendency to think of the Philippines as a place where it's fine to be late, this is no longer true. 'Businesspeople have gradually come to appreciate the importance of punctuality, and it's best to arrive on time.' He describes a pace of business that can be maddeningly slow to Westerners.

As one web blogger fumes:

I hate lateness. My whole family hates lateness. We consider it a disrespect of someone's time. I never understood the whole fashionably late thing. I thought it was rude. Who are we all kidding? If you really don't want folks at your house until 10 pm then for God's sake say show up at 10 pm. Don't do this, 'Oh, the party is at 8 pm but no-one will show up until 10 pm.' Don't play these passive-aggressive guessing games. At my house you show up on time or you don't get to eat.

SAVING TIME—TIME MANAGEMENT

In the morning when I get up, the first thing I do is think as though to myself: what am I going to do today? So many things: I count them, think about them, and to each assign its time.

LEON BATTISTA ALBERTI, *I LIBRI DELLA FAMIGLIA*, 1433

If time is the stuff of life, the time tactician's approach is to make sure he or she doesn't waste a moment. Time management is often aimed at businesses, with information like: if you can improve your time efficiency by 5 per cent, that's an extra three minutes an hour. For an organization of 20 working at that improvement, it represents the equivalent of an extra person's work.

Taking time is a thief's trade, says another time management consultant. An effective manager must be both thief and strategist, stealing time from less 'worthy' pursuits to get the job done. Sometimes it seems to take on its own mania: allot 15 minutes to clear the desk, another 15 minutes for a cup of tea with Joe, 10 minutes to order the flowers for Mrs Bloggs, 12.15 pm take personal organizer to be fixed. Some systems appear so complicated they seem to shrivel life up into little dried up pieces of time.

It's an approach with pitfalls as JE points out:

There's a perception that time management is about squeezing in as much as possible into any given period. Link this to the hullabaloo about how you must realize your full potential by making every second count and I think that's why we end up with a lot of fragile, stressed, exhausted and self-doubting people.

Perhaps we never quite get over the school report syndrome. We want gold stars and elephant stamps; our efforts acknowledged and rewarded. How well we perceive we manage our time can depend upon the types of progress reports we receive from those around us. Well Done! Could Do Better! Are we really choosing how we spend our time or merely seeking approval from others?

I'm not into strip programming my life. We're people, not television stations. Our activities do not need to be slotted into 30 minute spots with an update issued on the hour, every hour. We can't limit our heartbreak to fit in when the soapies screen, fun to the cartoon hour, and family time to prime-time.

Time management can take many guises, however, and being aware of time can help us use it in a way that is more in line with what we regard as important. 'Time, because it is invisible and intangible, doesn't get enough respect,' warns B Eugene Griessman, in *Time Tactics of Very Successful People*.

Effective time tactics, we are told, can make or break our careers, help us to better delegate and therefore manage the same job with less people, prevent burnout and an organization (or a home) that stops when you do. In a busy, complex life, managing time gets trickier and at the same time more important. Why is managing time such a challenge these days?

- Information overload. We have to choose what to look at and access, we can't possibly take in all that's available.
- Competition. B Eugene Griessman points to the advertisement, 'he who hesitates is lunch'. As economics professor Robert Frank says, the worker who stays the extra two hours at work is often competing for the top 10 per cent: the best 10 per cent of schools, houses and jobs.
- Finding balance: we talk of balancing family, career and social life. At other times, we would have been happy to keep a job and support a healthy family.

THE GIVE AND TAKE OF TIME

Given that time is finite, if you want to spend more time on one activity, it means spending less on another. It's the same idea behind much of the simple-living philosophy. You cannot do it all well. Choose the tasks that you want to take time over and you'll have more time for the important things in your life. Part of the appeal of time management books is the hope that there's just one little gem of advice that might unlock the time puzzle you've been struggling with.

In that vein, here are some tactics to take or leave.

- Watch less TV. You might have the time to write the letter, pick up the oil pastels or finish the assignment.
- Shop by phone or internet. You cut out time travelling and it's often very quick to choose what you want to buy too.
- Choose low-maintenance clothes and appliances. Avoid clothes that need to be dry-cleaned or hand-washed and ease off the ironing.
- Screen calls on the answering machine. Telemarketers don't even bother to leave messages; call others back at a better time, not 'prime' concentration time, for example.
- Put time aside. Take a day each month to catch up on bills, thank-you notes, stock up on kitchen cupboard basics and so on.

LEARN TO PRIORITIZE

Make sure you're putting your time and energy into what matters to you. It seems a part of modern life to have a 'to do' list that stretches on and on; people to call, applications to make, bills to pay and jobs that need to be completed.

To avoid feeling overwhelmed it's important to be able to set priorities. Which ones need doing now? Which can wait until next week with no ill-effect? Which would be 'nice' but shouldn't be high on the list of priorities? There's a business maxim that says about 20 per cent of customers bring in 80 per cent of the income. Or, the other way round, the large majority brings only a small part of the business. Eliminate the 80 per cent on your 'to do' list that is draining and gives you little 'return' says Griessman. Don't treat items on your list as equal and consider breaking down your list into two lists, one for the short term and one for the long term. Alternatively, you can number the tasks on your list and try to complete them in that order, or isolate the three most important and make them an immediate priority.

SYSTEMS AND LISTS

One person's list is another person's mania. Finding ways of managing your time that suit you can make life easier. And sometimes you need to change tack. Other time tactics include:

- Write down tomorrow's tasks before you turn off the light. Writing down helps you by not having to try to remember and helps garner resolve.
- Have a 'system': whether a diary or a large notebook; try to avoid writing on little scraps of paper that have a habit of becoming lost.
- Don't make today's list too long. Pick a realistic number of tasks each day that you can conquer.
- Time slots. If lists don't work for you, try setting a specific time against every job you must do.
- Schedule time for catching up and clearing up—your desk, dining table or the kids' room. These really do take time, squeezing them between 'real jobs' means they don't get done until it's urgent.
- Check lists. Create check lists for tasks that come up regularly, such as the packing for the weekend away or the camping trip.
- Doubling up. If you have an errand in town, wait till you have a few to do before making the trip and organize the jobs geographically so that you are not backtracking.
- Take advantage of windows as they open. If you're in town for a seminar, maybe you can catch up with a friend afterwards.

The art of managing time

Printmaker and textile artist, JB, takes a creative approach to using her time. She has lists of activities at the ready so that when necessary she can change jobs quickly. For example, she keeps a list of jobs she can do when she wants to listen attentively to a radio story; these could include garden jobs like weeding or pruning, mending or some artwork that doesn't need thinking about. 'A 10-minute interview I want to listen to means a 10-minute job, such as washing a window. I get the satisfaction of getting a job done almost without knowing. It's good for the soul!' she says. She'll often choose public transport over driving so that she can dip into her reading bag, a bag she made especially for the magazines and articles she intends reading. 'If I haven't read for a while, I know it's time to go somewhere,' says JB.

TREASURE YOUR DOWNTIME

The polychrons already do it. They make the most of times when you have to wait with activities such as:

- reading a book. Many people make sure they always have a book with them and that way they fill their waiting time happily and get the added bonus of having read those extra books. Alternatively you can read a work report or a business article.
- spot meditation. Make the most of a peaceful moment to find calm: practise mindfulness, slow down, count your breath.
- sketching. Carry a small visual diary or sketch book, pencil, sharpener and eraser and you're set for a creative moment.
- writing notes to clients or postcards to friends.
- listening to talking books or learning a language while driving.

CARVING OUT TIME

Interrupted time can be exasperating and ineffectual. Consider ways of creating streams of time. Some of life's unavoidables will take less time out of your day if you simply avoid doing them at the same time as the rest of the herd.

- Get up an hour or two earlier.
- Arrive at work early or stay later.
- Remove yourself from the source of interruptions by going to the library, excusing yourself for an hour of exercise. Avoid scheduling too much chauffeuring in a small period.
- Go to the post office mid-morning, before the lunch-time rush.
- If you catch public transport, travel off-peak so you get a seat and can read or work while on your way.
- Do the supermarket shop at a time when the queues are shortest.

FOCUS

Forget multitasking. When Thomas Edison was interviewed for *Success* magazine in 1898, and asked about the prerequisite for success, he said, 'the ability to apply your physical and mental energies to one problem incessantly without growing weary'. Most of us don't have the luxury of being able to put 16 hours a day into a

the value of time

project, even if we wanted to. Raising children, for a start, requires a broader outlook. But the ability to focus and put your energy and concentration into a job is a powerful one—even if it's only for a few hours at a time.

ROUTINES AND RHYTHMS

Life presents a blinding array of choices: What career? Which job? Which brand of tea or bread? Should you go for a walk or a swim? Watch the TV or a DVD? The blue T-shirt or the red one?

If you grappled with every tiny decision it would be exhausting, maybe even maddening. Routines cut out those choices and while you certainly wouldn't want all life to be mere routine, there is a reassuring rhythm to routine that gives the mundane a smoother, more comforting quality. Children like their routines, it's said, as it gives them a sense of security in knowing what's ahead.

DEADLINES

I love deadlines. I love the sound they make as they woosh past.
DOUGLAS ADAMS (1952–2001)

Writers and deadlines go hand in hand. Columnist Russell Baker, living in a world where time is forever running out said, 'Desperation is the newspaperman's normal state of mind'. But finishing a creative task to a time frame can be difficult. You can almost feel yourself buckling under pressure, as Mark Twain describes as he attempts to finish a book (from a letter published in Albert Paine's biography *Mark Twain*,1912):

The weather turned cold, and we had to rush home, while I still lacked thirty thousand words. I had been sick and got delayed. I am going to write all day and two-thirds of the night until the thing is done or break down at it. The spur and the burden of the contract are intolerable to me ... It is ten days' work, and unless something breaks it will be finished in five.

BREAKING PROCRASTINATION

The best time to plant a tree was 20 years ago.
The second best time is now.

CHINESE PROVERB

Putting off till tomorrow what should be done today is sometimes
wise, at other times it's called procrastination. The word comes from
latin, *procrastinare*, which literally means 'to put off until tomorrow'.
But does the task you procrastinate over really belong to tomorrow or
is it a job for today?

- Freezing the design. Engineers are taught to make a decision by a
  particular time and not keep looking for the perfect solution: this is
  called 'freezing the design'.
- Do it now. The best way to keep on top of some tasks is often by
  doing them immediately.
- Just do it. Don't waste your time getting ready to proceed and
  thinking about how a task can be done—plunge in and get going.
- Time and energy. Sometimes it's not lack of time so much as lack of
  energy that seems to make it impossible to wade through certain
  tasks. Yet other days you feel you could conquer anything. Try
  starting a difficult task when you've come back from an exhilarating
  walk that's allowed you to collect thoughts as well as energy. As MN
  describes, 'There are times I'll force myself to do something and it
  seems to take forever, yet other times, if I wait for the right moment,
  I can get on without resistance and sometimes even gusto.'

Let the subconscious do the work

The philosopher Bertrand Russell used to set his mind a task (a long
speech, for example) and let it work it out subconsciously for a few
months so that when he came to deal with it directly, he'd done a lot
of the thinking and had it all worked out in his head. Not everyone
has their subconscious under such iron control, but many of us
choose, wisely, to 'sleep on it'.

Losing time—losing things

Millions of hours are lost by people looking for things. The absent-minded may benefit from developing a foolproof survival system with a place for their keys, wallet, umbrellas and sunglasses. Usually the best place is the most logical—a key hook by the front or back door for car keys, perhaps a drawer in the bedroom for the wallet, umbrellas in a stand by the door and so on.

PARKINSON'S LAW AND OTHER TIME WASTERS

Parkinson's law says work expands so as to fill the time available for its completion. The 'law' comes from C Northcote Parkinson's book *Parkinson's Law: The Pursuit of Progress*, a satire based on extensive experience in the British Civil Service. He concluded that there was little or no relationship between the work done and the amount of resources devoted to it.

In private life as much as bureaucratic, we can be tempted to fill our time with trivia. Reviewing the real need for an activity might result in dropping it and having more time at your disposal for what really matters to you. As Ralph Waldo Emerson put it: 'A foolish consistency is the hobgobbling of little minds, adored by little statesmen and

Julio Iglesias (1943–)

Spain's most popular singer studied law then became a goalie for a Madrid soccer team. In 1963 he was involved in a car accident that almost took his life and near paralysed him for a year. While recovering in hospital a nurse gave him a guitar and he began writing songs. Five years later he won the Benidorm International Song Festival with a song, '*La Vida Sigue Igual*' ('Life Goes on Just the Same') and in 1983 he received a diamond disc from the Guinness Book of Records for selling 100 million records in six languages. He was a good goalie, but an even better singer, yet without the time in hospital he may never have discovered his talent.

philosophers and divines. With consistency, a great soul simply has nothing to do.'

In other words, you don't have to keep doing something that no longer means anything to you. Perhaps you don't have to finish every book that you start—only the good ones.

THE ART OF THE TIMELY CONVERSATION

The sticky area of how to tactfully set time limits to meetings and conversations is a universal tact conundrum. Experts recommend expanding your time-cue vocabulary with phrases like, 'I'm just about to dash out the door, but I can talk quickly now ...' or 'I can give you 10 minutes now, and if we need more time, we'll have to reschedule, is that okay?'

FG relates how her mother was very bad at being able to politely end phone calls. 'Jam's boiling!' her children used to help by calling out.

When you feel time's tight and looking at your watch seems rude, there are more sociable ways to curtail time. 'A quick cup of tea' or a 'cup of coffee' is about half an hour to an hour—time to make it and drink it; the empty cup reminds you of the time passed and the length of the invitation. 'Lunch' during the business day is an hour or so, whereas a meal in the evening is often longer.

A PATH IN TIME

This is our blessing and our curse: to count the days and weeks and years, to calculate the movement of the sun, moon and stars, and to capture them all in a grid of small squares that spread out like a net cast over time: thousands of little squares for each lifetime.

DAVID EWING DUNCAN, *CALENDAR*, 1998

Time management is not about filling up all the little squares. It's as much about making sure enough of them are empty. 'People on treadmills don't get very far,' Griessman says.

James Watson, co-discoverer of the structure of DNA and author of *The Double Helix* says it's necessary to be slightly underemployed if you are to do something significant. In his and Francis Crick's case, they needed parties, walks and drinks in the pub to reflect on what they were reading, hearing and seeing. The downside of being busy is missing out on that creative time to reflect.

Have we all become economists in time? asks Juliet Schor. Capitalism has raised the price of time and we're left in no doubt that we know the time price of everything, but not the worth. But as individuals, we can give back the proper value of time and give it another name: life.

TAKING STOCK:
THE VALUE OF TIME

1. Do you agree that time is money? In what ways are time and money interchangeable to you? In what ways are they utterly different? Which is more scarce in your life—money or time?
2. What are some of the ways you attempt to save time? Do these strategies bring the results you expect?
3. How does time change for you across a week or even a year. Is it all equal?
4. What time management system, if any, do you use? Does it work for you?
5. What stops you getting tasks done:
(a) lack of organization?
(b) lack of focus?
(c) lack of energy?
(d) lack of time?

She's got
Snow in her eyes, got
A tingle in her toes
And new red boots on
Wherever she goes

KIT WRIGHT, 'RED BOOTS ON',
FROM *POEMS* 1974–1983

10. HAPPY PEOPLE

SOME PEOPLE RADIATE HAPPINESS AND OTHERS SEEM TO OCCUPY A GRUMPIER PLACE. MANY OF US ARE SOMEWHERE IN BETWEEN ON THE TIDES OF EMOTION. ARE THERE HABITS WE CAN CULTIVATE TO IMPROVE OUR HAPPINESS, OR IS IT HAPPINESS ITSELF THAT CHANGES PEOPLE'S BEHAVIOUR? TO TEASE OUT THE ANSWER SCIENTIFICALLY REQUIRES A MEASUREMENT OF THAT ELUSIVE QUALITY, HAPPINESS. BUT JUST HOW RELIABLE ARE THE RESULTS?

HABITS FOR HAPPINESS

Are happy people different? Do they behave differently or think differently to the rest of the crowd? One group of researchers took a close look at studies of people who scored high in happiness surveys, (in the top 25 per cent). These weren't people who are always happy, and they experienced low moods too, but they seemed to have a certain joie de vivre. Such people are sometimes described as 'dispositionally happy'.

Happy individuals approach and respond to decisions in unique ways, say authors Allison Abbe, Chris Tkach and Sonja Lyubomirsky in the *Journal of Happiness Studies*. They analyzed a range of separate studies and found that happy people do indeed act differently.

- Happy people find 'good enough'. People who 'maximize' (that is, search exhaustively through every option before making a decision) don't tend to be happier. Even if maximizers might have objectively better outcomes, they are less content with them.
- Regrets make for unhappy people. Happy people, even if they do go through all the options first, are happier with the outcome and less likely to feel regret.
- Re-evaluating rejection. Happy people adapt and protect themselves by bolstering their self-esteem when rejected. For example, if turned down by their favourite college, a happy student might increase their assessment of a college that accepts them, and place the rejecting college lower in their estimations by telling themselves it has a worse social life.
- Curtailing comparison. Happy people are less influenced by the successes or failures of their peers. In one study, people were asked to do an exercise to teach people using hand puppets. They were then told they had performed well. That assessment lifted the mood of happy people, whether or not they were also told that others had done even better. Unhappy people, on the other hand, only felt happier if they were not told of a peer doing better. When the tables were turned and people told they'd performed badly, everyone felt a little deflated. But unhappy people felt slightly less deflated if they were told that a peer had performed even worse. The news of a peer doing worse did not affect the mood of a 'happy' person.

- Less is more. Happy people are less concerned with their emotions than unhappy ones and spend less time ruminating and reflecting on their thoughts and feelings. Individuals who engage in a lot of self-reflection may be wiser, but sadder too. 'Ruminative self-reflection appears to be a maladaptive coping response to both the hassles and tragedies of life,' conclude Abbe et al. The dispositionally happy may also avoid negatively biased thinking, poor problem solving, impaired motivation and concentration.

- Even more positive, even less negative. Happy people have different strategies in responding to life's events. When good things happen to 'happy' people, they see it more positively than unhappy people do. And when something bad happens, they don't view it quite as negatively as others might. In addition, happy people are more likely to use humour to cope with something unpleasant and dwell on improvements that have occurred.

- Positive sustains. Happy people more readily evaluate people and events in a positive light. And such an attitude is likely to help sustain happiness, bringing about positive outcomes and responses in other people.

In his book, *Authentic Happiness*, Martin Seligman points to a variety of studies that have drawn links between happiness and other characteristics. These show, in general, that happy people share many similar characteristics. Happy people:

- think they are much more skillful than others judge them to be.
- remember more good events than actually happened.
- forget more of the bad events.
- are more satisfied with their jobs.
- can hold their hands in icy water longer.
- are more altruistic.
- are more willing to donate money to those in need.
- display more empathy.
- are less self-focused.
- like other people more.
- want to share good fortune, even with strangers.

Are depressed people realists?

When it comes to making decisions and judgments, not everyone agrees that the happy person makes the best ones. 'Laboratory psychologists have given happy people a black eye,' says Ed Diener, Alumni Professor of Psychology at the University of Illinois. They claim that people in a positive mood use stereotypes more, are less logical and more biased. Is this a case of the opposite of the 'Depressive Realism' hypothesis, which suggests that depressed people are accurate, and happy people inaccurate in their judgments?

TOO HAPPY, TOO LONG

Is it possible to be too happy? Being 'chronically happy' may not be a good thing. People with hypomania (a high mood without justification) feel great, experience an 'elevated' mood, are very active, need little sleep and sometimes feel grandiose. Such buoyancy can fuel substantial achievements and creativity and can attract an expanding network of admirers. But such a positive outlook has its down sides. Too much happiness can subtly impair a person's judgment and overconfidence can hide the consequences of decisions. As a result, it's not uncommon to find those with hypomania sticking with untenable marriages or staying in jobs that do not even begin to use their potential. Hypomania also carries a risk of cycling into depression. Mania can be even more disastrous, like the story of the manic who gave away his life savings on a whim.

In theory at least, the ability to be aware of our own happiness and unhappiness, should steer us in the right direction as far as the survival of our genes: towards things that are 'good' for us (food, sex, enjoying friends and family) and away from 'bad' influences (danger, isolation). But of course it's not that simple. We are constantly faced with making decisions which affect our future—it's much easier to keep your perspective on the short-term horizon and do things which feel good now, even if it results in a harmful long-term outcome. Then there are people who look like they have it all but often feel unhappy. There's obviously more to the story.

Happy people

Happiness heavyweight, Ed Diener has found that happy people:

- on average have stronger immune systems, and may live longer.
- are more creative.
- tend to help others more at work and skip work less.
- are more 'successful' (his term): they earn more income, have better marriages and get more job interviews, for example.
- are more sociable and other people like them more.
- are better able to cope with difficult situations.
- like themselves and other people more; others like them in return.
- are, on average, more helpful and altruistic.

BORN HAPPY

When it comes down to it, what is happiness for? Robert Wright, writing the article, 'Dancing to Evolution's Time' published in *Time* magazine, is in no doubt: '… the laws governing happiness were designed not for our psychological wellbeing but for our genes' long-term survival prospects. That fact, when pondered at length, can induce unhappiness.'

So, we were not designed to be happy or unhappy. According to Professor Nesse, Professor of Psychiatry and Psychology at the University of Michigan in the US, writing about evolution and happiness in *The Science of Wellbeing*, these emotions are no part of the 'design' at all, but mechanisms that 'influence us to act in the interest of our genes'.

Wright agrees: 'Happiness is for getting us to use our intestines, ovaries and testicles,' he says. But genes also benefit when we help offspring and excel at work and play—so these actions bring joy too. The sobering news is that happiness is designed to evaporate. Permanent highs don't get people far. So Molière had a point when he said, 'unbroken happiness is a bore; it should have ups and downs'.

There is also much evidence to suggest a genetic component is involved when it comes to how much we experience happiness. More than half the variance in subjective wellbeing in individuals seems to lie in genetics, says Nesse.

The ways that we inherit degrees of happiness are not known, but are likely complex. For example, we might inherit tendencies, such as risk taking or a short temper, that have ramifications across our lives. The same goes, says Nesse, for things like depression, a tendency to hang on to ambitious and impossible goals, or even attaching to a partner so strongly that you won't leave, despite being abused.

THE HAPPINESS THERMOSTAT

Happiness depends, as Nature shows,
Less on exterior things than most suppose.

WILLIAM COWPER, 'TABLE TALK', 1782

Akin to the idea of a set weight that the body veers towards after each round of dieting, so too the idea of a happiness thermostat, or set level, that despite cause for celebration or commiseration, we swing back to.

David Lykken, emeritus professor at the University of Minnesota, believes that each person has a set range of happiness. This doesn't mean you can't change where you're at on the happiness scale, he claims, but it does mean there are happy people and happier ones—'… the set point around which happiness varies from time to time apparently differs from one person to another,' he says in a paper co-authored with Auke Tellegen, and published in *Psychological Science* in 1996.

Lykken studied over 4000 twins in middle age. Of the variation in happiness he found only 3 per cent could be attributed to socioeconomic status, educational attainment, family income, marital status or religious commitment. Between 44 per cent and 53 per cent of the variation in their happiness came down to genetics.

His study found that identical twins reared apart are more similar when it comes to happiness levels than fraternal twins who are reared together.

'The twin studies (and adoption studies as well) suggest that some portion of our happiness is likely to come from our genetics,' agrees Ed Diener. Adding weight to the genetics argument are studies of specific gene influences; for instance, there is little doubt that certain genes are linked with a propensity to depression.

NURTURE AND NATURE

The existence of a set level of happiness does not necessarily mean you can do nothing to improve how you feel about life. But it might mean that you change your view as to how devastating—or rewarding—a particular event on the horizon might be: a redundancy won't be the nightmare you're dreading, on the other hand, the promotion you're going for won't deliver everlasting peace either. People have a remarkable ability to adapt, both to bad fortune and to good.

But what sets the peak happiness point for each person? Genetics can play a role, then there are other factors, suggest experts, that might influence where our peak of happiness settles. Ed Diener and David Myers suggest other possible determiners, such as personal relationships, religious faith and a person's ability to experience flow in working towards achievable goals. 'Nurture' has an influence too on our ability to experience happiness. For instance:

- Family home. According to Ed Diener, the family home environment influences the degree to which you experience good moods as an adult; for example, how much you feel positive emotions, such as joy.
- Unemployed people are less happy. Longitudinal studies in Germany show that people who become unemployed are less happy—and remain so for many years.
- Marriage. Women who get married on average remain somewhat happier than woman who are unmarried.

Psychologist Mihaly Csikszentmihalyi, on the other hand, certainly does not agree that we're born with either a happy or sad temperament. 'This deterministic scenario is correct only insofar as the extroverted exuberance that is often mistaken for happiness is concerned,' he writes in *Finding Flow*. It depends on what you want to call happiness. But as far as he's concerned, you can significantly alter your experience of life by learning to engage and challenging yourself in deeply satisfying ways.

THE AUTOTELIC PERSONALITY

An autotelic activity is something you do for its own sake. It's the experience of it that is the main goal in doing it. For example, you meditate because you love where it takes you and the ripple effects on the rest of your life; you play the piano because it's challenging and satisfying to make gradual progress. In contrast, an exotelic activity, such as doing something for financial reward is performed to achieve an external goal.

Someone who is 'autotelic' has the ability to confront life with high involvement and enthusiasm. The term has Greek roots: *auto* meaning 'self' and *telos* meaning 'goal'.

No one is fully autotelic, says Csikszentmihalyi. Every one has to do at least some things that they'd rather not, but there's a gradation ranging from those who feel almost nothing they do is worthwhile for its own sake, to those who feel that almost everything they do is important and valuable in its own right. The autotelic person is not necessarily happier but they are often involved in more complex activities and feel better about themselves as a result. Some of the more typical characteristics of an autotelic person are listed below.

- They are not materialistic and generally need few possessions.
- They are less dependent on external rewards.
- They are less tied up in dull and meaningless routines.
- They are autonomous and independent.
- They have seemingly inexhaustible psychic energy.
- They have learnt to control their attention and have a high sense of curiosity, wonder and interest in life.
- They are interested in small 'breakthroughs' as much as major ones.
- They have an interest in the world that involves an attempt to understand it and solve problems in a non self-centred way.

MEASURING HAPPINESS

The utilitarian philosopher Jeremy Bentham proposed a 'felicific calculus', also referred to as hedonic calculus—a method of working out the sum total of pleasure and pain produced by an act, including its consequences. Outlined in his 1789 work, *Introduction to the Principles of Morals and Legislation*, he proposed it took into account variables such as how intense an act was, how long it lasted, the chance that one pleasure may lead to another and how many people were affected by the action. Bentham envisaged using

The autotelic teenager

Studies of the habits of autotelic teenagers show they:

- spend around 11 hours a week studying, almost twice as much as non-autotelic teenagers.
- spend twice as much of their time in hobbies.
- spend longer periods of time doing sports activities.
- spend less time than their non-autotelic peers watching television.
- spend a significantly higher amount of time interacting with family. The family may act as a protective environment in which to experiment without being self-conscious, defensive or competitive.

the calculus for criminal law reform but the idea was problematic —it was almost impossible to put human good and evil on a single scale.

Even when talking of subjective happiness, it is possible, researchers say, to be both happy and unhappy at the same time. At first that sounds ridiculous, but consider someone who is both happy but anxious, depressed but glad to see an old friend. Even in a single moment you can experience both positive and negative emotions.

SUBJECTIVE WELLBEING

There is no simple litmus test for happiness, although many people have attempted to capture its distribution. A term many 'happiness' researchers are more comfortable using is 'subjective wellbeing', often abbreviated to SWB. SWB is an umbrella term that covers all the various types of evaluations that people typically make, so it can include self-esteem, joy and feelings of fulfilment, for example. The key is that each person is making an evaluation about their own life and not relying on the opinion of an expert or a philosopher. SWB attempts to capture the quality of an individual's experience in terms of joy and life satisfaction; that is, the subjective side of wellbeing as opposed to the objective factors, such as income and health.

There's no doubt that happiness, or SWB, has a realm of different sources and causes. Can it be measured? Can it be measured with any sensible degree of accuracy? Says Ed Diener: 'Happiness is not something shallow, or just a gimmick or imaginary thing.' The point about SWB is that it's just that: subjective. It is a measure of how people think or report they feel. There are other ways it can be measured, says Diener: biologically, through what others see, and through measures such as health, work performance, and even the likelihood of committing suicide.

Different scales and measures that can be applied, the most obvious being to simply ask people how they feel.

Satisfaction With Life Scale

One of the most widely used measurements for happiness is the Satisfaction With Life Scale devised by Ed Diener in 1985. It asks people to score statements such as:

- In most ways my life is ideal.
- The conditions of my life are excellent.
- I am satisfied with my life.
- So far, I have gotten the important things I want in life.
- If I could live my life over, I would change almost nothing.

The Revised Oxford Happiness Inventory

The Revised Oxford Happiness Inventory asks people to nominate an answer from the statements below that best describes how they are feeling. It aims to take a measure from 29 different items, ranging from optimism and decision making to laughing and feeling rested. Here are two examples:

Example 1

a   I get by in life
b   Life is good
c   Life is very good
d   I love life

Example 2

a   I do not have a cheerful effect on others
b   I sometimes have a cheerful effect on others
c   I often have a cheerful effect on others
d   I always have a cheerful effect on others

Yet another measure, developed by Carol Ryff, is based on six factors: self-acceptance; positive relations with others; autonomy; environmental mastery; purpose in life; and personal growth.

The happiness formula
Happiness = Set Range + Circumstance + Voluntary Control
In Martin Seligman's equation happiness means an enduring level of happiness. This is different to your momentary happiness, which changes from moment to moment depending on whether you're in the middle of watching a side-splitting comedy or visiting a sick child in hospital.

The set range represents your barriers to becoming happier. Some of this comes from your genetic 'steersman', another significant barrier is the lure of the hedonic treadmill, with its ratcheting aspirations and expectations.

While some circumstances of your life make a little difference (wealth), others make more (living in a wealthy democracy is better than living in an impoverished dictatorship, for example). Some research shows married people to be happier, but does marriage make you happier, or do happier people get married? The same can be asked of people with a rewarding social life— do happy people generate a rich social life or does a rich social life make you happy?

Factors under voluntary control refer to things like insufficient appreciation and savouring of the good events in your past, or overemphasizing the importance of bad ones, which has the effect of undermining serenity, contentment and satisfaction. Seligman recommends cultivating gratitude and forgiveness, while challenging negative emotions, nurturing optimism and hope and building a 'good life'—one that uses your signature strengths in work, love, parenting and finding purpose.

THE TROUBLE WITH SELF-REPORTING

For good or bad, when people are asked how happy they are, they tend to make out they're happier than they really are. It's the same story when people are asked about their marriage. In Britain, most people say they are happily married when asked in surveys, yet half of them will divorce. And when it comes to comparing countries, there may be different cultural norms at play, which some commentators believe skew the results.

Are those countries that come out 'top' really the most happy, or is there a cultural norm which means people are reluctant to admit to negative emotions or to being unhappy some of the time because they think it's a sign of failure, or a weakness of character? One way to bypass the problem is to ask friends and family how happy a person is, but that too can be complicated by the nature of the relationship that might affect reporting. In the future, measures of chemicals such as serotonin or other 'good mood' chemicals might be used.

For Csikszentmihalyi, self-reported happiness is quite simply 'not a very good indicator of the quality of a person's life'. People are very resilient, he says, and will say they're happy even when they hate their job, have an almost non-existent home life and fill their life with meaningless activity. His point is not that such a person might or might not be happy, but that 'it is not enough to be happy to have an excellent life'.

EXPERIENCE SAMPLING

Another way that people attempt to measure happiness is through what's called the experience sampling method (ESM). People are given a pager or a hand-held computer that is beeped at random or at regular intervals during the day and asked about how they are feeling in that moment.

Nobel Prize winner, Daniel Kahneman has used such methods in his work and explained why they are so useful in a talk at the University of New South Wales in Australia in 2003. 'We have a different kind of access to our immediate core of experience and to our past experiences. All of us are memory impaired.' In other words, our memory plays tricks on us. If you stop and think about how you are feeling right now, your answer might differ to the one you'd give tomorrow if asked about the same experience.

Kahneman also differentiates between the 'remembering self' and the 'experiencing self'. The one that remembers is the permanent one that presents a narrative of life, with its significant and selected moments. Says Kahneman: 'There are beginnings, there are peaks, there are endings and that's how we think of our own stories and of our own life.' The experiencing self might be the one that's doing the living, but it's the remembering subject who keeps score and makes the decisions.

Kahneman's studies revealed that sleep quality also has a huge effect on how we feel. He believes that the mood people report is very closely related to the quality of their sleep. 'It's just about the strongest relationship that we find,' he says. People who report sleeping well, enjoy higher spirits throughout the day.

Asking someone about something in the past, for example, how they enjoyed a holiday, is different from asking them about something that's happening now, such as 'does this hurt?'. To answer about past events, we need to be able to retrieve our feelings about them, and we need to have 'integrated' the experience, he says. The bulk of happiness literature is based on questions like 'How happy are you these days?', which requires retrieval, integration and the evaluation of memories, says Kahneman.

CONFUSING MEMORY AND EXPERIENCE

A research report, 'What to do on a spring break?' by Derrick Wirtz and others of the University of Illinois in 2003, found that people's actual enjoyment of a holiday and their recalled enjoyment of the same holiday were quite different. When it came to wanting to repeat the experience, what mattered most was how they recalled it, not what they actually experienced at the time.

Kahneman developed something called the 'day reconstruction method' (DRM) which is a cross between a time budget study and other research, to capture how people felt about specific experiences the previous day. DRM captures the start and finish times of activities, the activity people were engaged in, where people were, who they

The Fordyce Emotions Questionnaire

Developed by Michael Fordyce in 1988, the Fordyce Emotions
Questionnaire consists of two questions.

I   In general, how happy or unhappy do you usually feel? Check the
    one statement below that best describes your average happiness.

    10. Extremely happy (feeling ecstatic, joyous, fantastic)

    9. Very happy (feeling really good, elated)

    8. Pretty happy (spirits high, feeling good)

    7. Mildly happy (feeling fairly good and somewhat cheerful)

    6. Slightly happy (just a bit above normal)

    5. Neutral (not particularly happy or unhappy)

    4. Slightly unhappy (just a bit below neutral)

    3. Mildly unhappy (just a bit low)

    2. Pretty unhappy (somewhat 'blue', spirits down)

    1. Very unhappy (depressed, spirits very low)

    0. Extremely unhappy (utterly depressed, completely down)

●   Consider your emotions a moment further. On average, what
    percentage of the time do you feel happy? What percentage of the
    time do you feel unhappy? What percentage of the time do you
    feel neutral (neither happy nor unhappy)? Write down your best
    estimates. Make sure the three figures add up to 100 per cent.

The average score of a sample of 3050 Americans was 6.92 out of 10.
On average, they felt happy 54.13 per cent of the time, unhappy
20.44 per cent of the time and neutral 25.43 per cent of the time.

were with and how they felt—with the latter being asked in a range
of scales. Some of the results of 1018 working women in Texas in
2004 found:

●   Most people reported themselves as in a moderately good mood
    most of the time (76 per cent of the time).

●   People reported negative emotions, such as anger, depression or
    frustration 34 per cent of the time.

●   The women felt tired most of the time.

- They were impatient for the episode (whatever task it was they were involved in) to end in more than half of the times recorded.
- How people felt changed according to what they were doing: they felt better when socializing, worse when with a boss.
- For those who reported work involving high time pressure, work was significantly less enjoyable than for those who reported their time as less pressured. But while people with high time pressure did not enjoy work as much when at work, they reported greater job satisfaction.
- Sleep affected how people reported feeling. Those with a generally good quality of sleep had a mean enjoyment level of 4.05 (on a scale of 0–6, with 6 being best), compared to 2.80 for those who said they had 'very bad' sleep.

Measuring subjective wellbeing

A combination of tests and measures may result in the most accurate assessment of subjective wellbeing. Some are more straightforward than others. To date, they include:

- informant reports—what do friends and family say about your subjective wellbeing?
- experience sampling—how happy are you over time when beeped at random moments?
- memory measures—can you quickly recall good events (and not bad events) in a timed period?
- interview or qualitative measures.
- frontal brain asymmetry ('happy' brains show different activity).
- facial electromyography. This measures the activity in different facial muscles that corresponds with a different emotion, such as sadness, anger or disgust.
- saliva levels of the stress hormone, cortisol.
- duration of a Duchenne smile.
- heart rate and blood-pressure responses to stress.
- illnesses, such as digestive disorders and headaches.
- skin resistance measures of response to stress.

● Personality, immediate circumstances and current activities had the most effect on their happiness, while income had much less of an effect.

PAY ATTENTION

Paying attention to when you're feeling good can have considerable rewards. Csikszentmihalyi describes how using the experience sampling method (ESM) dramatically helped a woman who was suffering chronic schizophrenia and had spent 10 years in a psychiatric hospital in Holland.

During a two-week period using the ESM, she twice recorded a positive mood. Both times, she'd been caring for her nails. The staff decided to seek training for her in professional manicuring. The woman was soon caring for the nails of all the patients. Her disposition changed drastically and she was released back into the community under supervision. Within a year she was self-sufficient and earning a living as a manicurist.

POSITIVE VERSUS NEGATIVE

In *The Science of Wellbeing* Randolph Nesse says, '… happiness and flourishing do not automatically emerge when the swamps of suffering are drained …'. This comment centres on the relationship between ill-being on the one hand and wellbeing on the other. But they're not considered to be a continuum with wellbeing at one end and ill-being at the other. It's more like a square divided into four, and each square can be more or less filled. On the wellbeing side there's positive moods and life satisfaction. On the ill-being side, there's anxiety and depression. It's quite possible to feel a mixture of all these. You can be generally happy with your life but in a bad mood, or sad because of a recent death; pleased about a promotion but anxious about the responsibilities it might bring, and so on. Some psychologists also differentiate between wellbeing from life as a whole (context-free) and wellbeing associated with a single area of life (context-specific). It's not hard to think of examples: happy with my life as a whole, but not happy about my bank balance; unhappy in general despite a good marriage.

TELIC VERSUS AUTOTELIC

Does wellbeing come from achieving a goal or from pursuing it? Is it about the destination or the journey? The telic theory says it's reaching the goal that produces subjective wellbeing; whereas the autotelic theory says it's the moving towards a set of goals that matters. This approach acknowledges that people can be proactive and choose goals and activities that they know to be rewarding in themselves.

One of the problems of trying to measure happiness is the gulf between individual situations—a new lease of life after falling in love, a personal nose dive after losing a job—and the mass of data that gives us averages to compare ourselves to.

VOX POP: What do you do to get yourself out of the blues?

I call people or see them if I feel unhappy with things. Professional help would be my best friend Poppy! AE

I try to remember how lucky I am and think of things I've done that have made me happy: watching beans and tomatoes grow in the garden, meeting up with friends, a cold beer at the end of a hot day. PN

Things I try: a walk by myself, a change of environment, a night away in a different place with the family, buying a nice bottle of wine rather than a cheap one. If it's a longer set downturn, I might arrange a few uplifting things, such as a lunch with a friend, to make sure I'm not isolated. AH

To avoid the blues I tackle the source of anxiety. For instance, just recently I was feeling way too anxious about money. It was keeping me awake at night. So I took it in hand, found out more, developed a plan and stuck to it. Instantly my anxiety dissipated. I also remind myself how fortunate I am in the scheme of things. FH

I give myself a good talking to! I feel strongly that the one person who can help me most is me. Sometimes it takes a while for me to 'snap out of it' but I think I am an optimist and so try to see the bright side of things. AS

When I am down I usually have a good cry. I find it works wonders. It relieves the tension and just gets it all over with. I might also buy a tacky magazine and go to a coffee shop alone if child minding is available—it feels so indulgent! SE

To get myself out of the blues I phone family and friends to just chat. Sometimes I go shopping. Cappuccino has great healing powers. Physical activity is good too: cleaning out cupboards, throwing out detritus—dumping things in the bin is good, sort of symbolic. EWB

I stop the negative thinking and replace it with a meditative kind of focus on positive things. ML

I don't get the blues, but my solution to stress or a difficult decision is to go walking and 'sort myself out'. LN

Blues? I hide under my doona. SG

I think of how lucky I am, how much I have that others may not have and wait for it to pass ... it always does eventually. CL

Friends, warm water and exercise are my blues exit strategies. So my favourite indulgence to change my mood is an evening at the Korean hot baths with my friends. Otherwise, a walk along the beach and cliffs on a crowded weekend watching all the funny things people do. KF

ARE PEOPLE HAPPY?

If I keep a green bough in my heart, the singing bird will come.
ANONYMOUS

Most people around the world describe their lives as 'generally happy'. But everyone has ups and downs. Nobody is happy every moment of the day and even the happiest people sometimes get unhappy. A significant number also experience depression: 16 per cent of people in the US say they've experienced serious episodes of depression and in any one year 6 per cent of adults will experience two weeks or more where depression is serious enough to interfere with their ability to function effectively.

HAPPY LIFE EXPECTANCY

Dutch sociologist, Ruut Veenhoven proposed a measure he calls a 'happy life expectancy' as a way of comparing subjective wellbeing between countries. Sociologists often use the term subjective wellbeing in the way that lay people might use 'happiness' and economists use 'utility'. Happy life expectancy, described as 'a very simple off-the-shelf measure of wellbeing', is average life satisfaction multiplied by average life expectancy.

So, how does happy life expectancy correlate with what we consider to contribute to the quality of life? It is strongly related to income per capita, rooms per dwelling, and negatively related to malnutrition and the proportion of people with safe water. It's also negatively related to the murder rate, lethal accidents, maternal deaths, corruption and (weakly) to income inequality and gender inequality. On the other hand, life expectancy is positively related to political freedom, personal freedom, self-perceived freedom and knowledge, and slightly to religious beliefs. It is quite strongly related to individualism, tolerance and trust in families and compatriots.

According to the latest World Values Survey (1999–2001), the most 'satisfied' people tend to live in Latin America, Western Europe and North America. Eastern Europeans are the least satisfied. (New

Zealand ranked 15th most satisfied, the US 16th, Australia 20th and Britain 24th.) Nigeria topped the list, followed by Mexico, Venezuela, El Salvador and Puerto Rico. The least happy countries were Russia, Armenia and Romania.

Confusingly, other surveys have shown Nigeria to be at the bottom! In a compilation of happy life expectancy values by Veenhoven in 1996, Iceland was top, followed by the Netherlands, Sweden and Switzerland, with Australia fifth. In the mid-range were Japan and a number of European countries, and at the bottom, Nigeria and Bulgaria.

Clearly, all is not straightforward when trying to compare satisfaction between countries. Daniel Kahneman is of the opinion that the differences between reported happiness are too large to be plausible, especially when you consider the relatively small contribution of circumstances to individual happiness.

The trouble is, he says, that one country could report low satisfaction with life but be consistently cheerful, while another can report high satisfaction with life but generally be grumpy or angry. If you're interested in how happy people are, which matters most: what they say or how they act? Despite reporting less life satisfaction, could people in a country like France (which reports being less 'happy') be objectively more happy than a country like America, which reports being happy?

Methodology and analysis too, affect the results. According to Diener, you can get different results by making a more fine-grained analysis. It might also depend on what exactly you're trying to measure. 'There are nations where lots of both positive and negative are felt, and there are nations where not much emotion of either type is experienced,' he says. But if you emphasize one over the other, you get a different picture.

He explains how in the Confucian nations of the Pacific Rim such as Korea, China and Japan, people regard negative emotions to be just as good as positive ones. So people don't place a high value on subjective wellbeing or being happy. Latin nations are much happier than you would expect based on their income, and the Pacific Rim countries are less happy.

Commentators seem to be able to pull out a survey to illustrate a variety of different arguments. In *Growth Fetish*, Clive Hamilton describes Japan and Taiwan as rich but unhappy, referring to the 'emptiness of Japanese affluence'. The Philippines and Argentina, he says, are poor but happy. 'While there is a tendency for wealthier nations to be higher on the scale of appreciation of life, there are many cases where a country with a much lower per capita GDP ranks higher than countries with much higher per capita GDP,' he concedes.

WHAT MATTERS?

Just as the very concept of happiness has many branches, so too its roots spread wide. Every 'expert' will have a slightly different take on what matters to being happy. But there's much common ground.

In the CSIRO's book, *Measuring Progress: Is Life Getting Better?*, Alexander Wearing and Bruce Headey from the School of Behavioural Science and Department of Political Science at the University of Melbourne in Australia, discuss how life satisfaction or wellbeing is related to a wide array of aspects and attributes. If you look at life domains, then close relationships are the most important, whether with family or other people. Other factors that are clustered around wellbeing are relations with parents, self-fulfilment, standard of living, marriage and sex. For example, while people in Australia do not perceive the government as being strongly related to wellbeing, 'the government has a powerful capability to change our level of wellbeing through its effects on life domains that are important to us'.

Martin Seligman, leader of the Positive Psychology movement, sees the following factors as important to happiness.

- Living in a wealthy democracy rather than an impoverished dictatorship has a strong effect on happiness.
- Getting married has a robust effect (but it may not be 'causal'— it could be that happy people get married).
- Avoiding negative events and emotion has a moderate effect.
- A rich social network has a robust effect, but like marriage it may not be causal.
- Religious belief has a moderate effect.

The factors that matter, he says, are inconvenient, if not impossible to change. Factors that make little or no difference to our level of happiness are money, health, education, race and climate. When Diener and Seligman looked at the happiest 10 per cent of college students they found the happiest always had two things in common—good mental health and good social relationships. Ed Diener's top three ingredients in the recipe for happiness are:

- Good friends and family. We need intimate, loving relationships with people who care about us, and about whom we care deeply.
- Pursuing activities we enjoy and value.
- We need to control how we look at the world by avoiding making a big deal of trivial hassles; focusing on working towards goals; counting our blessings and making a habit of noticing the good things in life.

Linus Pauling (1901–1994)

Two times Nobel Prize winner Linus Pauling was born in Portland, Oregon, in the US. His father died when he was nine years old, leaving the family impoverished. He was a voracious reader—at age nine he'd read the entire Bible and Darwin's *Origin of the Species*. By age 11 he was collecting insects and reading books on entomology and at 12 began to collect and read about minerals. He pursued these interests on his own, without recognition and with little support. He did not think he'd go on to tertiary education, but the parent of one of his friends almost forced him to enroll in college and he later received a scholarship to enter Cal Tech. During his college years he earned money by killing dandelions, chopping wood for the girls' dormitory, cutting beef and mopping the kitchen.

Pauling applied quantum theory to chemistry and in 1954 was awarded the Nobel Prize for chemistry; in 1962 he was awarded the Nobel Peace Prize. According to Mihaly Csikszentmihalyi, he showed a classic autotelic personality, approaching everything he did with bubbling energy. Even into his nineties, he maintained the enthusiasm and curiosity of a young child.

WHERE ARE WE HAPPIEST?

Are men happiest pottering in the shed? Where do you go for a bit of quiet? US experience sampling by Csikszentmihalyi came up with the following findings.

- Teenagers are happiest away from adult supervision, in places like parks. They feel most constrained in places like churches.

- Adults like public places where typically they might be with friends. For women, this can also mean being away from the drudgery of the house, while for men, it can mean being involved with work, so the preference is not so great.

- Cars give people a sense of control and freedom because they can concentrate on problems without interruption. For some families, in contrast to the scattered way they occupy the rooms in their homes, the car is a place for togetherness.

- Men report good moods most in places like the basement where they go for hobbies. In other countries, such stress-free space may be found in garages, sheds or spare bedrooms.

- Women report good moods in the bathroom—free from family demands—as well as the kitchen, where they often report enjoying cooking.

Play for satisfaction

A study of 265 retirees in inner-city Boston showed being able to play far outweighed financial security in the happiness stakes. The lifelong survey reported in the *American Journal of Psychiatry* in 2006, also found a good marriage was key to a satisfying retirement.

The largely working-class men had a socially disadvantaged upbringing and poor health, which had impacted heavily on their quality of life earlier on. But later in life, the importance of these factors receded. The longevity and satisfaction of their marriages was the largest contributor to their satisfaction. And their ability to enjoy their children and to participate in hobbies and community activities—which the authors termed 'play' because they were without financial ramifications—came a close second.

HAPPY WITH FRIENDS

Almost every list of ingredients for happiness includes good social relationships. When with friends, people report being happy, alert, sociable, cheerful and motivated. One explanation is that when we interact with others, our attention turns outwards, and other research seems to show that looking inwards, particularly navel-gazing, is more likely to lead to unhappiness than happiness. While intimate and loving relationships give us the deepest rewards, all levels of interaction and even superficial 'small talk' help ward off depression. Stimulating conversation is even better.

The most positive experiences people report in ESM are usually those with friends. This applies to tasks such as studying and household chores—they're depressing when carried out alone or with family—but enjoyable when with friends.

So, why do friends make us happy? Because ideally friendships:

- have mutual benefits: you help me by picking up my child from soccer training, I lend you my chainsaw.
- centre on an equal relationship without exploitation (unlike say, a doctor/patient or boss/employee relationship).
- are not static—they have changing dynamics that keep them interesting and provide new activities and adventures. AH encourages several friends to take up the tin whistle, LM gets some friends to go indoor rock climbing, LB emails friends about the film club showing each month.
- provide emotional and intellectual stimulation. RF's conversations often include information she's gathering for her assignments on Islamic studies; friends love hearing about PN's latest explorations around the globe.

A transient society makes long friendships a rarity. 'Lack of true friends is often the main complaint of people confronting an emotional crisis in the second half of life,' comments Csikszentmihalyi.

FAMILIES AND THE HAPPY LIFE

Good families are generally worse than any others.
ANTHONY HOPE, *THE PRISONER OF ZENDA*, 1894

Relationships with family members are far more complex than with friends. Perhaps because blood really is thicker than water—we test it more frequently and harshly, which may explain why people report being happier with friends than family. While you might not experience such highs at home, it is somewhere where you can release pent-up emotions. Families offer a very special environment where people can combine discipline with spontaneity, rules with freedom and high expectations with 'unstinting love'.

HAPPY SOLITUDE

The average time spent alone is about one-third of our waking time. Yours or my experience may differ widely. If you're a stay at home parent of four, it's fairly unlikely you'll have an hour alone, let alone more. And if you live alone, solitude is easy to clock up. Much more or less than the typical one-third can create problems: teenagers who always hang out with friends have trouble at school and are less likely to learn to think for themselves, while those who spend more hours on their own are prone to depression and alienation. Where that leaves people in cultures where it was believed you should never be alone is unclear. The Dobuan people of Melanesia were always accompanied by someone, even if they were relieving themselves in the bush, for fear that witchcraft could get them if they were alone.

People whose work isolates them, whether physically or emotionally, are also more at risk of suicide. A packed schedule can protect from the extremes, such as the life of a solitary monk or a privacy-free submarine sailor. In vocations such as these, schedules provide structure to the day, even if their quality and pace are very different.

We need a balance between engaging with people and being alone. It's often when we're alone that we can concentrate in the way that some types of learning in our society demand: for example, when studying complex maths problems or learning an instrument.

Happy at leisure

Anyone for tennis?

GEORGE BERNARD SHAW (1856–1950)

Sport and exercise puts people in a good mood very quickly, it enhances happiness and reduces depression if done regularly. Many other leisure activities also bring happy rewards.

- Religion enhances happiness, especially in the elderly, partly through the social support of the church community, but also through feeling close to God.
- Companionship, and other forms of social support from leisure groups, make people feel happy.
- Holidays produce good moods through relaxation.

HAPPINESS AND WORK

The world of work is full of paradox: many people think they'd prefer to avoid it if possible, yet in surveys, more than three-quarters of respondents say they'd still work if they inherited a sum of money that meant they didn't need to work. In ESM studies, people at work signal that they wish they were doing something else, yet people report more 'flow' (absorbed and engaged) moments at work.

In his book *Finding Flow*, Csikszentmihalyi describes the work of an eminent German social scientist who claimed that although German workers disliked work, those that disliked it the most were happiest overall! Another claimed that people disliked work only because they were brainwashed by the media, and in fact, those that liked their work lead richer lives.

Suffice to say, there is a deep ambiguity surrounding our working lives. It is one of the most important elements of our lives yet while we're doing it, we think we'd rather not be.

According to Csikszentmihalyi there are three main reasons people resent their jobs (when they do):

- when it is pointless or even harmful.
- when it is boring and routine, providing no variety or challenge.
- when it is stressful, especially from an emotional point of view, for example, when you are having problems with your boss or colleagues.

HAPPINESS AND HEALTH

How is happiness linked to health? Is a happy person more likely to be healthy? Is a healthy person more likely to be happy? Research shows it works both ways and health is a more important part of happiness for old people. When people are in good health, they can do more and feel better. And as you might expect, multiple and severe health problems that interfere with how you function on a daily basis can definitely lower your subjective wellbeing. It is, however, up for debate as to how strong the health and happiness link is.

Diener says that if people are satisfied with their health, they are more likely to also be satisfied with their life. That's a subjective measure. But if you look at more objective measures of health, for example, a doctor's rating, there's only a low correlation between health and happiness.

'There are plenty of healthy people around who take their health for granted, but for a variety of reasons are unhappy. And there are many individuals with bad health who are able to cope and adapt to their condition, and to be reasonably satisfied and happy,' Diener explains.

WORKING FOR WHAT YOU VALUE

Many persons have a wrong idea of what constitutes true happiness. It is not attained through self-gratification but through fidelity to a worthy purpose.

HELEN KELLER (1880–1968)

There is a lot of talk about goals—defined as 'the aim or object towards which an endeavour is directed'. Whether it's ancient philosophers, New Age spiritualism or financial planners, we're all encouraged to define and work towards our goals. The best goals are ones that are in tune with our deepest values—someone who feels strongly about the environment is unlikely to be happy working for a developer with no concern for it. If financial reward is a high priority and working with people low, then you probably won't find being a school teacher satisfying. Sometimes goals can conflict: pursuing a career while at the same time rearing children is today's classic conflict. When people put time and effort into things they value—whether it's recycling, raising money for refugees or running a scout group, people experience less internal conflict.

An overarching goal, such as a degree or a new landcare group, can ease the frustration over some of the preparatory tasks: the ringing around on the phone, letter writing or late night study. Achieving the goal in the long-run leads to satisfaction. If your goals are in line with your values, then, Diener says, 'being happy does not stand in contrast to basic values'. If you work towards goals that are in line with your values you are more likely to find happiness at the same time. Some people seem to think that you might have values on the one hand and happiness on the other, but in fact when the two sit together, you are more likely to be happy.

GOALS SET THE COURSE
According to Robert Emmons, Professor of Psychology at the University of California in the US, in a paper he co-authored, called 'Assessing Spirituality through Personal Goals: Implications for research on religion and subjective wellbeing', people's priorities are prime determinants of wellbeing. He explains how priorities set the course for your wellbeing; the goals you strive for and how you integrate the goals into a 'reasonably coherent framework' all influence how you feel about your life. The authors found that people whose goals were concerned with intimacy and 'affiliation with others' (reflecting a concern for establishing deep and mutually gratifying relationships) had higher levels of wellbeing.

'The task is not just to choose sensible goals; individuals must at every juncture make decisions that allocate effort to the pursuit of one goal and not another,' says Randolph Nesse. He tells us, reassuringly or not, that this is not just a human problem: most animals have to choose between allocating effort to feeding and watching out for predators. Too much watching results in starvation, too much feeding and youngsters might be the ones that get eaten.

'When there are sufficient time, energy and resources to successfully pursue current goals, life is good,' says Nesse.

A MEANINGFUL LIFE

The mechanisms that regulate human behaviour evolved in an environment that is wildly different to the one we live in now. Nesse believes that the size and duration of personal goals might account for much of our modern-day misery.

Even just a few thousand years ago, most people channelled their energy into a small range of tasks: gathering food, looking after their kin and being part of the group. But with bigger social groups has come great specialization, with the result that much of a lifetime's effort and energy is often taken up in a relatively small area of life. People who reach the top of their profession in the music, sport or corporate arena, often have to sacrifice much in other areas of their life.

Our brains are not designed to cope with such long-term efforts to big goals, especially one that is in many cases, an all or nothing aim.

Big ideas from small cultures

Robert Biswas-Diener (yes, he is related to Ed Diener, Robert is his son) is collecting data on life satisfaction among Amish communities. The picture emerging shows the Amish to be busy people who are rarely bored. For the Amish, satisfaction is in part a statement about their relationship to God. The Dieners have also looked at data from a number of other 'small cultures'. They've found the Masai in Africa report being extremely satisfied with their physical appearance—in contrast to most Americans. Californian homeless people miss close and trusting friendships more than they miss good housing. And the Calcutta homeless are not as dissatisfied with life as the Californian homeless—even though they have less food they are more likely to have a strong social network.

If you're foraging for nuts, says Nesse, it's relatively easy to give up looking for them after a few days of fruitless search. But it's much harder to give up on five years of study, for example, with the result that people either give up and feel bad about it, or persist and lose motivation.

Within the material world, it may be more or less easy to reach goals and aspirations—or possible, if not easy, to curtail such desires. But it's often much harder to come to terms with shortfalls that concern other people. As Nesse eloquently puts it: 'How many people spend their lives trying to get their mothers finally to love them, to get a spouse to want to have sex again, to stop a child from taking drugs, or trying to control their own habits? In such desperate enterprises that cannot be given up are the seeds of intense dissatisfaction that often precede serious depression.'

COMPROMISE WITH GOALS

A major problem in wellbeing surveys, says Nesse, is that they may overlook most of what is important. What seems to matter, he says, is 'the overall motivational structure'—the degree to which all major goals can be pursued successfully without unduly compromising others. People have different values and different commitments to a variety of goals, which can change over a lifetime.

PR has left the corporate world after a bout of ill-health and disillusion with corruption. But financially he's struggling and a part of him misses the feeling of being in the heart of the business world.

BL would like a career in arts administration but there's no local work, and housing's too expensive where there is work.

AM has fallen in love with India so much he's visited it several times over the last year, travelling for weeks at a time. The trouble is his wife is not so enamoured and thinks she may have fallen out of love with him.

Is the challenge working out what you're willing to give up? It might be possible to be a good parent and friend, especially if friendships centre around families, do some meaningful work and stay reasonably fit and healthy through exercise, but perhaps it's not possible to have the spotless house at the same time, or extensive

Helen Keller (1880–1968)

Helen Keller was born in the small farm town of Tuscumbia in Alabama, in the US. She lost her sight and her hearing at 19 months of age following a short but severe illness that was possibly meningitis or scarlet fever. She developed 60 hand gestures to communicate with her family, but life was frustrating—at six years old she threw tantrums, broke dishes and locked her mother in a cupboard. After some searching, her mother arranged for a tutor, and Helen wrote later: 'The most important day I remember in all my life is the one on which my teacher, Anne Mansfield Sullivan, came to me. I am filled with wonder when I consider the immeasurable contrast between the two lives which it connects.'

Anne began teaching Helen the hand alphabet, and a month after her arrival, she made a breakthrough by spelling W-A-T-E-R into Helen's hand as water from an outdoor pump poured over her hand. By nightfall Helen had learned 30 words. Helen soon learned to read braille and print English in block letters and after two years with Anne, Helen was ready to attend Perkins School for the blind. Helen graduated from Radcliffe College, Harvard in 1904 and was the first deaf and blind person to earn a Bachelor of Arts degree. She learned to read French, German, Greek and Latin in braille. Her first book, *The Story of My Life*, was translated into 50 languages. Helen also researched, gave speeches, and helped raise money for many organizations, including the American Foundation for the Blind and the American Foundation for the Overseas Blind, now known as Helen Keller International. She visited 39 countries from 1946 to 1957, speaking about the experiences and rights of blind people. She is remembered as an advocate for the handicapped, as well as numerous causes. She was a suffragist, a pacifist and a supporter of birth control.

trips overseas. Or maybe it's possible to take the sabbatical with the family and go abroad, but not own a home yet. Goals clash all the time, especially with regard to work and family, and examples can be found everywhere: the ambitious executive who feels the pull to have a baby, but wonders what will happen to her career; the father whose new promotion takes him interstate more often, just at the time when his wife suggests he take a more hands-on role with the children.

This constant struggle is part of the attraction of the simple life. The ability to develop coping mechanisms to deal with trade-offs between clashing needs and desires is an important life skill.

GOALS LARGE AND SMALL

The way our societies work today 'leave individuals sacrificing much in life to pursue major efforts to reach huge goals whose attainment is uncertain and whose alternatives are few and unsatisfactory', says Nesse. And what's more, whereas older, smaller kinship groups worked on commitment, today's groups work more on exchange and exploitation.

Eric Keverne, Professor of Behavioural Neuroscience at the University of Cambridge, has a similar perspective: for thousands of years we lived in small cooperative groups, finding food and rearing children, with a few relationships and a small range of decisions to make. Decisions centred on where to get the next meal, shelter and comfort and we were rewarded quickly with the result of good decisions. 'In modern societies, individuals are required to make decisions about careers, marriages and financial security for old age and pensions. These are some of the most important decisions we have to make, they are exceptionally long term, and there is no guaranteed way of getting them right.'

Act always as if the future of the universe depended on what you did, while laughing at yourself for thinking that whatever you do makes any difference.

BUDDHIST SAYING

Coping skills

Why do some people cope so well with what life offers us, while others, with a similar lot in life, suffer? What makes some people happy and healthy and others sad and sick? George Vaillant, Professor of Psychiatry at Harvard Medical School, drew on data from a study of 268 healthy and promising undergraduates recruited between 1939 and 1942 and followed thereafter in what became known as the Grant Study. Individual coping mechanisms were a significant factor, he found. What he calls 'mature defences' (as opposed to neurotic, immature or psychotic ways of coping) include traits such as altruism and the ability to postpone gratification and humour. Vaillant's theories are explained in full in his books, such as *Adaptation to Life and Aging Well*.

HAPPY IS AS HAPPY DOES

One of the puzzles that researchers set themselves to untangle is: Do happy people behave in a certain way or do certain activities make you happy? When people are severely depressed, particularly with illnesses such as bipolar disorder, for example, they tend to withdraw. And when their mood swings up again, they do the things that happy people do. Lykken and Tellegen believe it's more the mood that affects behaviour than behaviour affecting how you feel.

It's hard to know what's right to pour your life energy into, but if, for instance, you do it against a backdrop of supportive friends, perhaps you won't feel the sting of failure as sharply. Taking your eye off the destination and concentrating on the path can also help shift your emphasis. And to a degree, people can break cycles of mood … and mood can in turn change behaviour. Behaviour can change what you do with your life and putting your energy into what really matters makes you and the rest of the world just a little happier.

TAKING STOCK

1. Looking at the lists of happiness ingredients on pages 266 and 267, to what extent do you put energy into these areas?
2. When you look at your life, would you agree that these are important to happiness? If you look at where you put your time and energy, how do they match up with your values?
3. When you stop and think about it, what are the overarching goals in your life? To what extent do they clash? How do you cope with the problem of conflicting goals and aims?

Wherefore do ye spend money for that which is not bread? And your labour for that which satisfieth not? Hearken diligently unto me and eat ye that which is good, and let your soul delight itself in fatness.

ISAIAH 55:2

11. TIME WISE MONEY WISE

BY STRIKING A BALANCE BETWEEN TIME AND MONEY THE GOOD LIFE CAN BE YOURS. LIFE DOES NOT NEED TO BE ONE GREAT RUSH, IT IS POSSIBLE TO SLOW DOWN OCCASIONALLY AND PRACTISE LIVING IN THE 'NOW'. BY TAKING CARE OF WHERE OUR MONEY GOES, WE CAN MAKE SURE WE SPEND IT ON WHAT MATTERS MOST. BY GIVING TIME AND MONEY EACH ITS PROPER VALUE WE CAN FIND REAL WEALTH.

WHAT IS ENOUGH?

French philosopher Denis Diderot (1713–1784) was never a rich man. When he needed a dowry for his daughter, he sold his private library to Catherine the Great, Empress of Russia. Lucky for him, the Empress purchased his books but asked him to keep them in Paris and paid him a yearly salary as her librarian! A prolific writer, Diderot counted among his friends the poet and writer, Voltaire, and philosopher, Jean Jacques Rousseau. Among his works is the essay, 'Regrets on Parting with My Old Dressing Gown', written in the 1770s.

When a friend gave him a gift of a scarlet dressing gown, Diderot discarded his old and tatty gown. But when he sat down in his study in his new gown, he was struck by how shabby his desk was and decided to replace it. Compared to the new desk, the bookcases looked out of place. Then the chair ... eventually the entire study was transformed. But rather than feel pleased with the effect, Diderot found himself uncomfortable with his newly appointed surroundings in which nothing was familiar. His regret: 'This imperious scarlet robe [that] forced everything else to conform to its own elegant tone.'

Little did he know that centuries later scholars of consumption would talk of the Diderot Unity (that objects tend to get grouped together according to how new they are, where they come from, their size and so on); and the Diderot effect—the trickle down effect of consuming, that drives you to make another purchase. It's not hard to think of examples: the new modern house where the shabby but comfy furniture doesn't look at home; the new computer, which requires a new printer, then new software to go with it; the new dinner set which begs for matching cutlery when odd knives and forks did perfectly well before; the beautiful pair of shoes that makes the rest of your wardrobe look outdated.

Diderot's dilemma echoes some of the dissatisfaction described by those talking of 'affluenza'. Where should we stop? What is enough?

THE ELUSIVE 'ENOUGH'

Is it 'enough' to be able to feed and provide shelter for your family? Or does 'enough' include paying for a good education and the occasional stress-breaker holiday? What is 'necessary'? How do we differentiate our wants from our needs? Like Diderot, our benchmarks are continually ratcheting up. In 1973, 20 per cent of Americans said a second car was a necessity, by 1996 the figure had risen to 37 per cent.

Poverty tests often look at whether people experience any of the following (known as hardship indicators).

- Not being able to pay utility bills on time because of lack of money.
- Not being able to pay car registration or insurance on time.
- Having to pawn or sell something.
- Going without meals.
- Not being able to heat the home.
- Having to seek assistance from a welfare or community agency.

While these measures might help define a poverty line, they don't represent a benchmark against which we can measure what's enough. The measure is subjective and social, not objective or absolute.

In *Affluenza*, Clive Hamilton and Richard Denniss say: '... Australian households ... have an inflated, perhaps grossly inflated, understanding of how much money they need to maintain a decent standard of living.' But what is 'decent'? And what about someone who spends a fortune on an eccentric collection but lives without an inside toilet; or someone who lives to travel but runs an old car, or doesn't run a car at all. How many changes of clothing is enough in today's society? Are washing machines 'necessary' or not? What about the student who chooses not to heat the house so she has enough to go out once a week, or the family who forgoes holidays and restaurant meals so they can send their child to a private school.

On the one hand are personal needs, on the other are 'needs' you could argue are created by society, or culture. And beyond that, individual wants that are targets for desire control, especially if you're concerned about consumption and the future of the environment, your bank balance or where the energy you expend on earning is going.

Psychologists help compulsive shoppers work on the difference between needs and wants, then on removing the association between the acquisition of goods and a sense of self-worth.

What is a decent standard of living? What 'should' we aspire to? People are not the same the world over—we have different talents, needs and desires. Some of the attempts to put a finger on what is 'enough' are listed below.

Peak of fulfilment

In *Your Money or Your Life*, by Joe Dominguez and Vicki Robin, 'enough' is described as the peak of the fulfilment curve, it is past survival, past comfort and even includes a few luxuries. Beyond the 'enough' is the realm of over-consumption, where the clutter of possessions that you don't need can weigh you down. Beyond 'enough' lies over-consumption with material plenty but spiritual lack. For example, owning hectares of land, but yearning for a walk in the park, or being the proud owner of a shining yacht, with never the time to use it, unlike a group of friends who share an aging but serviceable boat they potter around in most weekends.

According to Dominguez and Robin, 'enough' has four components. The first is accountability, or knowing where you stand: how much money is coming in and how much flowing out. The second is the internal yardstick, where you make your own measure and don't take into account what other people have or think. The third is purpose, where you exercise your capacity to give—to your family or to a charity, for example—and get off the endless money-go-round at the same time. Finally comes responsibility—choosing limits and maintaining a sense of balance within yourself.

Aprovechar

The Spanish word *aprovechar* means to use time and possessions wisely, whether it's a wonderful picnic with friends, or turning old T-shirts into cleaning rags. It's about getting full value from life and enjoying each moment.

Budget standard

Australia's budget standards, developed by the Social Policy Research Centre (SPRC), estimate the costs for selected family types to achieve a defined standard of living at a particular time and location. They are calculated and built up by taking into account detailed items over nine areas: housing, energy, food, clothing and footwear, household goods and services, health, transport, leisure and personal care. The two most commonly used standards of living are the 'low cost' standard and 'modest but adequate' standard. The 'low cost' standard was intended to fall around the 20th percentile of Australian incomes (and was not considered to be a poverty line), while the 'modest but adequate' standard was to be closer to the median living standard.

The low cost budget standard developed for Australia is considered to represent a level, below which it is increasingly difficult to maintain an acceptable living standard, and there exists an increased risk of deprivation and disadvantage. Households falling into this category would need to exercise 'frugal and careful management of resources'.

When devising the standard, researchers listened to focus groups and their definitions of deprivation according to social norms. In the 1980s, for example, almost everyone in focus groups in Australia thought a television was a basic item, that buying alcohol was a social necessity linked to the capacity to participate in a community social life, a haircut was a necessity every six to eight weeks and parents needed cars to ferry their children between activities like sports and parties.

Ideas of time are creeping into considerations of poverty, and not only in regard to time poverty. 'For much of the [20th] century it has been customary to regard leisure expenditure as unnecessary expenditure,' writes Professor Michael Bittman in a Social Policy Research Council paper.

The luxury of a hot shower

Next time you feel 'poor', try this for a cure. Stand under a hot shower and consider that according to United Nations estimates, around 1.2 billion people in the developing world do not have clean drinking water. Half the people in developing countries don't have basic sanitation facilities. The hot showers don't warrant counting.

The pioneering study of poverty by Seebohm Rowntree of York in the UK in 1899, 'A Study of Town Life', specifically excluded leisure. Rowntree found a significant proportion of the population living below subsistence level, even below a standard of living that could only be managed on a very tight budget: not a single penny on a railway fare or omnibus, no halfpenny newspapers or postage stamps to write to absent family and friends, no beer, no tobacco, no marbles or sweets.

Living wage

Living wage differs from a minimum wage. The latter is set by law as an absolute minimum legal hourly wage that employers can pay a worker. A living wage generally aspires to a specific standard of living. (A standard used from time to time is the ability to live in 'frugal comfort'.) In developed countries, the idea is that a person working 40 hours a week, with no additional income, should be able to afford a specified quality or quantity of housing, food, utilities, transport, health care and recreation.

In Father John Ryan's dissertation, *A Living Wage*, published in 1906 in the US, among a workingman's family needs were listed donations to charity (US$2.80), religion (US$10.29) as well as food, (US$235) and rent (US$84). Amusements and vacations were listed at US$20 and 'intoxicating liquors' and tobacco came in at a total of US$18. 'Through the influence of habit or custom he comes to regard certain of those acquired needs as essential elements of a decent standard of life,' explained Father Ryan. 'They differ relatively to different races, communities, ranks and classes of men, but to the persons among whom they have been developed they are of vital importance.'

FRUGAL COMFORT

Spending carefully is a necessity on low incomes, and wise on higher ones too. Learning to make your money go further has a multitude of spin-offs: the potential to free up work time for something else; to ease anxiety over cash flow and to align consumption with a more sustainable way of life; putting it to better use that makes a difference to your life, whether it's being able to afford a year off in your forties, or to go on a working holiday in your twenties.

Learning tricks on the hedonic treadmill

If we command our wealth, we shall be rich and free;
if our wealth commands us, we are poor indeed.

EDMUND BURKE, *LETTERS ON A REGICIDE PEACE*, 1795

While our ability to continually adapt to good things—then enjoy them less and still want more—can take the gloss off life, the good news is we don't adapt equally to all good things. The pay rise or the new car will lose their power to thrill. But not so the comfort of friends, the pleasures of intimate sex, the companionship of marriage and the rewards of truly satisfying work. Put your efforts into these and you'll reap the benefits.

So, once we're well over the poverty line, do some spending patterns result in more happiness than others?

- Experience counts. A study published in the *Journal of Personality and Social Psychology* in 2003, concluded that spending money on experiences rather than 'things' made people happier. Researchers, Leaf Van Boven, from the University of Colorado and Thomas Gilovich, from Cornell University in the US asked the question, 'To Do or to Have?'. Experiences make people happier, suggested the authors, because they are more open to positive re-interpretations, are a more meaningful part of one's identity and contribute more to successful relationships. The findings back Aristotle's comment that, 'men fancy that external goods are the cause of happiness ... but leisure itself gives pleasure and happiness and enjoyment in life'. Individuals and communities alike would be better off, say the authors, if they adopted the slogan of the Center for the New American Dream: 'More fun, less stuff!'

- Making wealth work. You can make wealth work for your happiness if you spend the extra on the right things, says Robert Frank, professor of economics at the Johnson School of Management at Cornell University. Says Frank: 'As national income grows people do not spend their extra money in ways that yield significant and lasting increases in measured satisfaction.' The question is, are there alternative ways of spending our resources that could produce lasting gains in human welfare?

illustrate his point he asks us to imagine two societies. Society 'A' here people have a big house and spend an hour each day commuting work through very heavy traffic; or Society 'B' where they have a house at's a quarter less big, but only requires a 15-minute commute by apid transport.

If you moved from B to A, you might be thrilled with the extra space or a little while, then consider it normal. PN and AH can attest to this. loving out of a narrow inner-city terrace into a house with a garden and arage, at first they felt the relief of extra space—then filled up the arage and space started to feel tight again. You'd also find the ommuting stressful to begin with but your awareness of the stress it duced would wear off in time. But although you might seem to adapt, fact, the commute would continue to take its toll. Research around the orld shows symptoms caused by commuting include annoyance, creased levels of blood cholesterol and increased blood pressure—the nger the commute and the heavier the traffic, the greater the mptoms. Bus drivers show a greater and more severe range of mptoms and it's quite likely that commuters are suffering similarly. ociety B, with the smaller house and shorter commute time seems the ore appealing, yet it's not the way American society, for one at least, eems to be moving, says Frank. Commuting time continues to grow, oads are becoming more and more congested for longer periods of the ay, while at the same time houses are growing in size.

Conspicuous consumption (bigger houses) is favoured over nconspicuous consumption'—freedom from traffic congestion, time ith family and friends, vacation time and a variety of favourable job haracteristics. If we work longer hours to buy bigger houses further way from our work, then we don't end up any happier. But if we used xtra income to alleviate stresses then we might see greater happiness. The Science of Wellbeing Robert Frank says: 'The less we spend on onspicuous consumption goods, the better we can afford to alleviate ongestion, the more time we can devote to family and friends, to xercise, sleep, travel, and other restorative activities, and the better e can afford to maintain a clean and safe environment.'

YOUR MONEY OR YOUR LIFE

In the 1960s, in the US, Joe Dominguez devised nine steps to 'extricate himself from the shackles of wage slavery'. Once personally freed he began to present a seminar to groups of people, sometimes in church basements, entitled, 'Transforming your Relationship with Money and Achieving Financial Independence'. Ten years and 10,000 attendees later he wrote a book with his wife, Vicki Robin, called *Your Money or Your Life*. While Joe died in 1997 of lymphoma, Vicki has kept the message alive and become a spokesperson for frugal and sustainable lifestyles.

'Scratch the surface of almost any environmental or social justice issue, as well as many psychological ones, and you'll find a distorted relationship with money and stuff exacerbating it, if not driving the problem,' says Vicki.

What's in a word? Frugal

Be industrious and frugal, and you will be rich.

BENJAMIN FRANKLIN (1706–1790)

Frugal has roots in the latin words, '*frugalis*', meaning useful, and '*frux*', meaning fruit or value. It means being careful with material resources and with money, being economical and avoiding waste. It used to have a more positive spin, but has recently been associated with a penny-pinching approach to life. But perhaps that's changing again; the fastest growing trend in hospitality according to a *Los Angeles Times* journalist is frugal travel, or limited service hotels, which offer modest price accommodation, which provide quality comfort by forgoing large lobbies and 24-hour food services.

'Success at being frugal is measured not by your penny-pinching but by your degree of enjoyment of the material world,' say *Your Money or Your Life* authors, Dominguez and Robin. It's about enjoying, and not wasting, what we have.

The program claims to lower expenses by 20 per cent without feeling the pinch. It has helped many people find the balance of 'enough', and some call it a blueprint for simple living, which suggests that we connect with others, whether through parties, meals or just contact, to deepen experience, be less of a consumer and more of a human being. It also encourages people to get active—whether through civic organizations or 'outrageous' activism, party politics or writing to the media.

The old road map, write Dominguez and Robin, was 'nine to five till you're 65', pushing for a higher standard of living all the while. But over the past few decades, our material possessions first exceeded need, then enhanced comfort, and for many went from luxury to excess. Meanwhile, our relationship with money has taken over a major part of our lives. Some of the concepts in *Your Money or Your Life* are:

- Jobism. Our society has formed a caste system based on what people do for money.
- Social dis-ease. So-called successful professionals turning up for therapy with exhausted bodies and empty souls from focusing on the fruits of materialism, having money, position and success at the expense of personal fulfilment and meaning.
- The shackles of debt. Between mortgages, car loans and credit cards, people can't afford to quit unfulfilling nine to five jobs.
- Buying without thinking, often without really needing it, means the cash constantly runs dry.
- Upward mobility, downward nobility. Testing nature's limits with rocketing consumption; becoming consumers rather than citizens.
- Real hourly wage. When you look at the expense of getting to work, dressing for work, quick meals, a holiday from work and 'escape entertainment', how much are you really working for?

LG realized that half his wage was spent 'on the job': petrol, oil, repairs, lunches and so on. He realized that if he stayed at home and worked part-time, he'd save money. Once he and his wife started to rearrange their financial world, paying off debt and reducing spending, they realized they could manage on his wife's earnings and he trained for a new career.

Your Money or Your Life outlines a nine-step programme focused on financial integrity and financial intelligence to achieve financial independence; it aims to reduce monthly spending and debt, and increase income, especially investment income.

When monthly spending equals monthly investment income, at the cross-over point you become financially independent. Dominguez and Robin recommend keeping track of every single cent that passes through your life with a no-judgment approach—'no shame, no blame'—and hanging a very visible chart somewhere in your home showing your progress; assessing the satisfaction and fulfilment that spending brings, and developing an internal yardstick to alert you when you've reached 'enough' in any one category.

For instance, DG was a steady earner and a heavy spender. She reduced her spending by half by:

- cutting out some of the travel and entertainment.
- reducing automatic spending habits such as daily restaurant meals and buying clothes out of boredom.
- moving to an apartment that cost less to rent.
- taking budget ski trips rather than full price ones.
- trading a sports car for a fuel efficient car.
- learning to do her own car maintenance.

Perhaps the crux of Dominguez and Robin's viewpoint is understanding that money is something we choose to trade our life energy for. But life energy is more real than money. Money has no tangible value in itself, but life energy does. Not only tangible, but finite, and, say the authors, '... our choices about how we use it express the meaning and purpose of our time here on Earth'.

THE FRUGAL BUGLE

Being frugal means using what you have wisely so that your resources are put to good use. The more creative the better. Here are a few classic frugal approaches. If you run out of ideas, the internet is full of frugality sites.

- Sharing and borrowing. You don't have to own every possession you use. Friends lend and borrow drills, extra coffee pots for the big lunch, lawn mowers and books. And there's always the library for magazines as well as books. Putting on dinner for a dozen can be expensive, but get everyone to bring a dish and you have a fabulous spread, more variety and less of a cooking and financial burden at the same time.

- Cut your home running costs by adopting energy efficient practices. Turn off appliances at the wall, insulate ceilings to save on heating and cooling bills and so on.
- Don't go shopping unless you really need to. Beware retail therapy if it's cutting into your finances.
- Live within your means. 'This notion is so outmoded that some readers might not even know what it signifies,' comment Dominguez and Robin. Wait until you've got the money before you buy something. Delay purchases and save up for major ones.
- Look after what you've got: your car, your good coat, your shoes, your electrical appliances.
- Do it yourself. If saving money is the goal, mow your own lawn, do your own cleaning, take your trousers up yourself. But know your own limits too, and call in the experts for the jobs that are beyond your skills or resources.
- Learn useful skills. You can learn basic bicycle maintenance, car mechanics, carpentry and other useful skills, such as sewing, at adult education classes. And consider practising the skills you have within non-cash markets such as community-based local exchange systems.
- Think ahead. Make the most of sales, specials and good deals by anticipating your needs.
- Buy quality. When you have to buy a major item, research the features, decide what's really needed, shop around and buy quality that will last.
- Buy for less. Check out the seconds shops, factory stores, discount websites, wholesale prices ... only, of course, if you need the things in the first place. Do a bit of comparison shopping on major items and consider buying second-hand.
- Consider cutting the cost of transport. Try a bicycle or walking, public transport, second-hand cars or using a small and efficient

car. See what you can do without. For example, BA uses his bicycle in inner-city Sydney every day. He rides to work, carries his shopping home by bicycle and rides for pleasure on the weekends. He recently purchased a new bicycle. It cost him AUS$3000. But then again, the bicycle will last him at least 10 years and, as he says, 'what sort of a car could I buy for that?' BA is one of the few people he knows who doesn't run a car and he makes huge savings each year because of it.

- Consider cutting expensive habits like cigarettes and review your communications bills—are you paying top rates for distance calls or internet connections?
- Take a look at your food bills. If you must eat meat every day, check out cheaper cuts. Consider trimming the meat bill by cutting it out a few times a week. Keep an eye on seasonal pricing of fruit and veggies, look for specials and good deals.

The vegie co-op

Fourteen families in the Northern Illawarra district, south of Sydney in Australia, share fruit and vegetable shopping at a local supplier and buy them at half the cost of retail. Each fortnight two people, with two cars, go to the fruit and vegetable market and make a list of what they want. A representative from the market adds up the prices. Almost everything comes in full boxes: lemons, apples, broccoli and oranges. Potatoes and onions come in sacks and watermelons aren't packed. Assistants load the cars and the two shoppers take them back to one of their houses to divide 14 ways. The other families come to pick up their boxes later in the day, leaving money for the next shop. Each family has to shop once a quarter. Says AH, 'It takes half a day, but it's fun and all the boxes lined up look beautiful. It's a nice way to get to know people too.'

She calculates it saves her nearly AUS$900 a year. In addition, it encourages a more frugal approach to cooking.

The millionaire next door

Thomas J Stanley and William D Danko's bestselling book, *The Millionaire Next Door*, has sold more than one million copies. Millions of people want to know how to amass millions of dollars. Central to the theme of Stanley and Danko's research is that anyone can do it. And the people who you assume are wealthy are not necessarily: 'Many people who live in expensive homes and drive luxury cars do not actually have much wealth,' they explain. In contrast, the truly wealthy in America live well below their means—they are unlikely to be driving this year's car, more likely to be self-employed (one-third are employed) in businesses classified as 'dull-normal', wear clothes the authors describe also as 'dull-normal' and live in houses valued at an average of US$320,000. They have wives who are planners and meticulous budgeters (and are likely to have been married to the same woman for most of their adult life).

One story tells of a man who gave his wife $8 million worth of stock and then watched how she said thank you and without missing a beat, carried on cutting out grocery coupons from the Saturday newspaper. In addition, the authors describe truly wealthy people as working between 45 and 55 hours a week, fastidious investors and 'tightwads' who pocketed the sums offered for interviews for the book, rather than giving it to charity as suggested; one said he only drank two kinds of beer—free and Budweiser.

How wealthy should you be? Stanley and Danko pose this question to their readers, with their explanation of how to calculate the answer: Multiply your age times your pre-tax annual household income from all sources except inheritances. Then divide by 10. If you're total figure is a long way off, according to the authors, chances are you enjoy a 'high consumption' lifestyle.

Measuring money big time

Gross Domestic Products (GDPs) and Gross National Products (GNPs) measure the total amount of money changing hands within a country. GDP is the most commonly used indicator of national income. It attempts to measure the sum of incomes from the manufacturing, agriculture and service industries. Gross National Product is what happens when you add to the GDP the value of income from abroad. So it includes what domestic companies earn abroad but excludes what foreign companies earn. Both measures are seen as problematic because they are used as the primary indicator of prosperity and they take no account of non-market work, especially women's 'invisible' work. They also fail to take into account relevant measures of wellbeing such as family, community and the natural environment, counting a product only if it is exchanged for money.

GENUINE PROGRESS INDICATOR

Some alternatives suggested for measuring a nation's wealth are the Genuine Progress Indicator (GPI)—also known as the Index of Sustainable Economic Welfare. 'The rationale behind it is that a measure of national wellbeing that is confined to goods and services produced for the market makes no sense,' explains Clive Hamilton in *Growth Fetish*. Its starting point is consumption but also includes a value for household and community work, a broader estimate of the financial cost of unemployment and environmental costs.

Australian economist, Duncan Ironmonger, has suggested other measures:

- Gross market product (GMP), the traditional measure of an economy, such as GDP.
- Gross household product (GHP), the unpaid labour and capital bound up in the running of a household.
- Gross economic product (GEP), which is when you add together GMP and GHP.

Ironmonger's point is that you need to also look at hours spent to gain an accurate picture of the economy. He points to figures from the 1987 time use survey in Australia, which show that within the home, the greatest 'industry' was meal preparation at 76 million hours, with cleaning and laundry second, at 63 million hours. By comparison, in the market economy, the entire wholesale and retail trade involved 49 million hours, while manufacturing had the same figure.

HUMAN DEVELOPMENT INDEX

The United Nations Human Development Index (HDI) was developed in 1990 by Pakistani economist Mahbub ul Haq, and has been used since 1993. It is a comparative measure of poverty, literacy, education, life expectancy, childbirth, and a standard means of measuring wellbeing, especially child welfare. It considers three basic dimensions of human development to be a long and healthy life (life expectancy at birth); knowledge (adult literacy rate plus a ratio that refers to education enrolments) and a decent standard of living measured by gross domestic product (GDP) per capita at purchasing power parity (PPP).

The 2005 report shows HDI to be improving around the world with the major exceptions of post-Soviet states and sub-Saharan Africa. In the first case the causes are declining education, economies, and mortality rates and in Africa, HIV/AIDS is to blame.

AN ECONOMY OF WELLBEING

Ed Diener and Martin Seligman are among those calling for a shift in emphasis toward an economy based on wellbeing rather than economic outcomes. They define wellbeing as people's evaluations and feelings about their lives. They argue that as societies become wealthier, differences in wellbeing are less frequently due to income and more to do with social relationships and enjoyment of work. Non-economic indicators include social capital, democratic governance and human rights. In the workplace, they include work satisfaction and profitability.

TOWARDS A SIMPLE LIFE

In his book, *A Procrastinator's Guide to Simple Living*, Australian social psychologist, Jim McKnight, urges people to adopt 'a conserver way'. 'Not only are we caught in a swindle called over-consumption, but we are unhappy about it.' Changing is hard, he concedes, but flexibility and awareness will help. McKnight, head of the psychology department at the University of Western Sydney in Australia, and teacher of environmental psychology, has come up with a nine-step plan.

1. Distinguish between relative and absolute needs. Our absolute needs, such as shelter and health care, are in most cases quickly met. But our relative needs are under constant pressure to match the expectations of society.

2. Understand the difference between material and existential needs. We need the comfort of close personal relationships (existential), and we need material things like housing and clothing—but don't confuse the two and seek comfort from material goods while missing out on the personal bonds that count.

3. Review your own situation with regard to material versus existential needs: does the double-earning family really need to work those hours for a reasonable living standard?

4. Identify and eliminate sources of stress, such as large debt or a life that's so complex it starts to lose its shine. McKnight gives the example of a friend who had so many tools which were designated as 'labour saving' that he completely lost sight of the labour he was saving, and couldn't usually find the tool he needed in working order anyway.

5. Prune material possessions to free yourself from the stress of 'things'. Following a few rules might help the procrastinator in you avoid acquiring possessions that are expensive or difficult to maintain. Be suspicious of convenience items and consider why you are hanging onto things that you haven't used in the past year. (He suggests you store these items in a suitcase or crate if you can't let go just yet.)

6. Become a hard-minded shopper. Make purchasing a deliberate choice rather than one you're led into by retail psychology. Count the cost of each new addition, including the social impact, says McKnight.

7. Beware advertising that creates a 'need' and adds dollars to the cost of goods. Make a game of pointing out its absurd side and lessen its impact at the same time. (And if you want support, check out Adbusters, the Canadian anti-consumerist movement that makes a habit of spoofing ad campaigns.)

8. Review how you use your time. Notice where you concentrate your time and effort and compare this with what stresses you and what you'd like to be doing. 'If you are an average person, several things will jump out at you,' says McKnight. That you're doing too many diverse things, for one, that you're probably not doing them as well as you'd like and that you don't have the time to do all the things you'd like to.

9. Establish priorities in your commitments. This will involve abandoning some activities in favour of others. Which activities do you least like? asks McKnight. Perhaps it is dishwashing. A dishwashing machine's not the answer, he suggests, but finding someone else in the household who doesn't hate it as much, might be. As might reviewing the way you cook and serve meals.

OTHER CURRENCIES

One of the ways people do with less money is by bypassing the money economy through barter and exchanges, whether informal or administered systems. These have the potential to enrich in other ways as they tend to foster community relations at the same time. They include business barter, trade exchanges, local energy or exchange trading systems (LETS), time banks and skill pools. The philosophies behind such arrangements include:

- reducing reliance on free market forces. Dr Ted Trainer of the Department of Social Work, Social Policy and Sociology at the University of New South Wales in Australia argues that free market forces will 'allocate most of the world's wealth to the few, produce inappropriate development, destroy the environment, and ignore the needs of the majority'.

- valuing people. When money is scarce, valuations become distorted. Wanting to get as much out of someone for as little as possible becomes the norm.

Thor Heyerdahl (1914–2002)

The Norwegian marine biologist with great interest in anthropology, is best known for his 1947 Kon-Tiki Expedition, in which he sailed a raft 6920 kilometres (4300 miles) from South America to the Tuamotu Islands. A decade earlier, he and his new wife Liv began their honeymoon on Fatu Hiva, an island in French Polynesia, searching for the simple life. They wanted to escape civilization and 'return to nature'. For 18 months they lived in a small, almost abandoned valley on the island's mountainous interior, building a thatch-covered home.

At first the Heyerdahls found life on Fatu Hiva idyllic, with an abundance of fruit trees and clean river water. Elephantiasis-bearing mosquitoes and other tropical diseases intruded on the charm, however. Eventually the simple life wore thin and the couple found themselves longing to return to Norway.

Decades later, Thor wrote about their experiences in *Fatu Hiva: Back to Nature* and reflected: 'Progress today can be defined as man's ability to complicate simplicity. Nothing in all the procedure that modern man, helped by all his modern middlemen, goes through before he earns money to buy a fish or a potato will ever be as simple as pulling it out of the water or soil.'

- cheap champions. Money is a limited resource in its own right, so we try to spend as little as possible to get as much as possible, often in the form of imported goods produced at third-world pay rates using cheap raw materials and unsustainable methods.
- everyone can trade. Money solved the problem of the awkwardness of barter, but what do you do if you're short of cash? In alternative economies everyone has something to offer that they can trade with another.
- valuing work. This quote from a LETS website neatly sums up the issue of work: 'Work is currently defined as what one does to make money, and thus many things are considered work which are negative and destructive to the environment, society or the

human soul. Conversely, many useful, positive and constructive things that people do are not classed as work because they do not earn money.'

Business systems that fall outside traditional monetary systems include Bartercard, which combines traditional bartering concepts with a standard credit card structure. A business-to-business trade exchange, Bartercard was founded by Wayne Sharpe, Andrew Federowsky and Brian Hall on the Gold Coast, in Australia in 1991. Bartercard members now number 55,000 worldwide, with 100 offices in 16 countries—including Hong Kong, Jordan, the UK and Thailand, with billions of dollars exchanged in reciprocal transactions of Trade Dollars.

For example, a restaurant that needs $10,000 worth of printing could use a Bartercard member printer and then 'pay' for the printing over the next few months as Bartercard members come and eat at the restaurant. The printer in turn can use the earned Trade Dollars to buy office furniture, car repairs or stationery from other Bartercard businesses selling it.

Members have the advantage of an interest-free line of credit, conserving cash, using downtime or idle inventory to make purchases that their business is currently spending cash on. In addition, Bartercard says using the system brings extra business and more networking opportunities .

LETS: LOCAL ENERGY/EXCHANGE TRADING SYSTEMS

LETS are not-for-profit community groups in which people trade services and goods using an internal currency counter—often based on the local currency. According to LETS there are over 1500 groups around the world in 39 countries, with representation on all continents except Antarctica.

LETS enthusiast, James Taris, became involved because as an ex-photographer, he could only afford essential living expenses on his limited income: rent, gas, electricity, phone, petrol, food and clothes. Through his local LETS he swapped mowing lawns, removing rubbish and painting rooms, and later, designing business cards, brochures and newsletters for massages, piano tuition, restaurant meals, computer support, computer software, web design services, greeting cards, teddy bears and bonsai plants. Later, he travelled overseas among the LETS network.

BETTER THAN BARTER

'Barter is a type of exchange where we swap goods and services without using money—I give you a loaf of bread and you give me two cabbages. You fix my car and I'll cook you dinner. But you may not like my cooking … money overcomes the limitations of barter,' explains the LETS web page. Or, as another LETS member explains: 'I cook for John; John digs Mary's garden; Mary cuts Joe's hair; Joe fixes Lenny's car; Lenny sells me vegetables.' The details may vary from scheme to scheme, but in general they work like this: I pay you to paint my front door—$5 for the paint and $30 for your time. I give you a $5 note. We agree that I pay you the remaining $30 on our LET system. Your account rises by 30 LETS points and mine goes down by 30. You can now spend your 30 (or more, if you wish) with anyone else within the same system.

James Taris tells a heart-warming story of a dilemma in a Canadian LETS group. When helping with the administration, he noticed that one member was over 1000 LETS points in debit. Should he freeze the account? He asked the supervisor. Having ascertained that the person in question was a new homeowner (of an old run-down house), and a single mother with an eight-year-old child, the supervisor explained that LETS attracts two groups of people: those who like helping others and those who really need help. On the one hand, many of the members were natural helpers, mature age and comfortable with their lives; on the other, the woman in question was in need and after looking at what she'd offered: use of her piano and a holiday home and also gardening— it was decided she was not a freeloader, but someone who'd be paying back once her life was in better order.

It doesn't suit everyone, and each local scheme can differ, depending on the administration they employ and the people involved. For example, RU lost interest in his local LETS scheme when he got repeated requests to renovate a bathroom or build a shed, when he'd put 'labouring' down as a service on offer. But when it runs to plan, people can use the scheme for 'luxuries', such as a massage or 'extras', such as help in the garden, as well as more basic needs. The idea is that LETS units are supplementary to cash, not an alternative to it. People who use LET systems can often reduce their cash outgoings and make the rest of their money go further.

A MIDDLE WAY

A day without work, a day without food

PAI-CHANG HUAI-HAI (720–814)

The philosopher, Norman Brown—described as the 'playful philosopher'—once said that money reflects and promotes a style of thinking that is abstract, impersonal and quantitative. Maybe in some way that sums up our unease with it. There is no doubt we need it and the material things it buys, and we like some of the 'extras' it can bring, but we recognize its power, not just to shape human relationships, but also to alter the way we think and view the world.

It's all too easy to get sucked into thinking that money is more important than it is. A romantic's reaction to money has often been to turn their back on it and attempt to live without it—usually with a 'back to basics' vigour, focused on providing food and shelter. Because of the way our society works, it's a very hard decision to make and experiments to live without money often end before planned.

MONEY'S SOUL AND SHADOW

Thomas Moore, author and psychologist, calls money the coinage of our relationship to the community and environment in which we live—we are paid for our work, and we in turn pay for services and products. 'Money is central in our attempts to live a communal life,' he says in *Care of the Soul: A guide for cultivating depth and sacredness in everyday life.*

While some people's spirituality involves rejecting the money system—either working for nothing, or bartering services to avoid 'money's shadow'—that person might escape money, but also stands 'lonely outside the community that economics helps to sustain'. Losing the desire for wealth, one can also lose some of its joy, he believes.

ECONOMICS FROM THE HEART

Earth provides enough for every man's need, but not any man's greed.

ATTRIBUTED TO GANDHI (1869–1948)

Calls for a middle way—a sustainable and comfortable way to earn and spend money—are many. Some people have claimed to have found one.

The Greyston Bakery in Yonkers, New York opened in 1982 thanks to a Zen Buddhist meditation group led by aerospace engineer, Bernard Tetsugen Glassman, who borrowed US$300,000 to set it up. It originally sold muffins, but now the fare is more likely to be gourmet cakes—some of which have made it into the White House via its wholesale arm. One of the main ingredients of all products, says Greyston, is 'our dynamic social mission'. The bakery's profits support the community development work of the Greyston Foundation, which includes housing, childcare, health care and a computer learning centre, supporting low income individuals and families and helping them towards self-sufficiency. The Bakery also actively recruits and hires employees who have had difficulties finding employment in the past, giving them on-the-job training as well as a pay cheque.

SMALL IS BEAUTIFUL.

E F Schumacher's book *Small is Beautiful*, published in 1973, called for sustainable economics on a human scale, with appropriate technologies and a decentralized approach. Modern industry requires so much yet accomplishes so little, he believed. Schumacher wrote: 'Ever bigger machines, entailing ever bigger concentrations of economic power and exerting ever greater violence against the environment, do not represent progress: they are a denial of wisdom. Wisdom demands a new orientation of science and technology towards the organic, the gentle, the non-violent, the elegant and beautiful.'

TIME WISE

Traditional economic measures count money, they do not count time as would some of the alternative measures outlined above. Consequently there is a danger that productive activities are not valued when they involve spending time, yet do not produce cash. New Zealander, Marilyn Waring's 1988 work, *If Women Counted*, pointed out the shortcomings of this approach. She studied the United Nations Systems of National Accounts which sets out the 'rules' of what counts and what doesn't count when totting up national account figures used by organizations, such as the World Bank. While global economics might seem a world removed from a discussion of how individuals use their time, there is more common ground than might first appear. Both issues boil down to the question of how we value time. If our culture is one that doesn't see time as productive unless it involves money, where does that leave our vulnerable sense of the value of time? For Waring, the economic issue of valuing time as well as money is perfectly illustrated by cow dung.

Stuck for suitable gifts to take to Christmas parties soon after she bought her farm, Waring shocked her party-going companions by taking hosts bags of cow dung. Far from repulsed, her city friends were thrilled and enthusiastically put the fertilizing gift to work: in compost bins, in buckets to make liquid manure or straight onto their gardens.

When the farm became more established, collecting dung continued to be an important aspect of its running. In many parts of Asia and Africa, Waring has pointed out, women collect dung, sometimes following their herds, carrying heavy loads that will later be put to uses essential for survival. Dung is an important fertilizer, cooking fuel and building material. There's no 'market' at work here, so in official accounting eyes, no economic activity and no 'production'. '... dungwork is only women's work, so it is a safe assumption that in the official definitions of productive work it will be invisible,' writes Waring in *Three Masquerades: Essays on Equality, Work and Human Rights*.

There is a growing recognition that, even to understand how the 'market' or money economy works, you need to understand how the time economy works. Hence the interest in time use: measuring it and analyzing it to attempt to paint a real picture of the 'total economy'. If you count in housework, child rearing, 'reproductive work', voluntary work, caring work, household maintenance and subsistence agriculture, there's much valuable productive human activity that never gets a look-in when counting economic bottom lines. Waring describes this as, 'most of the work that most of the people do most of the time'.

Figures from India in the 1980s provide an apt illustration of the distortions that can occur when you count only money, not time. Census figures showed that almost three-quarters (73 per cent) of rural women did not work. Yet when researchers, Ankar, Kahn and Gupta questioned them they got a totally different picture. Most women reported housework as their main activity, many collected water and dung, some had earnt money in seasonal agriculture, made and sold preserves and tended a family vegetable garden. According to the researchers' estimations—reported by the International Labour Organization—93 per cent of rural women worked, not 27 per cent as the Census figures showed.

Now is a good time to pause

New York artist and designer, Dana Bishop-Root, works in public spaces, for example, writing on walls phrases like 'now is a good time to pause'. Practise the active pause she suggests: 'We are invited to wake up from a collective speed to practise a collective pause. Active pause is that one moment where you notice. Notice where you are!'

SLOW DOWN

If there are political reasons to value time, there are also personal ones. The Slow Food movement, with its snail logo, recognizes there are environmental reasons too. Founded by Carlo Petrini in Italy in 1986, Slow Food describes itself as 'an international association that promotes food and wine culture, but also defends food and agricultural biodiversity worldwide'. It is growing all the time and now boasts 83,000 members worldwide in 100 countries. In Italy alone there are about 35,000 members and 360 local Slow Food groups. The two strongest characteristics of the movement, says Slow Food, are its decentralized nature, and the fact it has roots in the local community.

HURRIED AND HARRIED

When we talk of feeling rushed, it's more than merely being busy— it's tinged with a feeling that we are not in control: that other forces are taking over our lives. It's akin to the feelings that the first workers to be 'clocked' felt about their working conditions. And that's where the stress comes in. Children as well as adults can feel the stress of being rushed.

David Elkind, Professor of Child Development at Tufts University, Boston in the US, believes there are many ways in which we are hurrying along our children, both literally and in their development. His 1981 book, *The Hurried Child: Growing up too fast too soon*, is now in its third edition. He sees problems in overscheduling children's time; overtesting children at school; in making children consumers and marketing violence to children in music, movies and video games. Much of what he says can be applied to many Western cultures: 'The contemporary parent dwells in a pressure cooker of competing demands, transitions, role changes and personal and professional uncertainties, over which he or she exerts slight direction,' he says.

For children this can lead to chronic stress that produces 'free-floating anxiety' (a sense of restlessness, irritation and a lack of being able to concentrate—all without being able to pinpoint what the trouble is); 'school burnout' (pressure leading to lack of enthusiasm, even hating school, truancy and eventually dropping out altogether); 'learned helplessness' (a feeling of being helpless, threatened and unable to take action which results in lethargy and listlessness); and 'premature structuring' (where character becomes structured so early that there's little room for personal growth and development of the personality).

We can't change the basic thrust of the society we live in, nor is there any point ignoring the social importance of being punctual, says Elkind. But we can watch out for certain behaviours.

- Calendar hurrying. When we ask a child to understand or make decisions beyond their capacity. Parents are more guilty of this type of hurrying with their firstborns, with the result that the oldest children are more likely to be hard working, driven and competitive.
- Clock hurrying. When due to the demands on our own time, we ask children to draw on their energy reserves. For example, when we take children on long trips. Children can accommodate these types of hurrying, but when they occur too often they're stressful. To reduce stress, either cut back on demands or provide more support. Acknowledging a child's feelings about going to day care and emphasizing how happy you are to see them at the end of the day, for instance, can help lessen the stress of hurrying.

Play is the perfect antidote to hurrying, believes Elkind. It's nature's way of dealing with stress, he says. And when it comes to playthings, those that allow most scope for the imagination offer the best relief. Showing your children that you can enjoy the here and now (which is where they 'live' mostly, too) means you enjoy better the time you spend with them, as well as giving them strategies for later life.

Elkind's concerns were echoed in a letter to the *Daily Telegraph* in the UK in September 2006, which expressed deep concern over rising childhood depression. More than 100 signatories, including neuroscientist, Baroness Greenfield and dozens of teachers, psychologists, children's writers and community organizations were behind the letter, which said: 'Since children's brains are still developing, they cannot adjust—as full grown adults can—to the effects of more rapid technological and cultural change. They also need time.' The authors bemoan formal school work starting too young, academically driven primary education and market forces which encourage children to act and dress like mini adults.

VOX POP: Is it important to slow down?

I do feel it is important to slow down at times. I am lucky because, as my parents live nearby, I can go and recuperate at their house for a weekend. I do this often as we're a close family and even if I didn't want to get out of the hectic pace of living in London, I would do this anyway. AE

It is vital. Sometimes we have a weekend away and I can relax with friends or family. Ideally it would be great to get all the work done beforehand, so I could just forget about it. But more often I can't finish it and it's hanging over me to be finished on Monday. PN

I like the idea of slowing down for an extended period and going back to basics: eating, reading, walking. Slowing down is when the 'I must ...' and 'I've got to ...' are suspended for at least a little while. I slow down when I go for an early morning walk on the beach, or when I decide just to blob on the sofa and read a book after the children have gone to bed. Children can make you slow down in that they push work out of centre stage and demand your attention on small things—eating, explaining the world, just being together—but as they get older their own lives become fuller and this takes more coordinating and running around for the parent. AH

Of course it is and we did spend an hour an evening meditating, but we've got so busy lately, that's gone out the window. AL

It's essential to slow down at times. I try to schedule 'people free' days each week, and sit around reading books, recharging the batteries. I even tell people I'll be away for a few days, and then hole up. EWB

It is important but it takes a concerted effort in this society to slow down. For me it means having time to breathe and reflect and not to be constantly distracted by something. I do live life at a slower pace and possibly achieve less, but I've chosen that for myself because I think it's healthier. But sometimes people don't approve of the slow approach. Soon after having my baby, for example, most people I knew were asking me when I was going to go back to work. ML

Slow down-time is time at home by myself, which I usually spend tidying the house. I find this quite therapeutic: putting things in order. SH

I am understanding more and more that it's essential to slow down at times. But when I give myself permission to do that, I feel guilty. Since my last bout of surgeries I have changed. Well, a little bit. I now say it's all right to lie down and rest when I am exhausted. It is all right to not complete tasks immediately. But it's hard to do. SG

Being both busy and doing nothing are vital to me and I have learned the art of knowing when one is more appropriate than the other. CL

THE PLEASURES OF SLOW

When you need reminding that there's more to life than speed, there are many ways to slow down. Slow down all day, every day, or occasionally as a conscious decision to step out of your more frenzied regular rhythm. Being able to slow down when you desire is a useful guard against stress, and brings you back a sense of control.

- Take up a slow activity. Activities that are slow in themselves, and demand your attention are absorbing and soothing: bookbinding, calligraphy, pottery and yoga as well as the popular and gentle art of gardening are just some slow activities you could try.
- Do nothing. Dr Stephan Rechtschaffen, co-founder of the Omega Institute for Holistic Studies in the US, sometimes gets people in his workshops to sit in a circle and do nothing for one hour. They don't talk or do anything else. They might feel uncomfortable for a while, but often end the session feeling deeply relaxed.

- Back to nature. Tune into the beauty of nature. Watch the night sky, take a slow walk in the forest, switch off the alarm clocks. Wake up to the sun instead of a clock.
- Stretch time. Bring back the long lunch at the weekend. Make a special time with family or friends. Take time over preparing food, share the cooking and let the meal take its course. Give yourself the occasional time periods without clocks and watches.
- Slow down with kids. Tap into children's natural rhythm. Yes, sometimes they're quick, but sometimes they're slow—happy to play the same game again and again or throw stones into a lake for hours on end. Computer games and television are 'fast'. Encourage slow time by reading with children and encouraging reading, limiting television and other screen time and making meals together.

LIVING IN THE NOW

The present contains all that there is. It is our holy ground.
ALFRED NORTH WHITEHEAD,
THE AIMS OF EDUCATION AND OTHER ESSAYS, 1929

In 1974 Thich Nhat Hanh, Zen master and peace activist wrote a letter to Brother Qang, a main member of staff at the School of Youth for Social Service in South Vietnam. After graduating, students of the school helped peasants to rebuild bombed villages, teach children, set up medical stations and organize agricultural cooperatives. The letter was to encourage the students through a dark time of kidnappings and even murders that took place against the school. Thich Nhat Hanh's letter reminded the students of the essential discipline of calm mindfulness—primarily through the simple discipline of following one's breath. It was later published in full as a book, *The Miracle of Mindfulness*, and has since been published in every continent and translated into several languages.

The book describes simply and directly many breathing exercises to accompany mindfulness—the presence of mind on the moment. But it also sends the more general message of paying attention to whatever task is at hand. While washing the dishes, we should only be doing that, concentrating on the warm water, the bubbles, each item of crockery and cutlery .... not cursing or moaning about the task while wondering what to do next. Writes Nhat Hanh: 'The fact that I am standing there and washing these bowls is a wondrous reality.'

When we attend wholly to what's at hand, life seems to fill up. When we give our full attention to our surroundings, they rarely appear bland.

Rushing the entire time has serious ramifications for the moment-by-moment experience of life. In a rushed state we take satisfaction from shorter moments and the intensity of an experience must be greater to feel a 'peak experience' in that time. But if we can maintain concentration over a longer period of time, an event of lower 'extensity' can give us a similar depth of internal experience.

If our attention span gets shorter and shorter, it can lead to seeking increasingly dangerous activities to get a 'high'—just like addiction. Get your highs from everyday activities by slowing down and expanding the moment. So, how do you 'expand the moment'?

- Breathe into now. Close your eyes, watch your breath and turn your attention to your breathing. There are endless ways to follow your breath: count up to ten, and start at one every time you lose count; feel it enter at the top of your body and leave at your feet; as you breathe, visualize a stone falling into a still lake.

- Honour the mundane. Don't fight the chores, enter them fully and enjoy sweeping, cleaning, folding laundry.

- Pay attention. Take notice of what's around now and pay attention to the sounds and smells. Are they distant or nearby? Focus your mind on your physical body and notice where you are holding tension.

- Mindful emotions. When feelings threaten to run off with your peace of mind, remember mindfulness. Remember that often there is no stress in the now, only stress caused by thinking about what might happen.

- Savour. Time stops, says Martin Seligman, when we're fully engaged in activities he calls gratifications, ones like rock climbing or reading a good book. Mere bodily pleasures fade and, worse, do not always give us repeat pleasure. We can become habituated to some pleasures and stop taking notice of them. 'The sheer speed of modern life and our extreme future-mindedness can sneak up on us and impoverish our present,' says Seligman in *Authentic Happiness.* In attempting to save time we lose it in the present. But through 'savouring'—applying a conscious attention to a pleasure—we may be able to prevent habituation. Like the tradition of mindfulness, it means drawing attention to the smallest details: physical feelings like textures, smells, feeling the heat of the sun, or lingering over a poem, for example.

Practising mindfulness is the way to exercise control over time rather than feel at its mercy. You don't have to slow down all the time, but it's a valuable skill to be able to move down a gear at will.

CONTROLLING ATTENTION

Only that day dawns to which we are awake.

HENRY DAVID THOREAU, *WALDEN*, 1854

To counteract the tendency for rushing to shorten the attention span, Mihaly Csikszentmihalyi, author of *Finding Flow*, recommends developing the habit of doing whatever needs doing with concentrated attention and skill rather than 'inertia'. Of time, he notes: 'One must learn to husband it carefully, not so much in order to achieve wealth and security in some distant future, but in order to enjoy life in the here and now.' Nurture curiosity and interest by fully engaging in a task and applying yourself with care, whether it's mowing the lawn or sewing on a button.

You have to find time in order to develop interest and curiosity to enjoy life for its own sake, he believes. Don't wait for things to grab your attention, learn some control over your 'psychic energy' and learn to concentrate at will. You'll have the feedback loop on your side: if you are interested in something, you focus on it, and with focus, it's likely that you'll become more interested in it.

To pursue mental operations to any degree of depth, believes Csikszentmihalyi, you have to learn to concentrate your attention, otherwise 'consciousness is in a state of chaos'. When you like what you do and are motivated to do it, he says, focusing the mind becomes effortless. Usually the mind's focus is divided and motivation and focus rarely coincide. Csikszentmihalyi gives a couple of good examples: the businessman who could be enjoying drinks with his friends after work but feels guilty about not being at home with his family, and is worried about all the money he's spending. Conflicts and contrary thoughts and intentions are a commonplace part of everyday life.

When heart, mind and will are together, we experience serenity because what we feel, what we wish and what we think are in harmony. This is what Csikszentmihalyi calls flow experiences; other interpretations of the same idea include the feeling some athletes call 'being in the zone' or that religious mystics call 'ecstasy' or 'rapture'.

FREE TIME

All day long no plans
And I remain at leisure.

WANG WEI (701–761) 'REPLY TO CHANG YIN'

We tend to plan work, but give less thought to how we fill our leisure time, however short. When it comes down to it, people are less in touch with what they really enjoy than they think, believes Csikszentmihalyi. Through a combination of habit and social pressure we plod or dash through life, not really knowing which components of our lives we actually enjoy and which contribute to stress and depression. To combat this, Csikszentmihalyi suggests keeping a flow diary for a while. Each night, reflect on the day's activities and write down the high experiences, after a while a pattern will emerge.

KILLING TIME

'Why do men die on average six years younger than women?' asked Leonie Bloomfield, an Office of Women Time Use Research fellow in

Australia. Could time use data shed any light on the question? Time use analysis shows men have more free time than women and their leisure time is more concentrated and less interrupted than women's. But perhaps more free time is not such a good thing.

In fact, free time for men is associated with boredom, Bloomfield told a seminar in Sydney in 2006 hosted by the Social Policy Research Centre. This so-called 'leisure boredom' is linked to loneliness, alcohol consumption, tobacco use and inactive leisure activities such as watching television, reading and listening to music.

Bloomfield looked at the time use diaries of 160 men between the ages of 20 and 75 living in Melbourne. (It took her seven years to analyze the data.) They had also recorded why they did an activity (and how motivated they were to do it, that is, did they want to do it), and rated each activity according to how meaningful it was and how lonely and bored they felt during the activity.

Unhealthy lifestyle habits, such as smoking, drinking and less physical activity go part of the way to explain earlier deaths, but don't account for all the variation. Her hypothesis: men have more free time because they don't do as much housework as women, and instead use the time unwisely.

Passive leisure accounted for 60 per cent of men's free time, but men were more bored and found the activities less meaningful— 25 per cent said at these times they 'had nothing else to do' and 15 per cent wished they were doing something else.

All the indicators were linked with an increased mortality risk, says Bloomfield. 'The gender division of household labour may be related to men's mortality risk.' In other words, men die early because they don't help in the house, have more free time that they use in passive leisure pursuits that are boring and meaningless and in which they feel lonely. These are linked with poor health and possibly explain why men die younger.

Passive leisure is inherently less engaging, more boring and less meaningful. And whereas it's active leisure that produces most flow, it's passive leisure that overshadows it for many. Shifting time from passive pursuits to active ones is likely to make you feel better—at no extra time cost.

THE VALUE OF SPARE TIME

If I ever think I've got spare time, I've forgotten an appointment.

PETER NEEDHAM (1950–), TRAVEL WRITER

Leisure time, free time and spare time can be very rewarding. Much scientific research, poetry, painting and musical composition used to be undertaken in people's 'free time'. So too, collecting, exploring and inventing. Although beware the concept of pushing important things into something called 'spare time', as JE asserts: 'Spare time? What a horrid notion! I find the idea that I can only do the things I really want to do in "spare time" abhorrent. Waiting for the moment when you can have a little spare time is like hanging out for the day you get to liberate the spare tyre from the car boot. What you find is usually disappointing. It's flat, bald and potentially useless. And it usually doesn't get you anywhere.'

A BAG OF TIME TRICKS

'Time stress has become one of the most popular complaints of the day,' says Csikszentmihalyi. You need to take control and put energy into organizing, prioritizing and streamlining routines, he adds. In the future we may be able to hibernate at will, or reduce, with the aid of drugs, how much sleep we need. Perhaps we will be able to change our perception of time, and slow it down like the king in one of Herodotus' stories. Herodotus tells the story of an Egyptian king who, on hearing from an oracle that he had six years to live, had lamps lit every evening, thus turning night into day and packing 12 years of living into the next six.

Try as they may to savour the taste of eternity, their thoughts still twist and turn upon the ebb and flow of things in past and future time. But if only their minds could be seized and held steady, they would be still for a while, and, for that short moment, they would glimpse the splendour of eternity, which is forever still.

AUGUSTINE OF HIPPO (354–430)

CREATE TIME BOUNDARIES

- Make time for spontaneity. Create windows of time every so often that are unstructured and free of plans so you leave room for the unexpected: the days when you let yourself go with the flow. Sometimes these are the best days, when you enjoy pottering around the house, or find yourself clearing out a cupboard or bumping into friends at the local park. Or perhaps just doing nothing.

- Take time seriously. Do something you like. Give yourself the freedom to do something just because you like doing it, not for other reasons, like getting fit, enhancing your skills or for other people. If you make time for other things in your life, why not make time for you.

- Rethink the multitasking. If you find doing lots of things at once adds to the feeling of being time-pressured and being rushed, give it a break. Or when you feel you're not achieving anything, try every now and then to simply do one thing.

- Work out your priorities for now. Priorities can change, but knowing that you can't do it all, (unless you really are determined to be superman or superwoman), can help you choose what you do put your time into. For example, SS purposely chose a job well below her qualifications and skill, so that she had the time for her child and for putting into her interest in making, decorating and firing ceramics. She might pursue the career option in another decade, but for now she has the satisfaction of making progress in an art form, and her sense of being pulled in different directions for time is reduced.

- Time retreat. Periodically stepping out of the mainstream rhythm, whether it's camping or partaking in island time, gives you a break from your habits and habitual rhythms. It gives you time to reflect.

REVISITING TIME

By trying to live efficient and productive lives we struggle against time's entropy, says Thomas Moore. The secret of time is that its loss and theft are part of the human condition, he says. It's not just an abstract structure into which life is poured, but also a quality of life, not a measurement of its units.

LIFE IS THE GIFT OF TIME

To wish for time is to wish for life, for the opportunity to live with fullness and vitality.

THOMAS MOORE, PREFACE TO *TIMESHIFTING* BY STEPHAN
RECHTSCHAFFEN, 1996

SEEKING MIDDLE TIME

The balance between fast and slow, event and clock time can be found in middle time. In some parts of the world two times rule, not just the one. For example, in the US children might be raised in a house on 'Mexico' time, but need to fit into an education or job world on US time, so are given training to adhere to clock time. Without it they are at a severe disadvantage when it comes to gaining an education and a job.

By recognizing the benefits of different approaches we can learn to timeshift. It's great to slow down, but to survive in society most people need to be able to speed up and adhere to clock time too. Some types of work call for slipping into the 'surge mode'—especially for short, critical bursts. Mark Twain wrote six of his best books in two summers; Mozart could work day and night when needed. Creative people—writers, musicians, scientists and designers—may use the surge mode rather than stop and start many different times.

Social psychologists, Jonathan Freedman and Donald Edwards looked at the relationship between pleasure and pressure in a paper called 'Time Pressure: Task Performance and Enjoyment' published in 1988. The greatest pleasure, they found, existed under an intermediate level of pressure. Too much 'temporal pressure' can be stressful, while too little can be boring. Csikszentmihalyi also found in his research that the least happy people in America are those with no time pressure at all.

Robert McCrum (1953–)

You will never get it, if you don't slow down.

PAUL ASTER, *SMOKE*, 1995

When, at 42 years of age, Faber & Faber Editor-in-Chief, Robert McCrum found himself in hospital rehabilitating after a stroke, his recovering body and mind gave him no choice but to slow down. He spent the next three months in hospital, paralysed on one side. He wrote about the 12 months that followed in a memoir, *My Year Off*, published in 1998.

'At times, my year off was one of all-pervading slowness, of weeks lived one day, even one hour, at a time.' Once back at home, walking to the front door could take three minutes. Dressing and bathing was slow, and the finishing touches—ties and shoes—impossible without help. He had to learn that 'everything takes time.'

'I became friends with slowness, both as a concept and as a way of life.' While in the past he was known for the speed at which he could accomplish any task, now he had to learn to be patient with himself. When he had the 'insult to the brain', as a stroke is sometimes described, he was two months into a marriage. The illness brought about an intimacy with his new wife that could have taken years to develop, McCrum believes. And although the experience left him frustrated, depressed and sometimes in pain, strangely, he writes: 'In the process I have been renewed in my understanding of family and, finally, of the only thing that really matters: love.'

Breathing in, I am calm,
Breathing out, I smile.

THICH NHAT HANH

VOX POP: Which is more important, time or money?

Time. With money and no time, there's no point in having the money. But vice versa, with time and no money, a great deal of satisfaction is possible. That's why I choose to work part-time rather than full-time. But I'm also realizing the value of my skills and am working towards earning a decent amount of money in the hours I allocate to work each week. So I think I'm finally achieving a happy balance between how much money I can earn and having the time to enjoy my life. It's taken a while to get there! ML

Money's nice, but there are lots of things I wouldn't do for it. One of them is work. To be in control of my own time is much more important, as is being in control of how I spend that time. I couldn't stand being an employee. EBW

I have never taken money for granted, but I have treated it shabbily. I used to think I had all the time in the world to do all the things I might wish. Now, with having a family and growing older, I value time so much more. Before I go to sleep, I mull over ways to avoid having to waste time on things I hate—and finding ways to free up a day here or there for specific pleasures. Sometimes I think this is what keeping a diary or a planner is really about: identifying the potential free time. LB

We all need money to live in society and most of us have to earn it. Time is a commodity that is given to us and we use it and appreciate it as we can. It will one day run out. Both time and money need to be treated with respect if we are to get the best out of them. I don't earn a lot of money. I think it is more important to be happy in your work than to be rich, but the more money we have, the more choice we have in doing more with the time we have and our enjoyment of it. As I get older, I realize the possibilities for using both time and money. I would like to have more money in order to open up my possibilities. CL

Rituals

Rituals can help timeshift, moving us from one pace to another or separating special moments from the more mundane. The word ritual comes from an Indo-European root, 'to fit together'. Rituals can help approach grief, celebration and life change, as well as help focus attention to appreciate and bless. 'In every ritual we connect to something higher than ourselves, evoking a higher force,' says Barbara Biziou in *The Joy of Ritual*.

Rituals come in many forms:

- Lighting candles at the beginning of a meal signals a special time for eating and being together.
- Incantation calms and unifies.
- Blessings and prayers focus attention, thanks and hope.
- Incense can symbolize cleansing, passage of prayers to heaven and other changes in mood.
- Song changes rhythm: think of farm labourers keeping up the pace or lullabies to soothe.
- A moment's silence collects thoughts.
- Taking a shower can wash away the day's cares.
- A warm bath with a candle can signal slow time.
- Meditating on rising reinforces the possibilities of a new beginning each day.

There are many examples of rituals in life that allow you to respect time and appreciate the moment. MK's full moon parties on the beach acknowledge friendships, the freedom of the sea and sand, as well as the rhythm of the moon. MH likes to decorate the Christmas tree as a family, playing Christmas music at the same time. Sometimes she asks a child to read a blessing for the tree, to mark the Christmas and New Year season.

AN spends a few moments in the early morning watering the nasturtiums, if she's up early enough, she might see pink clouds of sunrise. The birds are still singing and the light catches the distant hills. It's a quiet and special time, with a stillness that reminds her of the bigger forces of nature.

REAL WEALTH

Time is the one thing we all have. We do not all have market labour-force activities. We do not all have disposable cash. Many of us do not trade on the basis of money, we trade our time. Our economics is about how we use our time. And, even though we frequently do not have a choice about how we use our time, it is the common denominator of exchange. So time is the one unit of exchange that we all have in equal amounts, the one investment we all have to make.

MARILYN WARING, *THREE MASQUERADES*, 1996

Real wealth is about the riches of Earth and the people we love. It's about valuing people and our time here. We need to put money in its proper place and recognize the value of time: what we do with our time is what we're doing with our lives.

It is vital to creativity not to put too much emphasis on money, as *Rhythms of Life* authors Russell Foster and Leon Kreitzman so neatly put it: 'Modern science is driven by grant funding, which is directed towards the solvable.' Had Einstein asked for funding to study the nature of space and time by conducting thought experiments in an armchair, supported by esoteric mathemetics, it's hardly likely he would have found funding—especially if he'd said it would probably take a lifetime. It would have been the same story for Darwin who wished to study the problem of speciation by travelling for five years then thinking about it for another 15.

Not all activities that are useful have a cash value. It's one step away, in our systems, implies Marilyn Waring, to imply that something with no economic or monetary value has little value at all. This devalues much human labour and activity, tends to push us more towards work that pays in money and encourages thinking that values work for how much it pays rather than its inherent worth.

As Schumacher said in *Small is Beautiful*: 'Economy as a content of life is a deadly illness because infinite growth does not fit into a finite world.' When economy is the content of an individual life, it also has a deadening effect on the quality, richness and breadth of our life and time experience.

TAKING STOCK

It's very easy to find yourself stuck with the same old habits and attitudes when it comes to how you look at time and money. If you feel you need to shake up your approach, start with these questions.

MONEY WISE

1. Do you know where your money goes?
2. How much of it goes on 'needs'?
3. How much of it is spent on 'wants'?
4. Where could you cut back?
5. What does 'enough' mean to you? Does earning 'enough' money mean you don't have 'enough' time?
6. To what extent do you put a monetary value on time?
7. Do you ever think that someone's worth is related to what they earn or how wealthy they are?

TIME WISE

1. How do you treat your time?
2. Do you have time to let yourself become fully absorbed in an activity?
3. How do you spend your leisure time?
4. Do you feel like you have time you can call your own? If not, are there ways you can create some windows of time in your life?
5. Are there enough calm times in your life, when you find a quiet moment to read, enjoy silence or practise yoga, for example?

A time to get and a time to lose
A time to keep and a time to cast away;
A time to rend and a time to sew;
A time to keep silence and a time to speak
A time to love and a time to hate; a time of war and a time of peace.

ECCLESIASTES 3. 6-8

Do not say to yourself in advance, 'I should be happy if I could become absorbed in stamp collecting,' and thereupon set to work to collect stamps, for it may well happen that you fail altogether to find stamp collecting interesting.

BERTRAND RUSSELL,
THE CONQUEST OF HAPPINESS, 1930

12. NURTURING HAPPINESS

NEW RESEARCH INTO THE PLASTICITY OF OUR BRAIN IMPLIES WE *CAN* CHANGE FOR THE BETTER. ALTHOUGH SOME THINKERS SAY IT IS FUTILE TO PURSUE HAPPINESS FOR ITSELF, A GROWING VOLUME OF RESEARCH SHOWS THERE ARE MANY WAYS TO MAXIMIZE OUR ENJOYMENT OF LIFE.

MEDITATING ON HAPPINESS

Born in Paris in 1946, Matthieu Ricard studied at the Institut Pasteur. After completing his doctorate in cell genetics in 1973 he decided to become a Buddhist monk and concentrate on Tibetan studies. He moved to the Himalayas and now lives in Nepal at the Shechen Tennyi Dargyeling Monastery. He's an accomplished photographer, works on projects to build and maintain clinics, schools and orphanages in Tibet and since 1989 has been the Dalai Lama's interpreter on his visits to France.

Ricard is a scientist who's switched his focus to the 'contemplative science of Buddhism' as he calls it. He became a subject for scientific study when he agreed to have his brain scanned by neuroscientist, Dr Richard Davidson, director of the Laboratory for Affective Neuroscience in Wisconsin-Madison, in the US. Ricard was one of 150 people studied by Davidson for brain activity—Davidson put electrodes on people's heads and measured the electrical activity in the prefrontal area of the brain. He found that activity in the left was associated with 'happy' moods such as joy, enthusiasm and happiness; while activity in the right was associated with anxiety, fear and depression. By looking at the balance of activity in the prefrontal areas, left and right, he found a very good measure of wellbeing, which changed as people's mood changed.

Most people in the study fell into the middle ground between positive emotions and negative emotions. But Ricard, who had been deeply meditating on compassion when his brain was scanned, was almost off the chart—he had the highest level of happiness ever documented.

Ricard does not use the word 'meditation', preferring the term 'familiarization', which he says is closer to the Tibetan word. 'You familiarize yourself with a new way of being, a new way of thinking. Familiarization over years of practice is like a musician that becomes well trained in his instrument. In the beginning you have to be very attentive but then, after some time, it becomes second nature—you are the helm of your own mind, to be much less vulnerable to, say, thoughts of animosity ...'

Davidson also practises meditation. But it's one thing to experience changes in your own mind, and another to measure the changes in other people's. 'When I spend time with these people it reinforces my belief that there is something important and very positive that can be derived from these kinds of practices and it transforms our notion of the mind as not a fixed entity but rather as something that can be sculpted and shaped through the systematic cultivation of these kinds of practices,' Richard Davidson told the Australian Radio National programme, *All in the Mind* in 2003.

Daniel Kahneman (1934–)

Daniel Kahneman was born in Tel Aviv, but spent his childhood in Paris, moving to Palestine in 1946. A psychologist by education, he is a key pioneer and theorist of behavioural finance, a branch of science which attempts to explain seemingly irrational risk management behaviour. In 2002 he won the Bank of Sweden Prize in Economic Sciences for his work in prospect theory and is currently involved in hedonic psychology—the study of what makes life and experiences pleasant. Kahneman wrote of his childhood that like other Jews 'I grew up in a world that consisted exclusively of people and words, and most of the words were about people. Nature barely existed, and I never learned to identify flowers or to appreciate animals.' But the people his mother talked about with her friends and with his father seemed fascinating in their complexity: 'Some people were better than others, but the best were far from perfect and no one was simply bad.' In 1941 or 1942 in Paris, he remembers having to wear the Star of David and observe a 6 pm curfew. One evening he'd stayed too late at a friend's, and walking home, turned his brown sweater inside out, hoping the star wouldn't be noticed. On the way home, an SS soldier approached him, beckoned him over, picked him up and hugged him. He was terrified the soldier would see the star, but instead, he showed him a picture of a boy from his wallet and gave him some money. 'My mother was right, people were endlessly complicated and interesting,' he later wrote.

Happiness and compassion are skills, Davidson believes, that are no different from learning to play a musical instrument or learning golf or tennis. 'Like any skill, it requires practice and time,' he says, 'but because we know that our brains are built to change in response to experience, it is possible to train our minds to be happy.'

In one study, Davidson and colleagues tested eight Buddhist practitioners and a control group of 10 'healthy' students. The Buddhists had meditated—or 'undergone mental training' as the authors also called it—for between 10,000 and 50,000 hours, over periods ranging from 15 to 40 years, in a mixture of daily practice sessions and meditative retreats. Control subjects, on the other hand were interested in meditation, but had no experience of it. They were given training for a week before the trials.

The subjects were asked to enter three meditative states and it was during the last, 'objectless' one that measurements were taken. Subjects meditated to generate a state of 'unconditional loving, kindness and compassion'. This is sometimes described as 'an unrestricted readiness and availability to help living beings'.

The results showed changes during meditation but also differences between the control group and the practitioners' brain patterns at rest. In other words, not only does meditation bring about changes in the brain while it's occurring, but it also seems to affect the brain over the long term.

WHAT DOES MEDITATION DO?

If your mind isn't clouded by unnecessary things,
This is the best season of your life.

WU-MEN

Meditation is a set of practices that have been around for more than 2500 years. There are many schools, methods and interpretations. Some say it's like the settling debris in a shaken glass of muddy water. Let it become still and the water—or your mind—will become clear. For others, meditation is a way of becoming more deliberate about what you are doing, avoiding knee-jerk reactions in daily situations.

Just a few of the types of meditation practices are:

- Concentration practices. Attention is focused—or concentrated—on an object, a mantra, or the sensation of the breath. Every time your mind wanders, bring it back to the focus.

- Mindfulness meditation. You pay attention on purpose, deeply, and without judgment to whatever arises in the present moment, either inside or outside of you, shifting aside the 'automatic pilot' in regular practice or everyday life.

- Walking meditation. Walking to enjoy the walk, not to arrive anywhere particular. Being in the present, enjoying each step, a little slower than normal walking, perhaps breathing rhythmically with the steps—three steps while breathing in, three steps as you breathe out. Be aware of the contact between your feet and the ground and walk in the spirit of peace.

- Telephone meditation. This is described by Thich Nhat Hanh in *Peace is Every Step: The path of mindfulness in everyday life*. Instead of feeling a victim of your telephone with its insistent ring, when you hear it, stay where you are, smile to yourself and say 'Listen, listen—this wonderful sound brings me back to my true self'. Practise smiling, breathing and repeating the phrase to yourself for three rings—by then you will be your own master.

Opinions seem to differ as to how long you need to practise meditation to reap benefits. There are two main approaches:

- Setting aside special practice time. Common suggestions are for a minimum of 15 minutes a day, some say 30 minutes, some people say two episodes of 20 minutes. To start seeing changes, you'd have to practise for at least a couple of weeks, maybe more. Some people report significant changes months into their practice. A comfortable sitting position is the usual recommended stance for beginners.

- Daily 'life' time. Another way of meditating is to try and incorporate aspects of it throughout your everyday life: while walking between business meetings, waiting at the traffic lights, chopping vegetables, having a shower and so on.

Alice Walker (1944–)

Pulitzer Prize winner, Alice Walker, the American novelist and poet, was born into a family of sharecroppers in Georgia in the US. She worked as a social worker, teacher and lecturer and is best known for the novel about two black sisters in the segregated world, *The Color Purple*. In her late thirties she came to meditation out of, 'intensity of pain. Loss, confusion, sadness. Anxiety attacks. Depression. Suicidal inclinations. Insomnia,' that descended after she divorced her husband. Although she sat on her cushion thinking 'this will never work', she gradually realized that she wasn't quite so jumpy. She didn't want to just draw the covers over her head in the morning and found she could allow herself to listen to music again—'in general it began to seem as if my inner vision had cleared'. Meditation has been a loyal friend, she says. It has helped her write books, made losses bearable and raise a child as a single parent. *The Color Purple*, she says, owes much of its humour and playfulness to the 'equanimity of my mind as I committed myself to a routine, daily practice'.

MEMORY TRICKS

While Davidson's work with meditation shows how an activity can alter the basic emotional patterns of the brain, Daniel Kahneman's work highlights the different ways people experience and recall events.

In one of Kahneman's experiments, he observed 682 patients who were undergoing a colonoscopy. Half the patients had the 'usual' treatment—where the 'scope' on the tube is moved around the bowels and removed as soon as the results are captured—and the other half received treatment with an extra minute added on, but during which the tube was not moved. The first group's was shorter, and the second group's was longer—but the last section of it was less uncomfortable.

The surprise is that when people were asked to rate the experience, those who'd had the longer treatment did not feel as negative about it as the ones who'd had the shorter episode. Endings, so to speak, are very important to how we recall an event.

A CURRICULUM FOR HAPPINESS

Over the course of his 30 plus years in happiness work, Dr Michael Fordyce, professor of psychology (now retired) developed several psychological tests of personal happiness and carried out many studies on the effects of strategies designed to make people happier.

He observed increases in happiness in the participants during the studies and in follow-up investigations. Many participants continued to report the increases over time, in periods ranging from several months to two years.

Fordyce identified fourteen traits—through his own studies and by review of 'the literature'—that again and again were associated with increased happiness. The premise for the 'course' is, 'if you can be like happy people, you can be happy too'. Each of the fundamentals is based on numerous studies, he says.

Fordyce's Fourteen Fundamentals

1. Be more active and keep busy. Get involved in happy activities. These are considered to have a tendency to be:
   - enjoyable ones (sort of obvious, but when participants sit down to think about which activities they enjoy, as opposed to which they don't enjoy, sometimes they learn something new about themselves).
   - exciting and physically active rather than sedate and tranquil ones (but there's a place for both).
   - new and novel, rather than familiar activities.
   - social rather than solitary activities.
   - meaningful rather than trivial activities.

2. Spend more time socializing. Formal clubs and organizations and informal relationships (family, friends, spouse) contribute strong feelings of satisfaction, support and a sense of belonging.

3. Be more productive at meaningful work. Choose careers wisely; persevere towards commitments and goals; try to find meaning in work, or outside work in the voluntary sector.

4. Get organized. Crack procrastination and take some time management lessons to help work towards and refine goals.

5. Stop worrying. Spend less time worrying and you'll be happier (spend more time in enjoyable activities and you'll be happier, is the corollary). List your worries daily for a few weeks to observe your worry patterns: most don't come true and many are beyond your control anyway. Learn to distinguish between worry and planning and see the planning ease the worry.

6. Lower expectations and aspirations. 'How pleased we are with life is not merely determined by what happens to us—it is also determined by what we expect to happen to us,' says Fordyce.
    *   Don't set yourself up for disappointments: cultivate a modest expectation of daily life.
    *   Recognize that 'success' may not be as important to your happiness as you've been led to believe.
    *   Don't wait to be happy, it's a way to travel, not a place to arrive: it's the present, not the postponed future that matters most.
    *   Select life goals that are within your ability to attain.

7. Think positively and be optimistic. It's not what you have, it's how you look at it. Take a real situation (you didn't get the house you wanted to rent/you missed the train and will be late for the film) and look at it in its most positive light, and its most negative, and you'll get the picture. If you expect a good outcome, it's more likely to happen. Ultimately, being an optimist, says Fordyce, is believing you can be happy no matter what.

8. Be present-orientated. Aim to be fully present in the moment to squeeze the most out of each day. There's more happiness in the 'here and now' than the 'there and then'. Savour the moment with meditation and focusing techniques and keenly appreciate the pleasures of life.

9. Work on a healthy personality. To get going in the right direction try to:
    *   like yourself—analyze your views about yourself and consider how these affect your happiness.
    *   accept yourself, shortcomings and all.
    *   know yourself: you need insight and understanding to make good decisions about what to do in your life and your day.

- help yourself: cultivate self-sufficiency and being 'inner' rather than 'outer' directed.

10. Develop an outgoing social personality. You'll likely expand your social life with small changes, such as smiling more, acknowledging others and initiating conversations.

11. Be yourself. Get comfortable with expressing yourself honestly and sincerely and you are more likely to find others who like you 'just the way you are'.

12. Eliminate negative feelings and problems. Seek help with problems, such as substance abuse or severe mood problems. It's hard to work with your happiness, says Fordyce, if your unhappiness is too encumbering.

13. Close relationships are number one. Healthy loving relationships are critically important to happiness, whether with close friends or family, and particularly with a marital or romantic partner.

14. Value happiness. Fordyce says people who regard happiness as important, are happier. In some ways this seems to go against the folk wisdom of not pursuing happiness for its own end, but here the emphasis is on not pursuing it directly, but being aware of it and sensitive to being 'happy'.

No more navel gazing

Dwelling on failure and ruminating over misfortunes leads down the spiral staircase of happiness, and absorbing thoughts and activities on the other hand, help climb back up the stairs. Do distractions help? The answer appears to be 'yes'. It does seem to help to distract the mind and then come back to solving problems. Drawing attention away from the self is a strategy that can boost moods. Activities that are engaging and provide quick positive reinforcement are best: bike riding, seeing a film with friends or learning a new language, for example. A whole range of activities can do the trick, as long as they absorb attention and help a person slip out of self-consciousness.

HAPPINESS IN ACTION

*Chase after money and security
And your heart will never unclench
Care about people's approval
And you will be their prisoner
Do your work, then step back.
The only path to serenity.*

LAO TZU

Whether you're happy or not depends on what you're doing. Some things make us happier than others. It sounds transparently obvious. Not so obvious, though, is which types of activities have a greater happiness payoff.

When we have free time, our minds wander. A wandering mind is often an anxious one, observes Mihaly Csikszentmihalyi. The usual response is to seek out stimulation that screens out the anxiety—watching TV, reading a trashy novel, obsessive gambling, getting drunk or being promiscuous.

THE ANXIETY/ENERGY PAYOFF

If we can muster the initial 'investment' of gathering our attention, what Csikszentmihalyi calls 'disposable activation energy', to both organize in a practical sense and prime our minds, we can find deep satisfaction in challenging and engaging leisure activities—the ones that Csikszentmihalyi defines as producing 'flow', usually involving skills and attention.

Sometimes however, fatigue or anxiety, or both, get in the way. Without the discipline to go against natural tendencies, we'll settle for second best—passive leisure. Not that there's anything wrong with a bit of sheer relaxing, but too much (for example, when it's the principal way you use your free time) is a waste, he believes, and worse, will mar your quality of life.

Active leisure activities are more demanding and difficult and sometimes create their own anxiety even though they are a source of 'extremely positive experience': things like getting involved in

331

exercises, playing a musical instrument or going out to see a film tend to include flow states.

Passive leisure activities don't cause anxiety, any more than they provide challenges. But this, says Csikszentmihalyi, 'is a bargain that many find worth making'. It takes energy to achieve optimal experiences, and too often people are unable or unwilling to put in the initial effort.

THE SKILLS AND 'AROUSAL' RELATIONSHIP

One way of portraying a person's various states of mind can be to imagine flow at one extreme, and apathy at the other. Between these extremes fall worry, anxiety, arousal, control, relaxation and boredom.

Flow occurs when the challenge is high and the skills that are needed to perform the activity are also high. Apathy occurs with situations that present little challenge and also low skill level. Anxiety surfaces when the challenges are high but the skills available are low. The two nearest states to flow are 'arousal', where someone is mentally focused, active and involved, and 'control', where you feel happy, strong and satisfied.

To move from 'arousal' to flow, you need to learn new skills, while to move into flow from control you need to step up the challenges. If the challenge is too great, frustration and worry set in, making you anxious. If a task is not challenging enough, at first the task is relaxing, then boring.

PAYING ATTENTION

Paying attention can be the turning point that tilts the experience towards 'flow', both in leisure and at work. By paying fine attention to what's needed and how it could be improved, you can see a job in its larger perspective, and make it more meaningful. Many of the world's major discoveries—like penicillin and radiation, for example—came about because people paid attention, says Csikszentmihalyi.

FRAMING WORK FOR SATISFACTION

How can you avoid the danger of polarizing life into work that is meaningless because it is unfree, and leisure that is meaningless because it has no purpose? asks Csikszentmihalyi. When we spend so many of our working hours at work, it makes sense to try and make them rewarding. He offers the following suggestions.

- Weave work and play together, making work as enjoyable as leisure and giving both more meaning. Highly productive and creative people, such as artists, entrepreneurs, statesmen and scientists, tend to experience their jobs as completely integrated with their lives, as did our hunting ancestors.
- Pay attention and reduce entropy, or, in simpler terms, start to see order and meaning in the work you are doing.
- Question the steps involved in a job and try to improve it, especially if it's a dull one.
- Find ways of accomplishing more and you'll probably enjoy your time more.
- Make a game of the aspects of jobs you don't like—like the man who liked his job, bar two points: waiting at airports and grant proposals. But when he combined the two, with the aid of a tape recorder, and worked on the grant applications while waiting at airports, he lost his distaste of the job and instead felt energized.

HAPPY ATTITUDES

... everything can be taken from a man but one thing, the last of human freedoms—to choose one's attitude in any given set of circumstances.

VIKTOR FRANKL, *MAN'S SEARCH FOR MEANING*, 1946

When you don't appreciate the good events in your past and overemphasize the bad ones, you can undermine the present, says Martin Seligman, author of *Authentic Happiness*. Two major ways of reconciling feelings about the past involve gratitude and forgiveness. The first 'amplifies the savouring and appreciation of the good events gone by'; while forgiveness 'loosens the power of the bad events to embitter'.

GRATITUDE

Robert Emmons from the University of California, and Mike McCullough from the University of Miami in the US, randomly assigned people to keep a diary for two weeks. They were asked to record happenings for which they were grateful. Another group was asked to record hassles, and another, life events. The people recording gratitude began to score much higher for joy, happiness and life satisfaction.

Give gratitude a chance to blossom by keeping a gratitude diary. Every night for two weeks record up to five things that you're grateful for—whether it's simply 'waking up' or 'good health' or a particular kind act from a friend.

FORGIVING AND FORGETTING

Dr Everett Worthington, a psychologist and author of *The Power of Forgiving*, learnt to forgive the murderers of his aged mother, who had been beaten to death with a crowbar and baseball bat. He describes a process he calls REACH:

- R stands for recall of the hurt—as objectively as you can. Breathe deeply and calmly as you visualize the event.
- E is for empathize. Try to recreate a plausible story as to why a person hurt you—how they might explain themselves if challenged, for example.
- A stands for altruistic—recognizing the altruistic gift of forgiveness. Rise above hurt and vengeance and give forgiveness for the other's good.
- C stands for commit, and involves being able to forgive publicly.
- H stands for hold—Worthington encourages you to hold onto forgiveness.

OPTIMISING OPTIMISM

If you're prone to pessimism, try shifting the balance by disputing your pessimistic thoughts—argue them even if you don't quite believe what you're saying to yourself. The first step is to recognize the pessimistic thoughts, then dispute them as if they were uttered by someone else who's out to make you miserable.

THE INNER AND THE OUTER LIFE

Are extroverts happier than introverts? Is the 'good life' secured by a strong inner life or one that is outwardly directed? We're often led to believe people are one or the other; Carl Jung described extroversion and introversion as fundamental and opposite traits of the psyche.

Many Greek philosophers saw the *vita activa* as the ultimate fulfilment: the active life of the doer, expressing himself in the public arena by engaging in politics and taking public stands.

On the other hand, the idea of the thinker, or *vita contemplative* gained popularity under the influence of Christian philosophy. It involved solitary reflection, prayer and communion with God.

Current research shows that the outgoing extrovert is happier, more cheerful, less stressed, more serene and more at peace with themselves. (Although extroverts tend to put a more positive spin on things, while introverts are more reserved—so it could be it's the reporting that's different.) Creative people show signs of being both extrovert and introvert—they need the hours of solitude to carry through projects whether they are film scripts, flower breeding or fine art. But at the same time, they usually find people a vital means of exchanging ideas, hearing other people, learning about their work and so on.

Rather than one or the other, it seems a yin and yang relationship between extroversion and introversion is the healthy one and there's nothing to stop us experiencing and enjoying the full spectrum of the continuum between the two.

A DESIRE FOR HAPPINESS

The secret of contentment is knowing how to enjoy what you have, and to be able to lose all desire for things beyond your reach.

LIN YUTANG

From an evolutionary point of view, suggests Randolph Nesse, Professor of Psychiatry and Psychology at the University of Michigan in the US, 'an excessively direct pursuit of happiness is likely to lead to frustration and paradoxically, unhappiness, because happiness is not a

The politics of happiness

That a government should nurture happiness is an idea that comes and goes in varying forms.

GNH In the 1970s the King of Bhutan announced his interest in a GNP that was the Gross National Happiness. 'It is based on the belief that the ultimate pursuit of every human being is happiness,' explained Lyonpo Jigmi Thinley, former prime minister. During a workshop exploring the idea in 1999 he suggested that GNH was being pursued through four platforms: economic development, environmental preservation, cultural promotion and good governance.

THE WELLBEING MANIFESTO Developed by the think-tank, The Australia Institute, the Wellbeing Manifesto has more than 6000 'signatures' (it's an online signing), including numerous well-known Australians such as Reverend Tim Costello and epidemiologist and Australian of the year in 2003, Professor Fiona Stanley. It outlines nine areas where governments should enact policies to improve national wellbeing, from providing fulfilling work and reclaiming time (reduce the maximum working week to 35 hours, it says), to promoting responsible advertising and measuring what matters.

PEACE AND DEVELOPMENT Johan Galtung, director of the international network, Transcend, a non-government organization for mediation in protracted conflicts, believes it is impossible to implement a formula for a single peak experience of wellbeing. A single experience for a plurality of humans would spell totalitarianism, would not be sustainable and could only apply to a small elite. A 'multi peak' approach is better, he says in an essay in *The Science of Well Being*. 'A suggested formula would be: take worries out of people's lives.' But don't expect them to proclaim happiness, he says, or be grateful. From there, is a simple bridge to subjective happiness—learning to appreciate the pain not suffered: 'Enjoy sitting warm and dry with cold rain pouring down outside.'

reachable goal, but a state that emerges when an individual is making good progress towards his or her individual life goals'.

What is the secret of happiness? That there is no secret? While we find ourselves lured to hedonistic pleasures, that path to happiness has its limits because of the way we adapt to pleasures. Avoiding temptations might be another route, but it's hard to give up or control desires. The golden mean makes good sense but people who pursue it 'nonetheless lurch from unbridled desire to restraint and back again,' observes Nesse. He says, 'although it is disappointing to recognize that there is no formula for happiness, at least not one that applies to everyone, it is reassuring to understand the origins of the emotions in whose loops we dance'.

But it seems there are many ways we can make the dance more harmonious and perhaps even more joyful. Minds are not made to remain static, we can learn new ways of thinking and behaving. We can choose work and other pursuits that are meaningful. We can choose to respond to and care for the people in our lives.

What matters, says Csikszentmihalyi in *Finding Flow*, is how people manage to join all experiences into a meaningful pattern: 'When that is accomplished, and a person feels in control of life and feels that it makes sense, there is nothing left to desire.'

Happiness is a process not a place, it's a way of life, not a goal in itself, a state we can hope for when we're living lives of real wealth. Meaning outshines the material in the pursuit for happiness, and it's the way we use our time that determines our chances of ever finding it.

POSTSCRIPT

Around three years ago my family moved out of an inner-city terrace that seemed to be shrinking around us, to a weatherboard cottage with a garden in a coastal village. We were seeking space, but we found much more.

Like everyone else I know, I live and breathe the issues I've explored in this book. Since we moved, we've bought a house, sold a house—with big decisions and negotiations along the way; we've grappled with the uneasy knowledge that sometimes we seem to spend money like water: violin lessons, a new 'old' car and its repairs, new socks for children that apparently go down the drain, phone bills … As fast as it comes in, money's on its way out again. But spending money is a fact of life—it's just that the choices are broad, and those that have enough money get to choose where to spend the rest. In our case we're not interested in a big house or a new car, and even find ourselves procrastinating over whether to upgrade our hand-me-down TV (that is so small that visiting children consider it freakish!). Yet we do spend on travel. Living in Australia with half our relatives in New Zealand and the other half in England, I want my children to know their family and I regard it as important. We buy lots of books and regularly buy from local artists. In these ways, perhaps we are extravagant, but I guess eventually we put our money where our values are.

Then there's time. At times I wish for a simpler life. I try to rein in that feeling of being in a race heading too fast towards the next hurdle. Being the linchpin in the family happenings—the one who oils the organization cogs and usually drives them too—life gets very complex: helping with homework, fixing up quotes for house renovations, making sure the music practice happens and the home readers are read; ensuring the birthday gifts are bought and parties arranged; that the house is in a vague semblance of order and cleanliness; helping at school and soccer; all quite apart from anything on my personal agenda of keeping sane and fit and meeting writing deadlines. But I also make a point of having 'quiet' time in our lives, when it doesn't matter what time it is and we can all potter in our own ways: drawing, playing the tin whistle, planting seedlings.

I do take heed of the call of less clutter, however, and that's something I'm working on, although anyone who's seen our house, will realize it is quite a challenge. But it's all about the journey, they say, not the destination ... maybe one day I'll have the perfectly neat house. Maybe it won't matter!

Out of the city we've found gardening. Snake beans did well last year. We've also found many people who for various reasons are managing outside the 'nine to five' framework. Significantly for us, we've met lots of families who've become good friends and we can get together in ways that are stimulating for the adults and children as well. I really value my friends and the feeling of support and connection they bring.

What matters to me is the magic that statistics and studies can't capture: the little things that make my life worth living. That I can laugh with my husband, enjoy timeless walks on the beach with my sons and we can all be amazed at a particularly beautiful sea anemone, or the fact the wind has sculpted a giant sand hill. I may not earn much, but in the summer for a lunch break I can jump on my bike, flippers in my hand and take a quick dip in an ocean pool and marvel at the fishes. For me, that's priceless.

Alison Haynes

BIBLIOGRAPHY

CHAPTER 1

Duncan, David Ewing, *Calendar: humanity's epic struggle to determine a true and accurate year*, Fourth Estate, London, 1999

Foster, Russell G and Kreitzman, Leon, *Rhythms of life: The biological clocks that control the daily lives of every living thing*, Yale University Press, New Haven and London, 2004

Landes, David S, *Revolution in time: clocks and the making of the modern world*, Viking, 2000

Langone, John, *The mystery of time: humanity's quest for order and measure*, National Geographic Society, Washington, 2000

Lippincott, Kristen, *The Story of Time*, Merrell Holberton, London, 1999

McCready, Stuart (ed.), *The discovery of time*, Naperville, Sourcebooks Inc, 2001

Seligman, Martin E P, *Authentic happiness*, Free Press, New York, 2002

Wiseman, Thomas, *The money motive: what you unconsciously reveal about desires and fears every time you handle money or talk about it*, Random House, New York, 1974

CHAPTER 2

Csikszentmihalyi, Mihaly, *Finding flow*, Basic Books, New York, 1997

Godbey, Geoffrey and Robinson, John P, *Time for life: the surprising ways Americans use their time*, Pennsylvania State University Press, University Park, 1999

Pember Reeves, Maud, *Round about a pound a week,* Virago, London, 1979

Schor, Juliet, *The overspent American: why we want what we don't need*, Harper Perennial, New York, 1998

Schor, Juliet, *The overworked American: the unexpected decline of leisure*, Basic Books, New York, 1992

CHAPTER 3

Denniss, Richard and Hamilton, Clive, *Affluenza: when too much is never enough*, Allen & Unwin, Sydney, 2005

Zelizer, Viviana, *The social meaning of money: pin money, paychecks, poor relief, and other currencies*, Princeton University Press, 1997

CHAPTER 4

Argyle, Michael, *The psychology of happiness*, Routledge, London, 2001

Cutler, Howard C and His Holiness the Dalai Lama, *The art of happiness: a handbook for living*, Hodder, Sydney, 1998

Csikszentmihalyi, Mihaly, *Flow: the classic work on how to achieve happiness*, Rider, London, 2002

Honderich, Ted (ed.), *The Oxford companion to philosophy*, Oxford University Press, Oxford, 2005

Marinoff, Lou, *Plato not prozac!: applying eternal wisdom to everyday problems*, Harper Perennial, New York, 1999

Solomon, Robert C, *The joy of philosophy: thinking thin versus the passionate life*, Oxford University Press, New York, 1999

White, Nicholas, *A brief history of happiness*, Blackwell Publishing, Oxford, 2006

Wiseman, Richard, *The luck factor: change your luck — and change your life*, Century, London, 2003

CHAPTER 5

Argyle, Michael and Furnham, Adrian, *The psychology of money*, Routledge, London, 1998

Cope, Wendy (ed.), *Heaven on Earth: 101 happy poems*, Faber and Faber, London, 2001

Layard, Richard, *Happiness: lessons from a new science*, The Penguin Press, New York, 2005

Salerno, Steve, *SHAM: how the self-help movement made America helpless*, Crown, New York, 2005

CHAPTER 6

Cockburn, Linda, *Living the good life: how one family changed their world from their own backyard*, Hardie Grant Books, Melbourne, 2006

Elgin, Duane, *Voluntary simplicity: toward a life that is outwardly simple, inwardly rich*, Harper Paperbacks, New York, 1998

Hamilton, Clive, *Growth fetish*, Allen & Unwin, Sydney, 2003

Shi, David E, *The simple life: plain living and high thinking in American culture*, The University of Georgia Press, Athens, 2001

Smith, Robert Lawrence, *A Quaker book of wisdom: life lessons in simplicity, service and common sense*, Harper Paperbacks, New York, 1999

CHAPTER 7

Dement, William C with Vaughan, Christopher, *The promise of sleep*, Macmillan, London, 1999

Lamberg, Lynne and Smolensky, Michael, *The body clock guide to better health: how to use your body's natural clock to fight illness*, Henry Holt and Company, New York, 2000

Sturt, Mary, *The Psychology of Time*, Kegan Paul Trench, Trubner & Co Ltd, London, 1925

CHAPTER 8

Birth, Kevin K, *"Any time is Trinidad time": Social meanings and temporal consciousness*, University Press of Florida, Gainesville, 1999

Csikszentmihalyi, Mihaly and Rochberg-Halton, Eugene, *The meaning of things: domestic symbols and the self*, Cambridge University Press, New York, 1981

Kasser, Tim, *The high price of materialism*, The MIT Press, Cambridge, 2002

Levine, Robert, *A geography of time*, Basic Books, New York, 1997

Schwartz, Barry, *The paradox of choice: why more is less*, Harper Collins, New York, 2004

CHAPTER 9

Griessman, B Eugene, *Time tactics of very succesful people*, McGraw-Hill Inc, New York, 1994

CHAPTER 10

Baylis, Nick, Huppert, Felicia A, Keverne, Barry (ed), *The science of wellbeing*, Oxford University Press, Oxford, 2005

Eckersley, Richard (ed.), *Measuring progress: Is life getting better?*, CSIRO Publishing, Melbourne, 1998

CHAPTER 11
Danko, William D and Stanley, Thomas J, *The millionaire next door: the surprising secrets of America's wealthy*, Pocket Books, New York, 1996

Dominguez, Joe and Robin, Vicki, *Your money or your life: transforming your relationship with money and achieving financial independence*, Penguin Books, New York, 1992

Elkind, David, *The hurried child: growing up too fast too soon*, Da Capo Press, Cambridge, 2001,

Honore, Carl, *In praise of slow: how a worldwide movement is challenging the cult of speed*, Orion, London, 2004

McKnight, Jim, *A procrastinator's guide to Simple living*, Melbourne University Press, Melbourne, 2001

Moore, Thomas, *Care of the soul: A guide for cultivating depth and sacredness in everyday life*, Harper Perennial, New York, 1994.

Rechtschaffen, Stephan, *Timeshifting: creating more time to enjoy your life*, Doubleday, New York, 1997

Schumacher, E F, *Small is beautiful: economics as if people mattered, 25 years later ... with Commentaries*, Vintage, London, 1999

Waring, Marilyn, *Three masquerades, essays on equality, work and human rights*, Allen & Unwin, Sydney, 1996

CHAPTER 12
Hanh, Thich Nhat, *Peace is every step: the path of mindfulness in everyday life*, Bantam Books, New York, 1992

Russell, Bertrand, *The conquest of happiness*, Liveright, New York, 1971